IMAGES
of America

JEWISH READING AND BERKS COUNTY

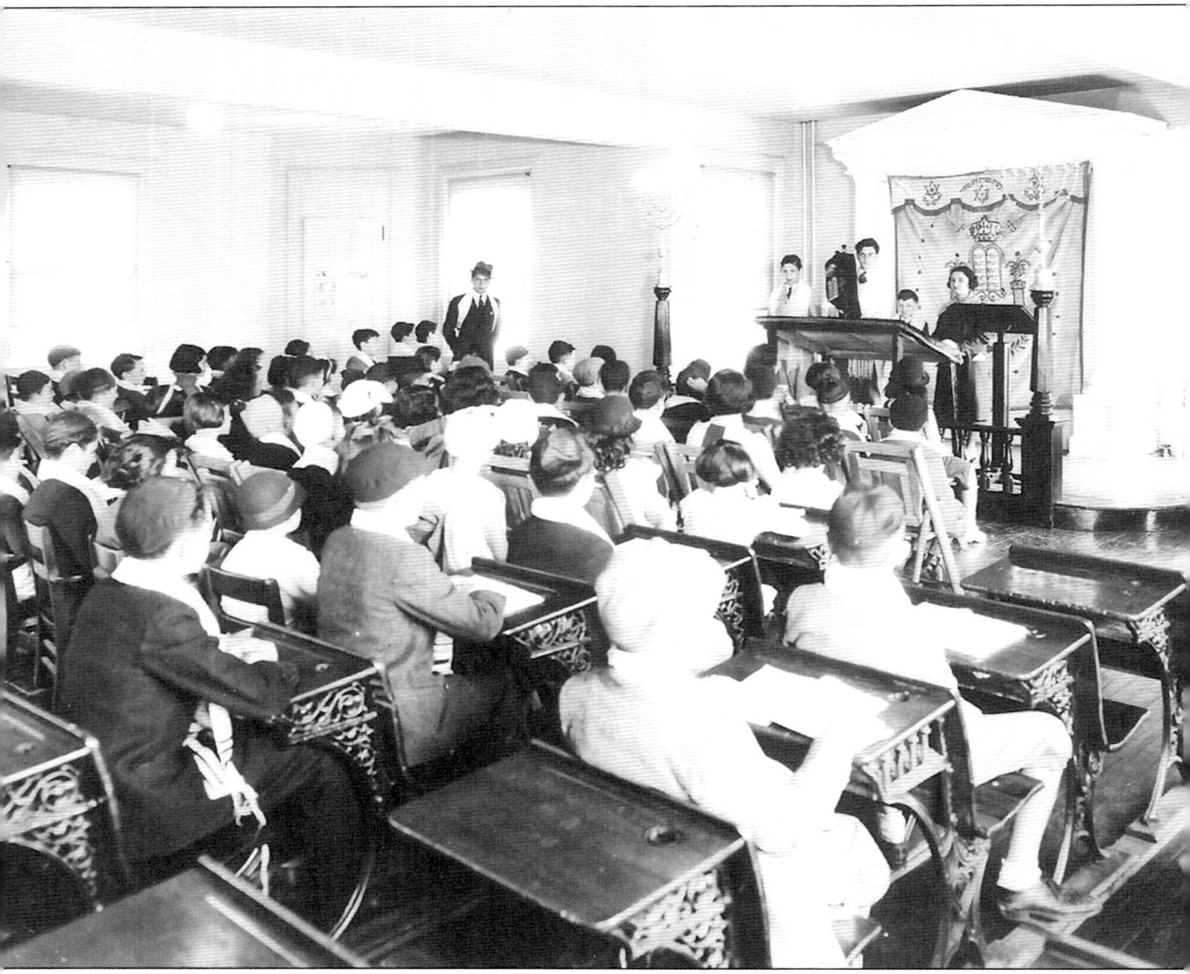

On the Cover: This is a Saturday morning junior congregational service in 1934. Students are participating in reading from the Torah while standing in front of the Ark in the old Kesher Zion building. Kesher Zion Synagogue was first established in 1929 as a result of the merger of B'nai Zion and Kesher Israel. The synagogue was located at Eighth and Court Streets in Reading. (Courtesy of Kesher Zion Synagogue [KZ].)

IMAGES
of America

JEWISH READING AND BERKS COUNTY

Laurie Grobman and Jessica Didow
Foreword by Tammy K. Mitgang

ARCADIA
PUBLISHING

ISBN 978-0-7385-7600-8

Published by Arcadia Publishing
Charleston, South Carolina

Printed in the United States of America

Library of Congress Control Number: 2011923577

For all general information, please contact Arcadia Publishing:
Telephone 843-853-2070
Fax 843-853-0044
E-mail sales@arcadiapublishing.com
For customer service and orders:
Toll-Free 1-888-313-2665

Visit us on the Internet at www.arcadiapublishing.com

To the students at Pennsylvania State University, Berks

Contents

Foreword

It seemed obvious after reading an article in the Penn State Berks journal *Research* (Winter 2009–2010) that I had to contact Dr. Laurie Grobman, a professor of English and women's studies. Dr. Grobman's work brings teaching and research together as a classroom experience, melding collections of local histories into celebrations of multiculturalism. To my knowledge, the last effort to compile a comprehensive history of the local Jewish community had been in 1990, when Dr. Paul A. Leisawitz, a local physician, wrote *A History of the Jewish Community in Reading and Berks County*.

The hard work of the students is admirable. Dr. Grobman's class was comprised of students from other communities juggling challenging course work, many with little or no knowledge of the area's local history or the intricacies of Jewish ritual and tradition. Ultimately, the students were challenged to join in an undergraduate research effort destined to become a published book that would tell the story of the Jews of Berks County through pictures and expanded captions, a photograph album for readers.

It was not until I began to see and experience the interaction of the students with members of the Jewish community, its synagogues, and institutions that I understood the paramount success of this project—the shared experience before the written word and image. Dusty photographs were retrieved from cardboard boxes and family records gathered while students and their interview subjects sat side-by-side, paging through family photograph albums and fading recollections. The creation of this book represents an exchange of more than historical information and oral histories; it is a work bound with relationships—community-building.

Although anti-Semitism was a painful reality in our local history, the true success of the Jewish community in Berks County was the ability of its members to successfully open the doors that were at one time closed to them. Jews created neighborhoods and built businesses, synagogues, religious schools, civic organizations, and social clubs that celebrated their religion and culture. And they built relationships that reached beyond hatred and ignorance. Our neighborhoods today are rich and diverse, reflective of the multicultural communities shaped by the immigrant populations who settled here.

Mazel tov to Dr. Grobman and her students; your work is appreciated and important. You challenge us all to write our stories, share our history, and celebrate our communities.

The student writers are Caitlin Bonner, who will graduate in May 2011 with a BA in communication arts and sciences; Barry Foster, who will graduate in May 2011 with a BA in professional writing; Aaron Griffith, who will graduate in December 2012 with a BA in professional writing; Michael Henderson, who will graduate in May 2011 with a BA in communication arts and sciences; Christine James, who will graduate in May 2011 with a BA in global studies and a minor in professional writing; Britany Maack, who will graduate in May 2012 with a BA in communication arts and sciences; Robert Quinter, who will graduate in December 2011 with a BA in communication arts and sciences; Kristen Rulli, who will graduate in December 2012 with a BA in communication arts and sciences; Razvan Viteazu, who will graduate in May 2011 with a BA in American studies; Jeffery Watts, who is majoring in American studies and plans to take a year off from his studies; Alyssa Williams, who will graduate in May 2011 with a BA in professional writing; and Sara Williams, who will graduate in May 2011 with a BA in American studies.

—Tammy K. Mitgang

Acknowledgments

This book is a collaborative effort between many people, but most of the credit goes to the 12 students in an interdisciplinary, upper-level course taught by Laurie Grobman at Penn State Berks in the 2011 spring semester. The students enrolled in Jewish Representation in History and Photography have spent much of their time in the course producing the book, including gathering over 200 photographs, obtaining permission to print the photographs, selecting and arranging photographs for each chapter, and finding information and writing captions for the photographs. The intellectual framework of the course focused on photography as history, art, and truth.

Many people deserve thanks, including everyone who went through their family photograph albums and contributed pictures to the book. In addition, the images in this volume appear courtesy of Jewish Federation of Reading (JFR), Reform Congregation Oheb Sholom (RCOS), Kesher Zion Synagogue (KZ), Shomrei Habrith Synagogue (SH), Chabad-Lubavitch of Berks County, and George M. Meiser IX and Gloria Jean Meiser. Jennifer Goss, Jeffrey Gernsheimer, and Bernie Gerber were especially helpful. But Irving Fidler became our close friend and classmate, spending countless hours working with all of us in and out of class.

We thank the Jewish Cultural Center, and especially Tammy Mitgang, Barbara Nazimov, Jayne Kleinman, Brenda Seidel, and Fame Brubaker.

Many people helped with writing captions for the photographs and images. We are especially appreciative for the *Reading Eagle*, archived on Google Archives. Much of the history for the captions was written by students in this and other classes, including Ryan Edwards, Barry Foster, Aaron Griffith, Stephen Groller, Michael Henderson, Christine James, Rattanpreet Kohli, Erin Koller, Kara Lindley, Lacey Lott, Tiffine Malamphy, Meghann McGuire, Allison Owens, Andrea Stennett, Blaine Turner, Razvan Viteazu, Jonathan Rivera, Alyssa Williams, and Sara Williams.

Our class photographer, Jeffrey Watts, a student in the class, has a bright career as a photographer. Christine James voluntarily took on the task of writing the book's introduction. Christine has been awarded a Fulbright Scholarship and will be teaching in Taiwan.

INTRODUCTION

An October 7, 1923, article in the *Reading Eagle* titled "Progress of Jews in this Community—Leading Factor in City's Growth—Their Organizations, Houses of Worship and Cemetery" states, "The Hebrews of Reading have long been a factor in the city's growth. Although the members of this faith have been located here only three quarters of a century, they have always been recognized as useful citizens, figuring in the civic and business life of the community ever since their arrival here."

Actually, there is evidence that people of the Jewish faith have been present since the mid-1700s. According to Dr. Paul Leisawitz, the names of three Jewish men can be found on a property deed that is from the 1700s. But the 1923 article is right in stating that the Jewish community has left its own mark on the area and continues to do so. From the Boscov's department stores to the Knoblauch Bank, which is no longer open for business, Reading would not be what it is today without the Jewish community.

Through the photographs, we hope to portray just how much the Jewish community has changed and adapted throughout the years. This book starts by displaying pictures of the immigrant families and the loved ones left behind. Chapter one depicts those who persevered and impacted both the Jewish community and the larger community of Reading, Pennsylvania. This is a chapter of family and growth, individuals who went above and beyond, and more importantly, how they interacted with each other.

Chapter two reflects the stories of the synagogues and how they have grown and changed over the history of the community. Starting as small congregations, these synagogues have been places of worship as well as places for coming together and finding a community. In times of extreme anti-Semitism, these places offered understanding and a safe house from such intolerance. One of the most important aspects of synagogue life is religious education. Many Jewish children attend Hebrew school from one to three times a week.

Chapter three demonstrates the significance of religious education though Hebrew school, Bat and Bar Mitzvahs, and other educational activities. This chapter focuses on the education of children in religious and cultural traditions and the recognition that the children are the future of the Jewish community.

Chapter four depicts other formal Jewish organizations and their activities. These include the Jewish Federation of Reading, the Jewish Cultural Center of Reading, the three newspapers (one that no longer exists) that are the voices of the community, and the Albright College Holocaust Resource Center.

Chapter five illuminates the interconnectedness of the Jewish community from its beginnings. For instance, many Jewish business owners who still remain on Penn Street or in the community will say that at one time, almost all of the businesses lined along both sides of the street were Jewish-owned. These businesses leaned on each other for help when they struggled. Jewish businesses also sought out other Jewish businesses to fill the needs of their companies.

Chapter six is about how the community found ways to have fun. This chapter includes a lot of smiles. Much of the recreational activities were the result of the Jewish Community Centers (at their various locations). Other activities, especially performances, were sponsored by sisterhoods. It was through these social outlets that the Jewish community bonded on levels beyond that of religion.

In creating a pictorial history, though, a few issues arise, especially selectivity. All history is selective simply because it is impossible to create an entirely comprehensive history of anything, including any community. When people document history through pictures or through writing, they are being selective, choosing what to use or to write about. Another layer of selectivity is added when the pictures are chosen. In many instances, when asked for photographs, individuals selected pictures that appealed to what they thought should be put in a book. Then, from that collection of pictures, the students and editors selected the final pictures. These pictures were chosen to portray the overarching narrative of how people have made the community what it is and how those same people have given back and contributed to the entire Berks and Reading communities.

In putting this pictorial history together, Dr. Laurie Grobman, professor of English and women's studies; coeditor Jessica Didow, program assistant for the Laboratory for Public Scholarship and Democracy, and Grobman's 12 undergraduate students worked closely with the Jewish Cultural Center (JCC) in Reading to obtain many photographs. The students also contacted individuals in the Jewish community directly and were given some access, but not a great deal, to private collections of photographs. Students divided the JCC directory of over 900 members and attempted to call each person. Despite difficulties of disconnected lines and numerous lines without answering machines, the students obtained a variety of incredible photographs that individually and collectively tell fascinating stories. Each student was also assigned to collect photographs from different locations, from the synagogues to the JCC to the Albright College Holocaust Resource Center. We learned that the different institutions' archives are very different. Reform Congregation Oheb Sholom, for example, has many photographs of individual leaders throughout the temple's history; on the other hand, Kesher Zion Synagogue's collection is dominated by photographs of religious services and education. Moreover, due to the Shomrei Habrith Synagogue's sale of its former building, photographs from those archives are limited. Students aimed to create the most comprehensive pictorial history possible, but due to these and other constraints, some people and places are better represented than others.

Despite the issues that arise from creating a pictorial history, one thing is clear: the Jewish community in Reading has long been active in the city's affairs, has had a significant impact on how the city and county are shaped, and will continue to play an important role in the future.

One

COMMITMENT, COURAGE, AND CREATIVITY

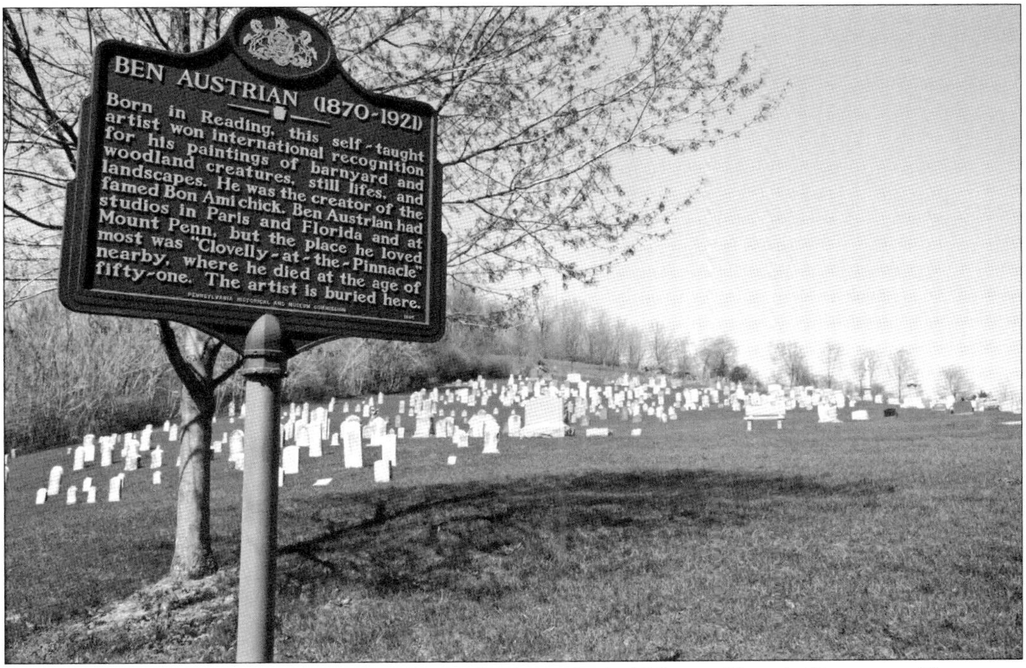

The Ben Austrian historical marker is located at New Bethel Union Church Cemetery, Kempton, Pennsylvania. Austrian was born on November 22, 1870, in Reading. His family helped to found Reading's Congregation Oheb Sholom Synagogue in 1864. His father, Raphael Austrian, was a German immigrant who owned a dry goods store in Reading. Austrian's art achieved acclaim in the United States and internationally. (Photograph by Jeffrey Watts, courtesy of Jeffrey Watts.)

This Indenture

Shown here is a deed for a property bought by Meyer Josephson and his wife, Esther, on October 4, 1764. Christopher Sauer's Germantown newspaper for July 8, 1758, carried an ad stating that "Meyer Josephson, formerly occupying Moses Heyman's store, Reading, has opened a new store in Steinmetz's house, at the market place." (Courtesy of the collection of the Historical Society of Berks County Museum & Library, Reading, Pennsylvania.)

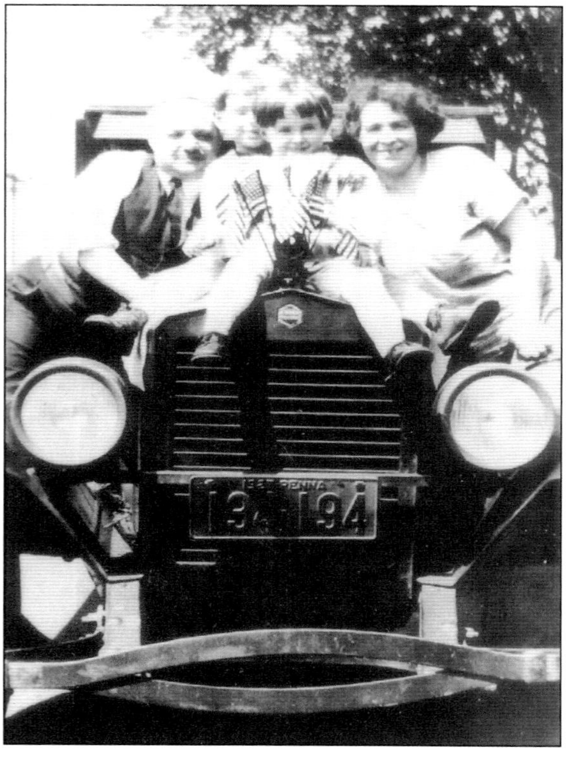

In 1910, fifteen-year-old Samuel Bascovitz was conscripted to serve in the Russian army for 20 years. Bascovitz's parents, fearing that the young 4-foot, 11-inch Jewish boy could not survive in the Czar's army, gave him his brother Solomon's birth certificate and helped him flee the country. Coming through Ellis Island, immigration officials changed his name to Bosco. He later added the "v" to better reflect his heritage. Here he's pictured in 1927 with his wife, Ethel, and children Shirley and Joseph. Daughter Reba was born later in 1927, and son Albert was born two years later. (Courtesy of Ken Lakin.)

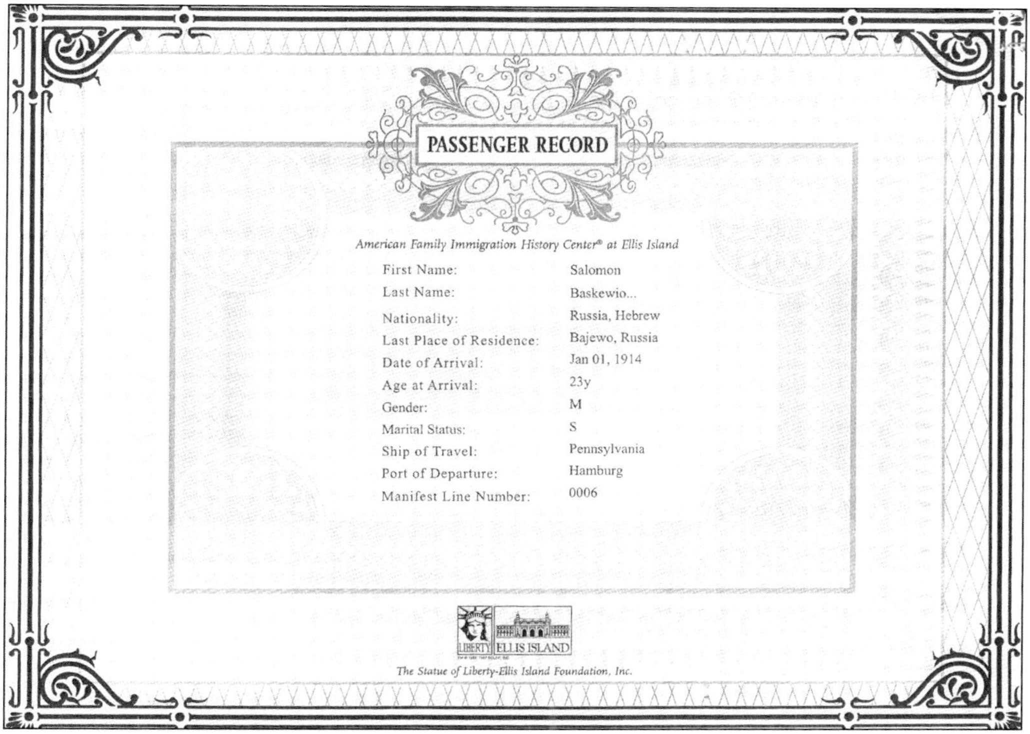

PASSENGER RECORD

American Family Immigration History Center® at Ellis Island

First Name:	Salomon
Last Name:	Baskewio...
Nationality:	Russia, Hebrew
Last Place of Residence:	Bajewo, Russia
Date of Arrival:	Jan 01, 1914
Age at Arrival:	23y
Gender:	M
Marital Status:	S
Ship of Travel:	Pennsylvania
Port of Departure:	Hamburg
Manifest Line Number:	0006

LIBERTY ELLIS ISLAND

The Statue of Liberty-Ellis Island Foundation, Inc.

Solomon "Samuel" Bascovitz sailed on the SS *Pennsylvania*, pictured below, from Hamburg, Germany, to Ellis Island. The ship, built by Harland & Wolff Limited in North Ireland in 1897, set sail on December 19, 1913, and arrived in New York on January 1, 1914. Above is Solomon Bascovitz's (Boscov's) passenger record. After trying his hand as a lemonade vendor and Western Union Telegram delivery person, Boscov moved to Berks County, where he heard everyone spoke Yiddish. In fact, what they spoke was Pennsylvania Dutch, a derivative of German close enough to Yiddish making it easy to communicate. He first established himself as a peddler, selling dry good to the farmers outside the city. He continued to expand his territory and purchased a horse and cart to carry his wares. He ultimately became a partner in a general merchandise store before opening his own store at 1401 North Ninth Street in 1921. This small retail store and his philosophy of honest value was the foundation for Boscov's, now the nation's largest family-owned department store chain. (Both, courtesy of Ken Lakin.)

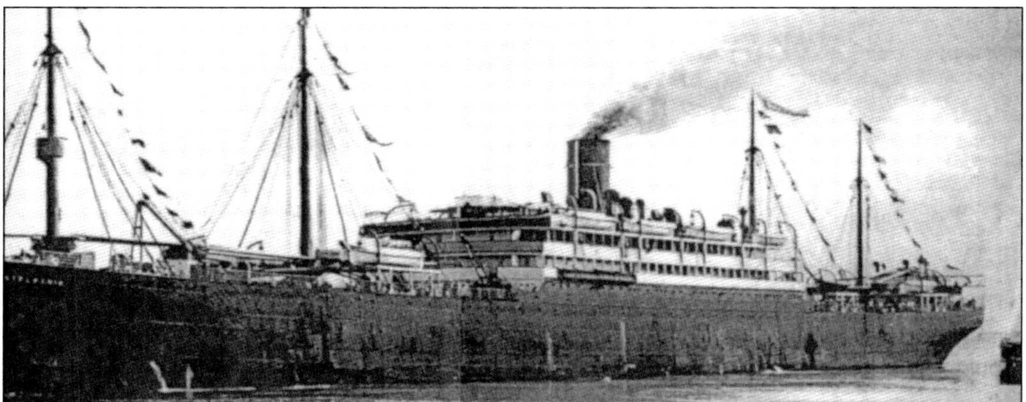

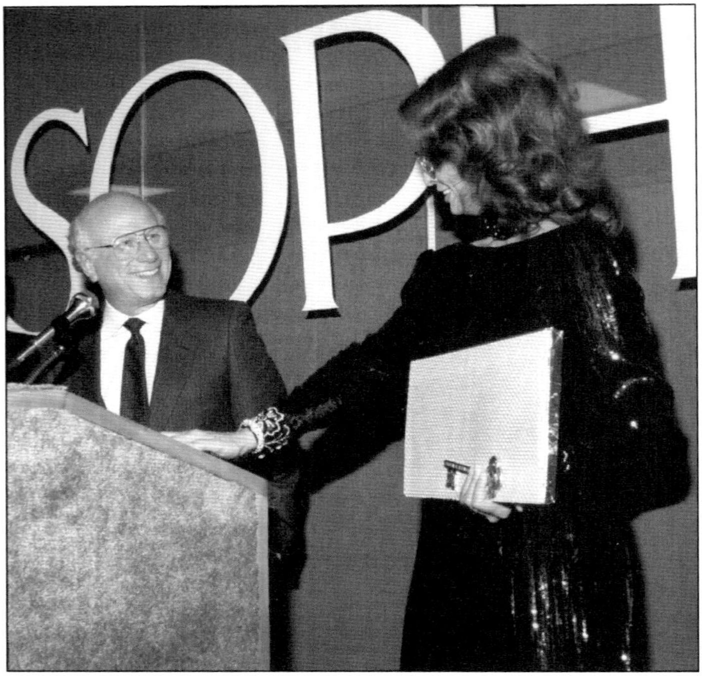

Edwin Lakin, president of Boscov's Department Stores, Inc., promotes renowned actress Sofia Loren's perfume line at a Boscov's event. Lakin graduated with a master's degree in business from New York University and joined Boscov's in 1956. Lakin married Albert Boscov's sister, Alma. At right, three-year-old Ken Lakin, son of Edwin and Reba Boscov Lakin, models for Reading's Pomeroy's department store in 1957. He graduated from Boston University with a bachelor's degree in journalism and received a master's degree in business administration from George Washington University, as well as completing the Federated Department Stores' executive management training program with Foley's in Houston, Texas. He joined Boscov's in 1984, and he has served as vice chairman, chairman and chief executive officer, and chief of operations. (Both, courtesy of Edwin and Alma Lakin.)

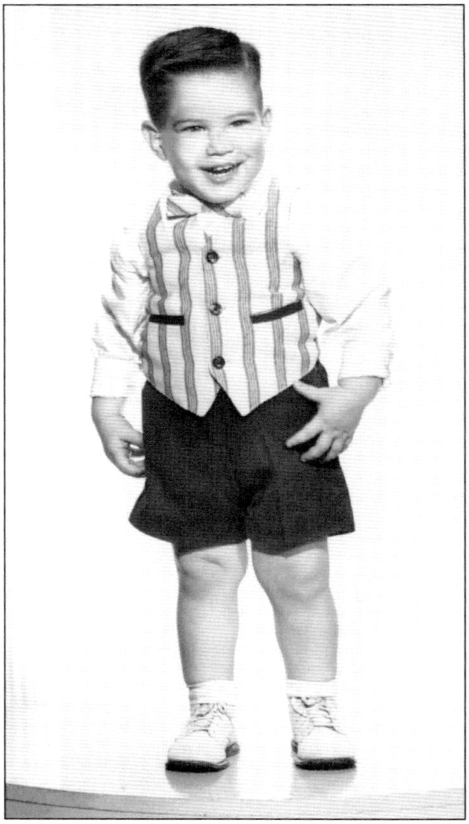

Pictured here is the original naturalization certificate presented to Tobias Knoblauch on August 4, 1900. Though it is unknown when exactly Knoblauch emigrated from Austria, living relatives believe that becoming a naturalized citizen took Tobias at least a year. After that, Tobias was determined to help other Jewish immigrants make a new start in America. (Courtesy of Eileen Knoblauch-Wagner.)

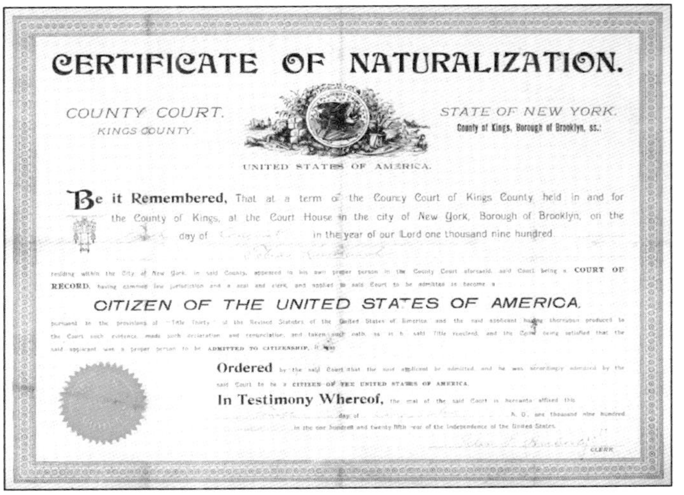

CERTIFICATE OF NATURALIZATION.

COUNTY COURT.
KINGS COUNTY

STATE OF NEW YORK.
County of Kings, Borough of Brooklyn, ss.:

UNITED STATES OF AMERICA.

Be it Remembered, That at a term of the County Court of Kings County held in and for the County of Kings, at the Court House in the city of New York, Borough of Brooklyn, on the day of in the year of our Lord one thousand nine hundred

residing within the City of New York, in said County, appeared in his own proper person in the County Court aforesaid, said Court being a COURT OF RECORD, having common law jurisdiction and a seal and clerk, and applied to said Court to be admitted to become a

CITIZEN OF THE UNITED STATES OF AMERICA,

pursuant to the provisions of Title Thirty of the Revised Statutes of the United States of America, and the said applicant having thereupon produced to the Court such evidence, made such declaration and renunciation, and taken such oath, as is by said Title required, and the Court being satisfied that the said applicant was a proper person to be ADMITTED TO CITIZENSHIP, it was

Ordered by the said Court that the said applicant be admitted, and he was accordingly admitted by the said Court to be a CITIZEN OF THE UNITED STATES OF AMERICA.

In Testimony Whereof, the seal of the said Court is hereunto affixed this day of A. D. one thousand nine hundred in the one hundred and twenty fifth year of the Independence of the United States.

CLERK

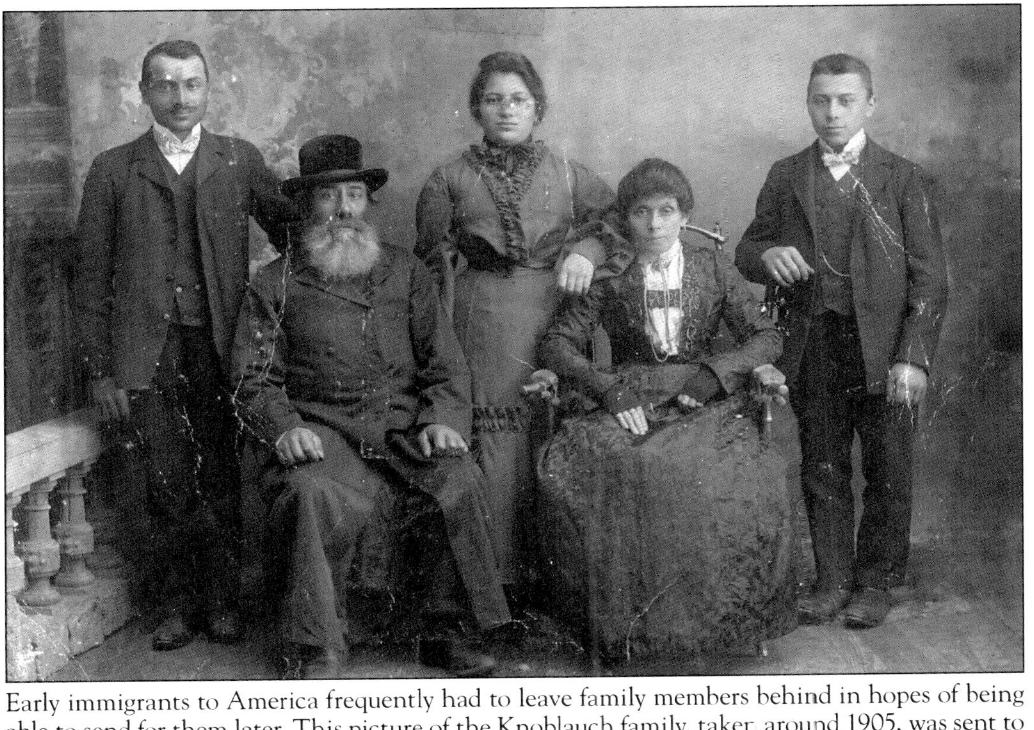

Early immigrants to America frequently had to leave family members behind in hopes of being able to send for them later. This picture of the Knoblauch family, taken around 1905, was sent to Tobias Knoblauch so that he would not get homesick. Standing from left to right are his siblings Philip, Esther, and Morris Knoblauch; seated are Simon, Tobias's father, and Bincha, his mother. (Courtesy of Eileen Knoblauch-Wagner.)

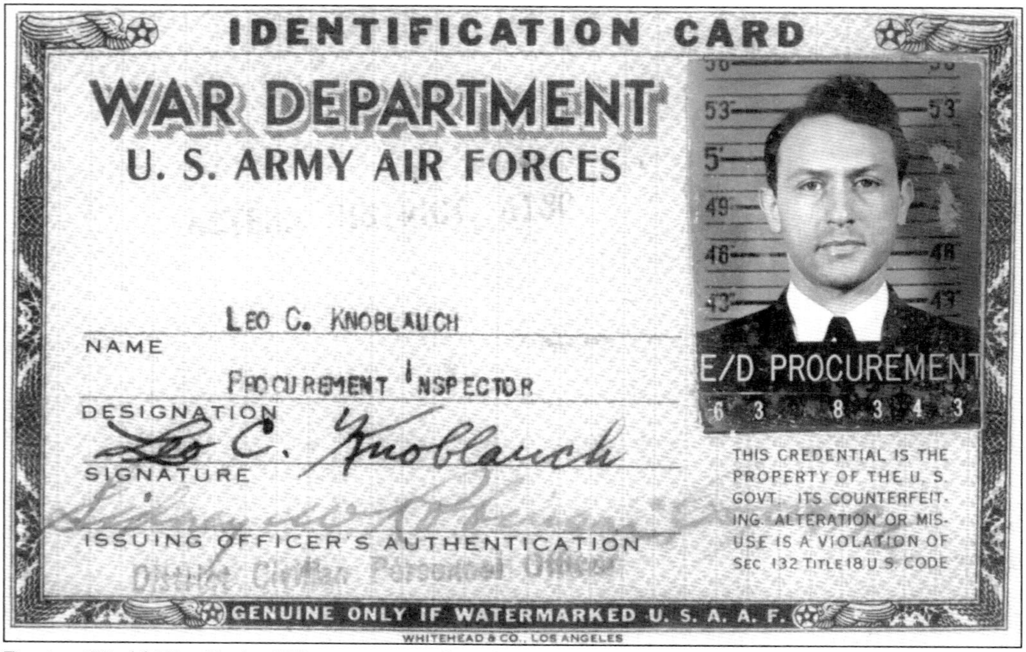

IDENTIFICATION CARD

WAR DEPARTMENT

U. S. ARMY AIR FORCES

LEO C. KNOBLAUCH

NAME

PROCUREMENT INSPECTOR

DESIGNATION

Leo C. Knoblauch

SIGNATURE

ISSUING OFFICER'S AUTHENTICATION

District Civilian Personnel Officer

E/D PROCUREMENT

6 3 8 3 4 3

THIS CREDENTIAL IS THE PROPERTY OF THE U. S. GOVT. ITS COUNTERFEITING, ALTERATION OR MISUSE IS A VIOLATION OF SEC 132 TITLE 18 U. S. CODE

GENUINE ONLY IF WATERMARKED U. S. A. A. F.

WHITEHEAD & CO., LOS ANGELES

During World War II, the US government hired many people. Leo C. Knoblauch, who later ran his father's business, the Knoblauch Bank, was secretly hired by the US government as a procurement inspector. Above is his military ID card, which Leo kept hidden from everyone except his family until now. Leo Knoblauch passed away on August 3, 2011, at the age of 102. (Courtesy of Eileen Knoblauch-Wagner.)

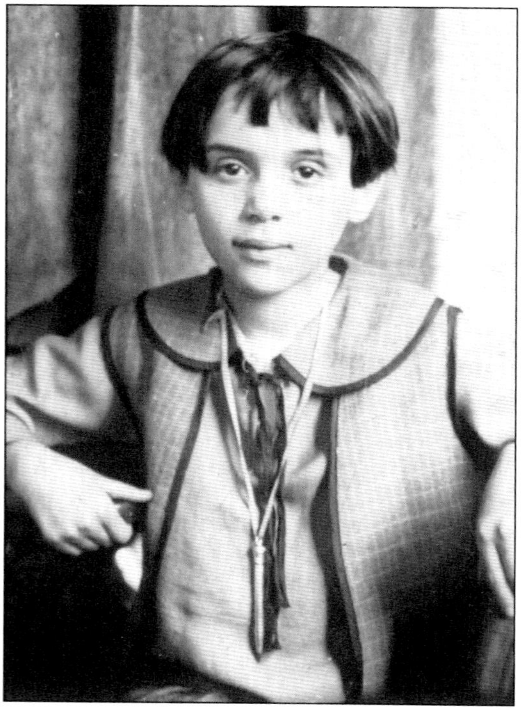

Kathryn Strom Charnoff is pictured in 1915 at seven years old. This photograph was taken after getting a haircut from her uncle, Shaya Markowitz, a barber. Strom's mother wanted her to have it cut to the tip of her earlobe, but he cut it above the ear. Markowitz left for Poland a few years later to find a wife; they were both killed in the Holocaust. (Courtesy of Diane Charnoff Fidler.)

Anna Charnoff stands with husband Abraham in approximately 1880. Anna Charnoff was born in Lithuania. The Charnoffs have seven children, including Herman, pictured here. They were members of Shomrei Habrith Synagogue, and Anna Charnoff was a member of its sisterhood. Herman Charnoff grew up in Reading and owned and operated a men's clothing store, the United Workmen's Store, on Ninth Street. (Courtesy of Diane Charnoff Fidler.)

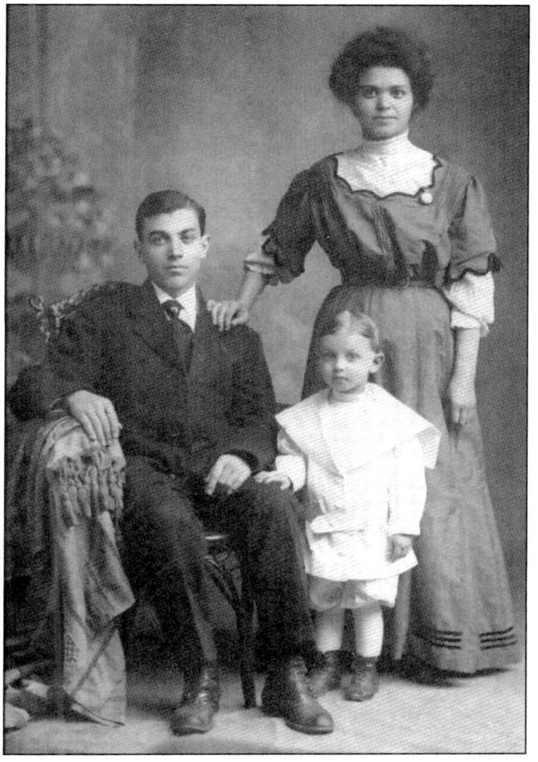

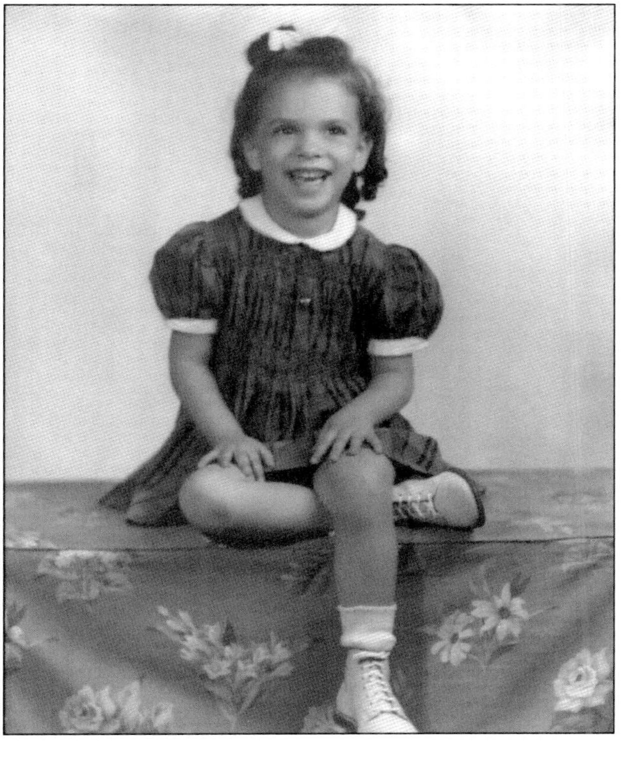

Rosalyn Charnoff, daughter of Meyer Charnoff and his wife, Kathryn, was born in 1942, exactly one year after Pearl Harbor. On March 23, 1954, Rosalyn sang in a Purim play sponsored by Shomrei Habrith Synagogue. In 1957, she was the campaign manager for Joanne Gallas, a candidate for student council at Southern Junior High School. Rosalyn Charnoff was a school nurse in Reading. (Courtesy of Diane Charnoff Fidler.)

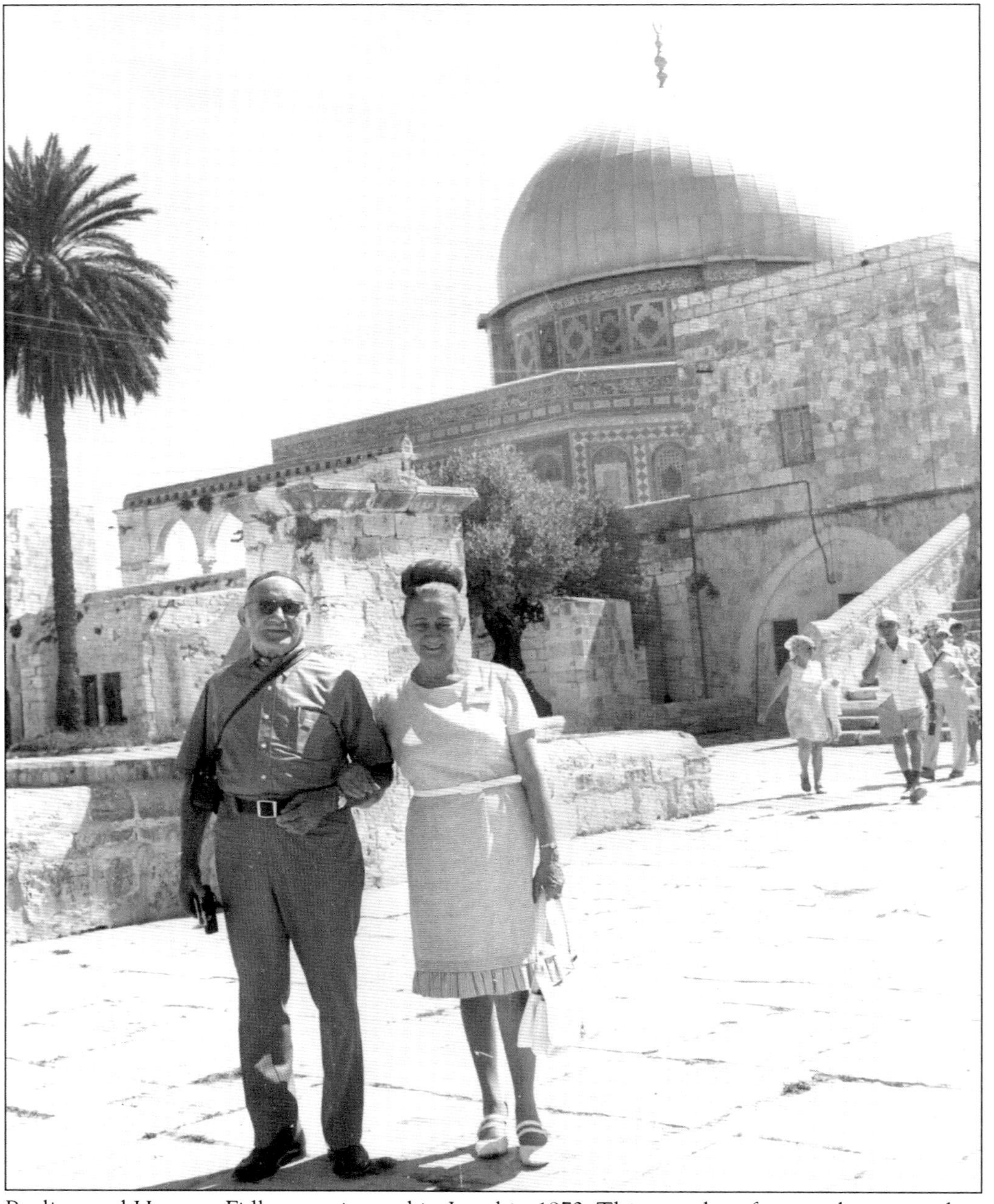

Pauline and Herman Fidler are pictured in Israel in 1973. This was their first airplane trip; they went to Israel with a tour group and visited many holy places, including the Western Wall. This picture was taken at the Dome of the Rock, where they partook in prayer. Herman Fidler's brother Leon and Leon's wife, Bella, accompanied them on this trip. Herman Fidler, son of Isaac and Freda Fidler, was born in Elmira, New York, but grew up and spent the rest of his life in Reading as a salesman. Pauline Fidler, daughter of Isaac and Ida Cohen, was born in Leeds, England, and spent a short amount of time there as child before coming to Reading with her mother. Pauline Fidler operated the former Pauline's Card Shop in Pennside. Pauline and Herman Fidler were married in 1934. Their son, Irving, was born in 1937. (Courtesy of Irving Fidler.)

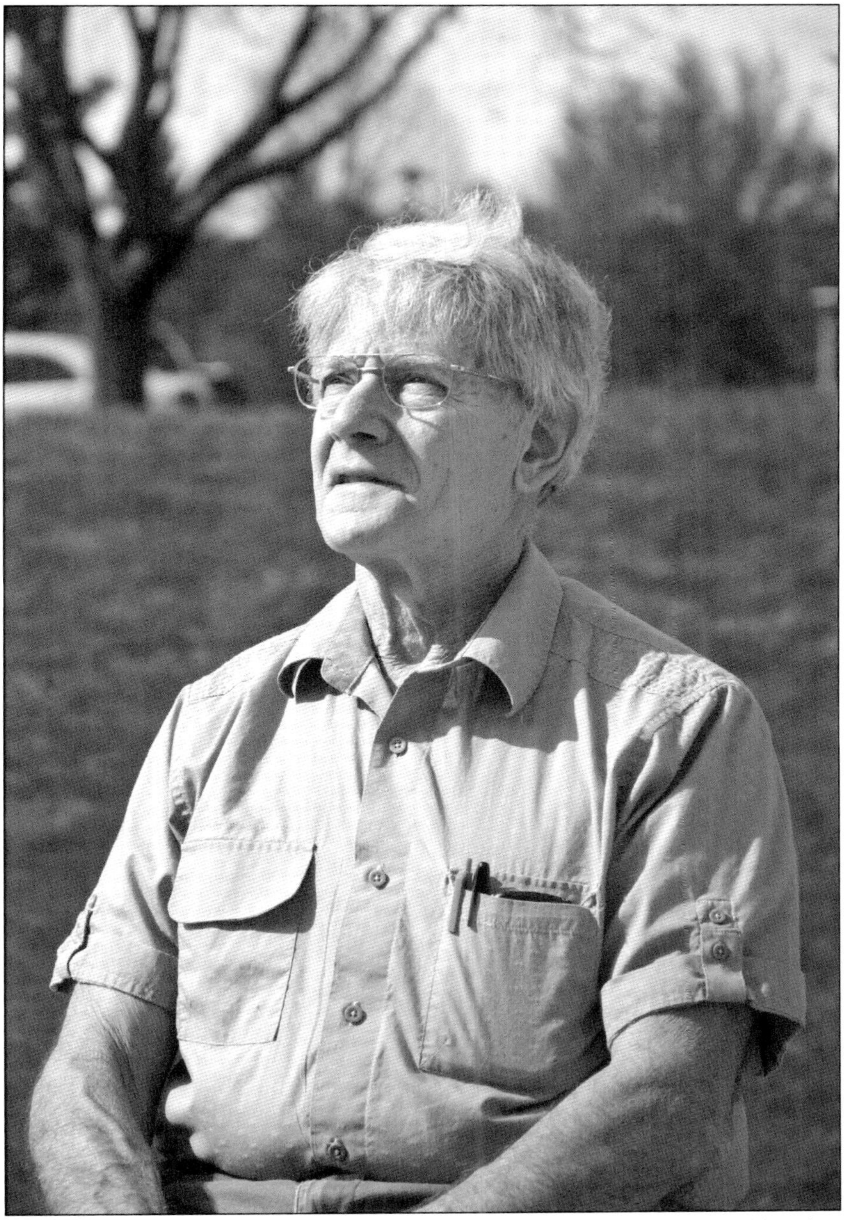

Irving M. Fidler was born on February 1, 1937, in Reading. He has grown up and lived in the area all his life. He graduated from Reading High in 1954, at which point he worked various jobs. He worked at Henry's Radio & TV Repair Shop in 1954 and at George D. Barbey Company, which specialized in electronics, from 1956 to 1968. Fidler was a radio repairman for the Reading Railroad from 1968 until 1973. He worked at Carpenter Technology from 1973 until his retirement in 1999. Fidler is also a military veteran, having served in the Army from 1960 to 1962. He and his wife, Diane Charnoff Fidler, married on June 28, 1970. Together, they have three children: Michael, 40; Joseph, 37; and Rachel, 31. Fidler's hobbies include electronics, railroads, and collecting radios and microphones. He recently received his motorcycle license and is an avid rider. (Photograph by Jeffrey Watts, courtesy of Jeffrey Watts.)

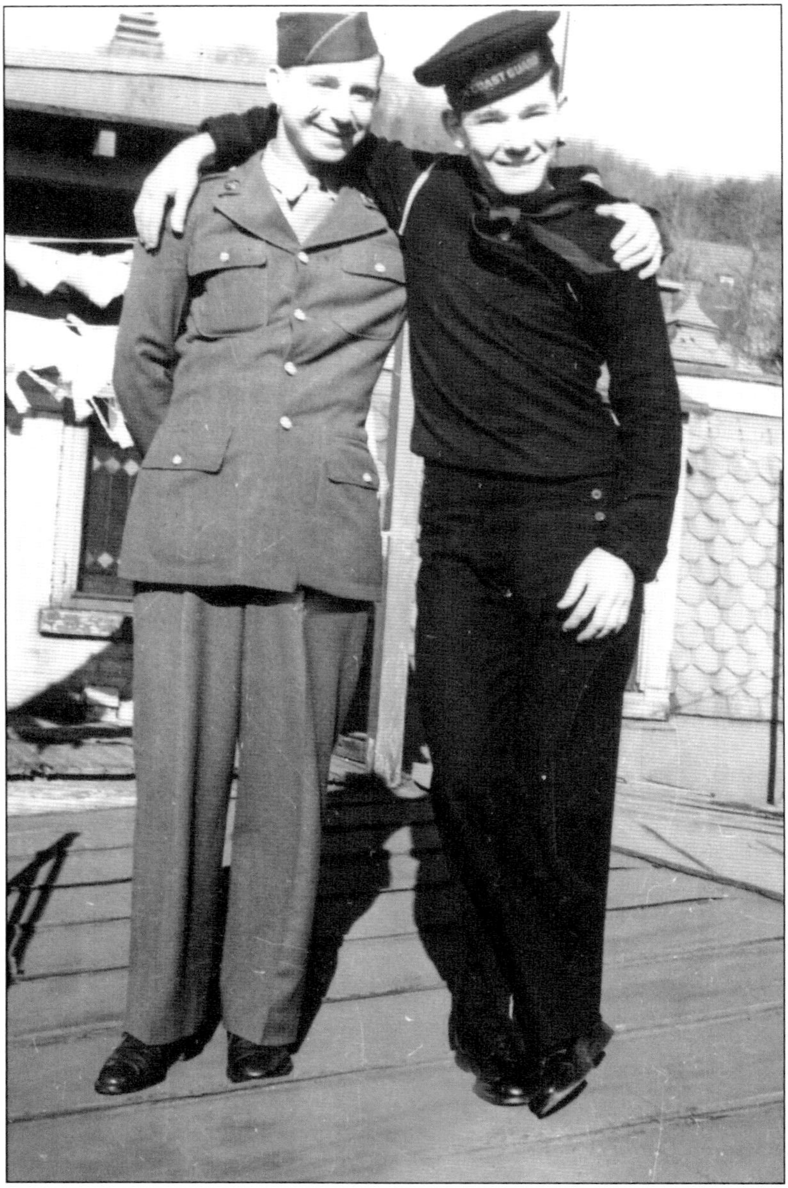

Henry Scher, right, chose to serve two tours of duty in the Coast Guard before also serving in the Navy. Scher and Irving Fidler are cousins. Scher owned Henry's Radio & TV Repair Shop and moved the business to four different locations before retirement. His first store was located at 136 North Ninth Street, a family-owned property where they also lived. He then rented a storefront on 404 North Front Street; however, he was called to duty and had to serve the Navy in Japan. This forced him to sell his store. After service, Scher opened a store at 552 North Front Street and stayed there shortly before buying his last store at Seventeenth Street and Perkiomen Avenue. Scher stayed in this location until retirement. He also was a vice president of the radio club at Reading High School. Harry Goldberg, left, served in the US Army. Goldberg was married to Anna Cohen, Irving Fidler's mother's sister. Goldberg was in the jewelry business. (Courtesy of Irving Fidler.)

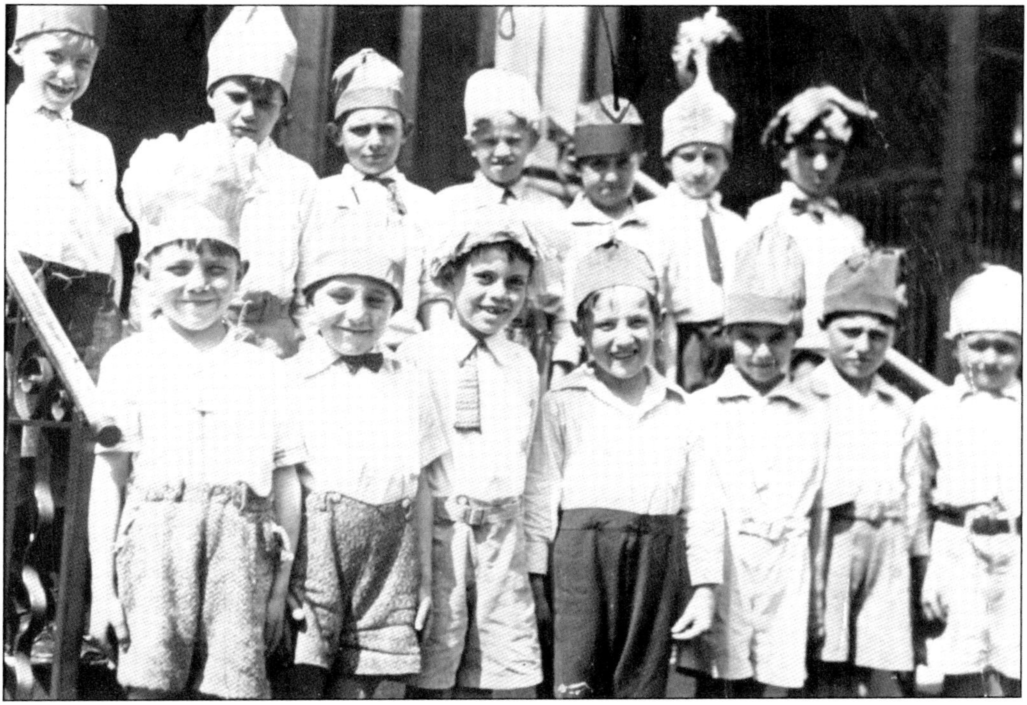

Here is David Moyer's Tenth and Green Elementary School picture in 1933. He is the son of Annie and Abraham Moyer. He served in World War II in the US Army, from 1943 to 1946. Upon his return, Moyer worked at the Campbell Soup factory in Maidencreek Township until his retirement. David is in the front row at the far left. (Courtesy of Marjorie Moyer.)

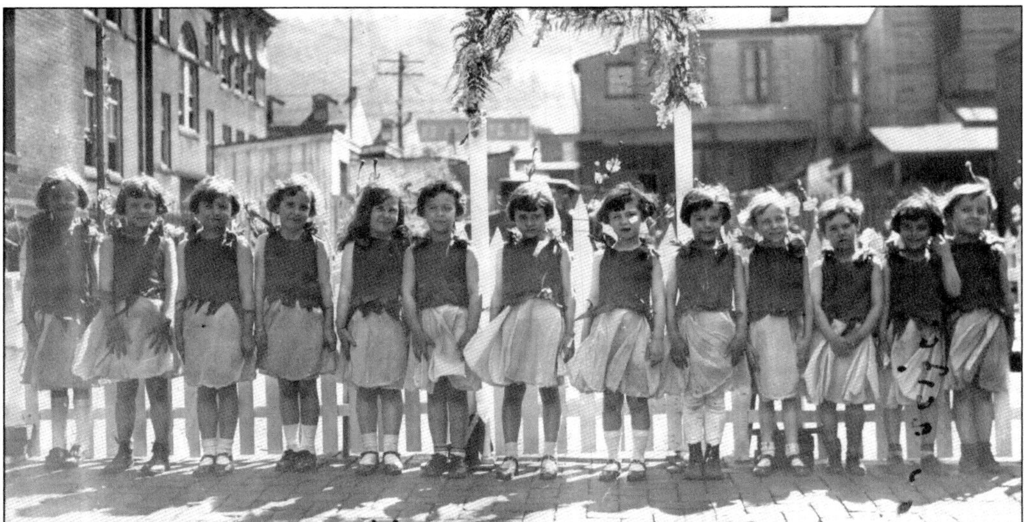

Marjorie Sulman Moyer and her classmates from Reading's Tenth and Green Elementary School are celebrating May Day in 1929. She married David Moyer in 1946, after he returned from World War II. Moyer worked for Berkshire News and Cards and was involved in several women's leadership groups, including Shomrei Habrith Sisterhood. David and Marjorie Moyer have four children. Marjorie is fifth from left. (Courtesy of Marjorie Moyer.)

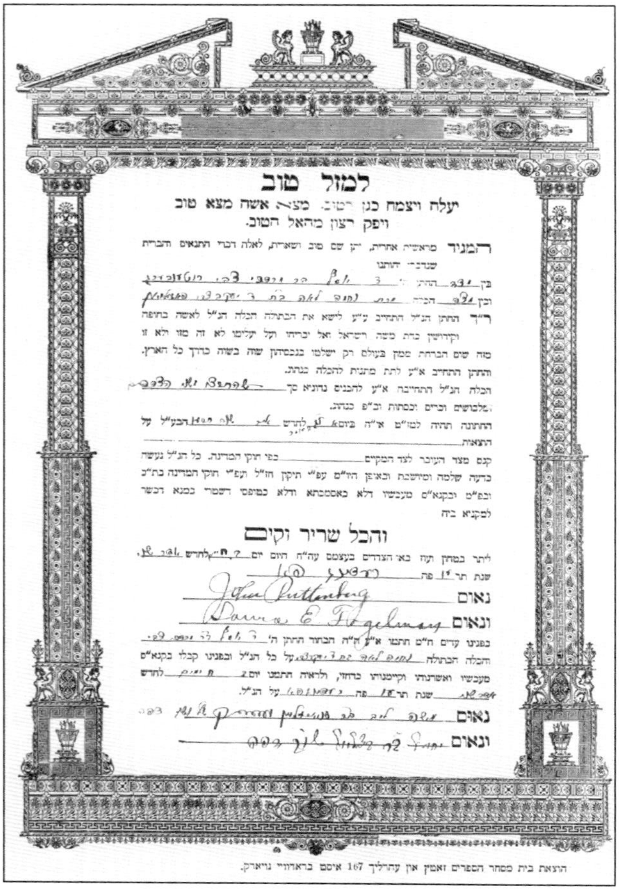
למזל טוב
יעלה ויצמח כגן רטוב. מצא אשה מצא טוב
ויפק רצון מהאל הטוב.
והכל שריר וקים

This dowry written in Hebrew is between John Ruttenberg and Laura Emma Fogelman when they were married in 1916. Ruttenberg was born in Russia and immigrated to the United States. Fogelman, a Reading native, married John in her home at 1009 Buttonwood Street in Reading. John Ruttenberg operated John Ruttenberg and Sons, an auto glass store. Laura Ruttenberg was active in B'nai B'rith Women of Reading. (Courtesy of Mildred Ruttenberg.)

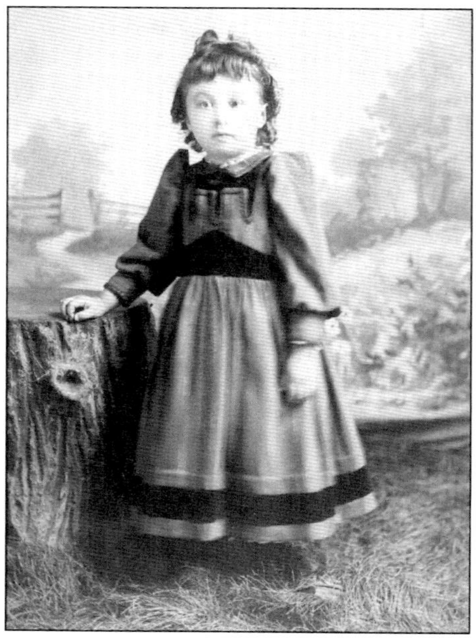

Here is a picture of Laura Emma Fogelman taken when she was four years old at the Saylor's New York Gallery located at 411 North Sixth Street in Reading in 1893. The Ruttenbergs were members of Shomrei Habrith Synagogue, and Laura Ruttenberg was a member of the sisterhood. She was also a member of the young women of the Army Auxiliary Corps of the Berks County Junior Council. The Ruttenbergs had two sons, Melvin and Floyd Ruttenberg, and a daughter, Mildred Ruttenberg. (Photographs courtesy of Mildred Ruttenberg.)

The Goodman family is pictured in approximately 1924. In the photograph are, from left to right, (first row) Abe, Pauline, and Danny; (second row) Morris, Ben, and Sam. Their father was Israel Goodman, husband of Frannie Goldberg Goodman. Pauline Goodman served as president of the B'nai B'rith Girls Club in 1939. Morris Goodman owned the London Shop on Penn Street. Sam and Abe Goodman owned Manson Billard, a manufacturer of barbells. Danny and Ben Goodman owned the Embassy Bar on Penn Street. (Courtesy of Pauline Goodman Goldberg.)

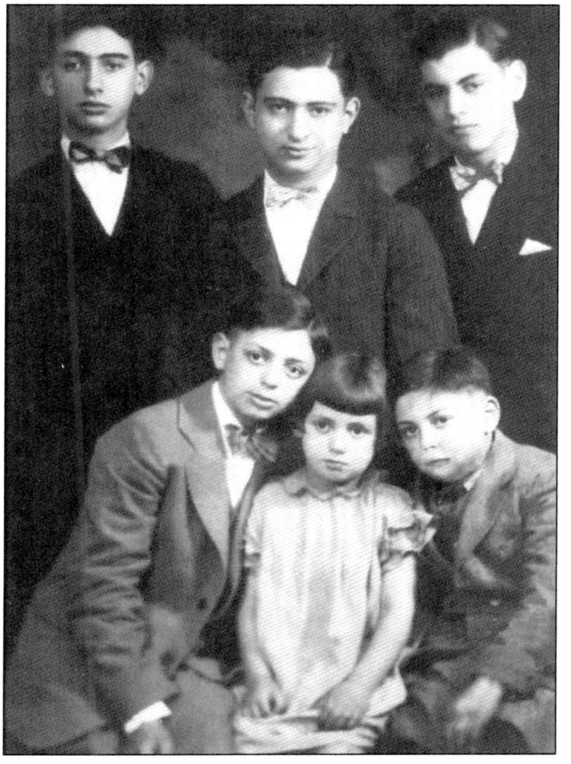

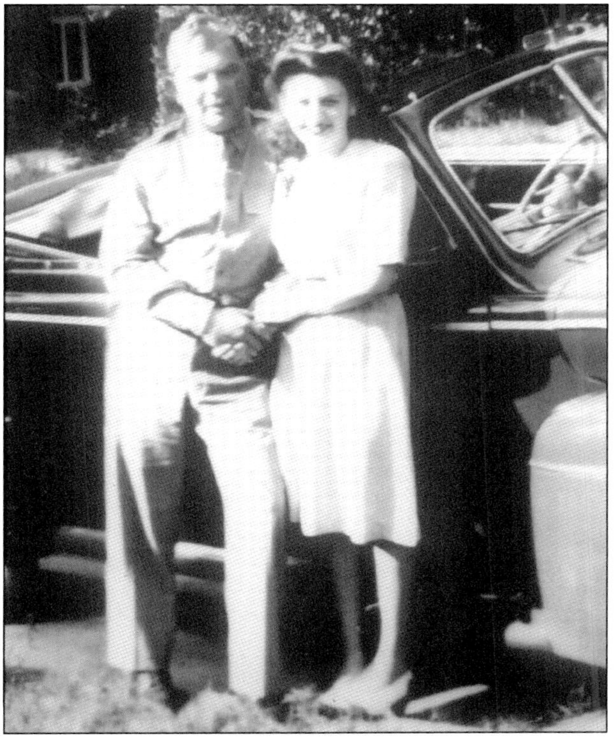

Pictured in front of their 1941 Ford, Bernie and Pauline Goodman Goldberg were married a few months before Bernie Goldberg left for the Army in 1941. While Bernie Goldberg was overseas, Pauline Goldberg stayed with family in the Reading area. Pauline Goldberg was involved with the Ladies Auxiliary of the Jewish Community Center, the Thirteenth and Union School Mother's Club, and the Kesher Zion Sisterhood. (Courtesy of Pauline Goodman Goldberg.)

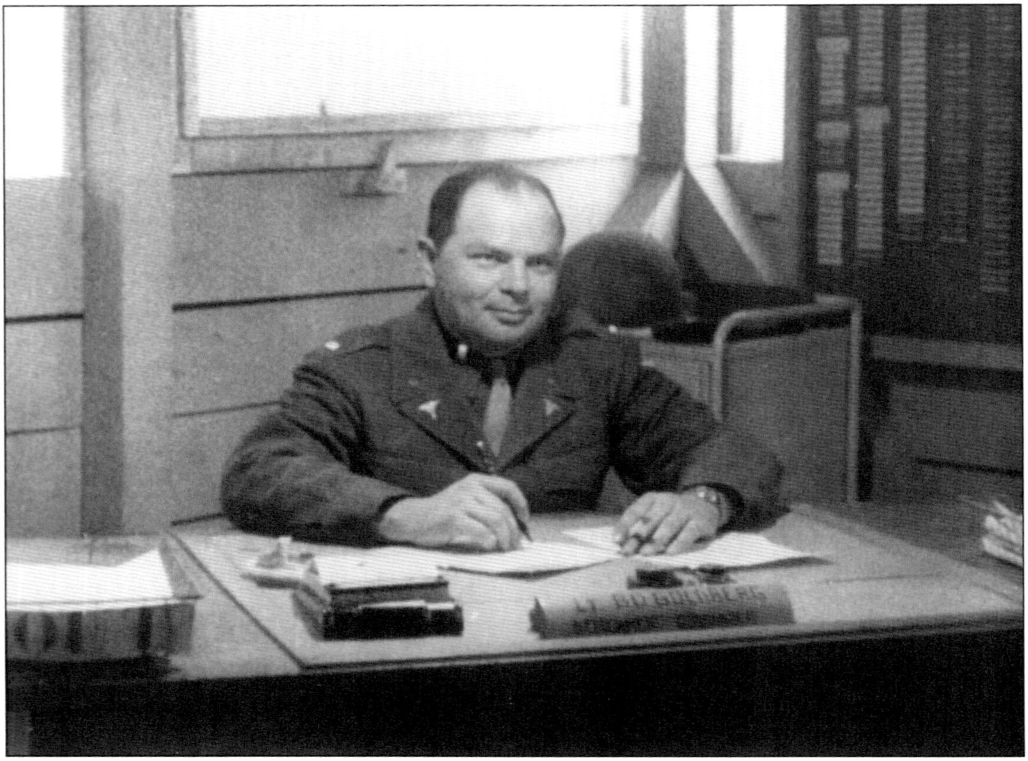

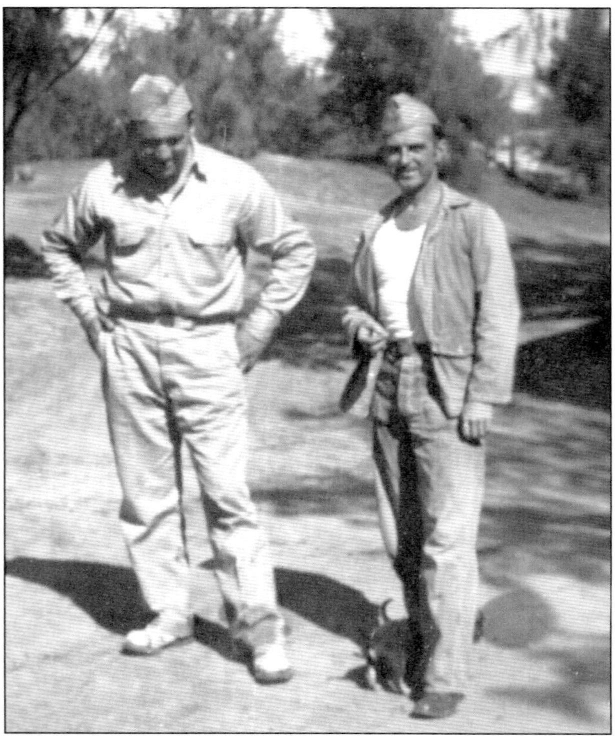

Bernie Goldberg, pictured above in 1943, is sitting at his desk in Italy, where he served as a first lieutenant in the Army. He worked in hospitals and was overseas from 1942 until the end of the war in 1945. Goldberg was in charge of enlisted men who were non-medical personnel. He organized sporting events while stationed in Africa and Italy. (Courtesy of Pauline Goodman Goldberg.)

Solly Gernsheimer (on the left) played on a Jewish boys' soccer team in Hanau, Germany. After immigrating to the United States in 1934, Gernsheimer served in the US Army from 1940 until 1945. His estimated termination of service was December 8, 1941, but after Pearl Harbor, he was sent to Hawaii and served as a mess sergeant at the Scofield Barracks until the end of the war. (Courtesy of Hilde Gernsheimer.)

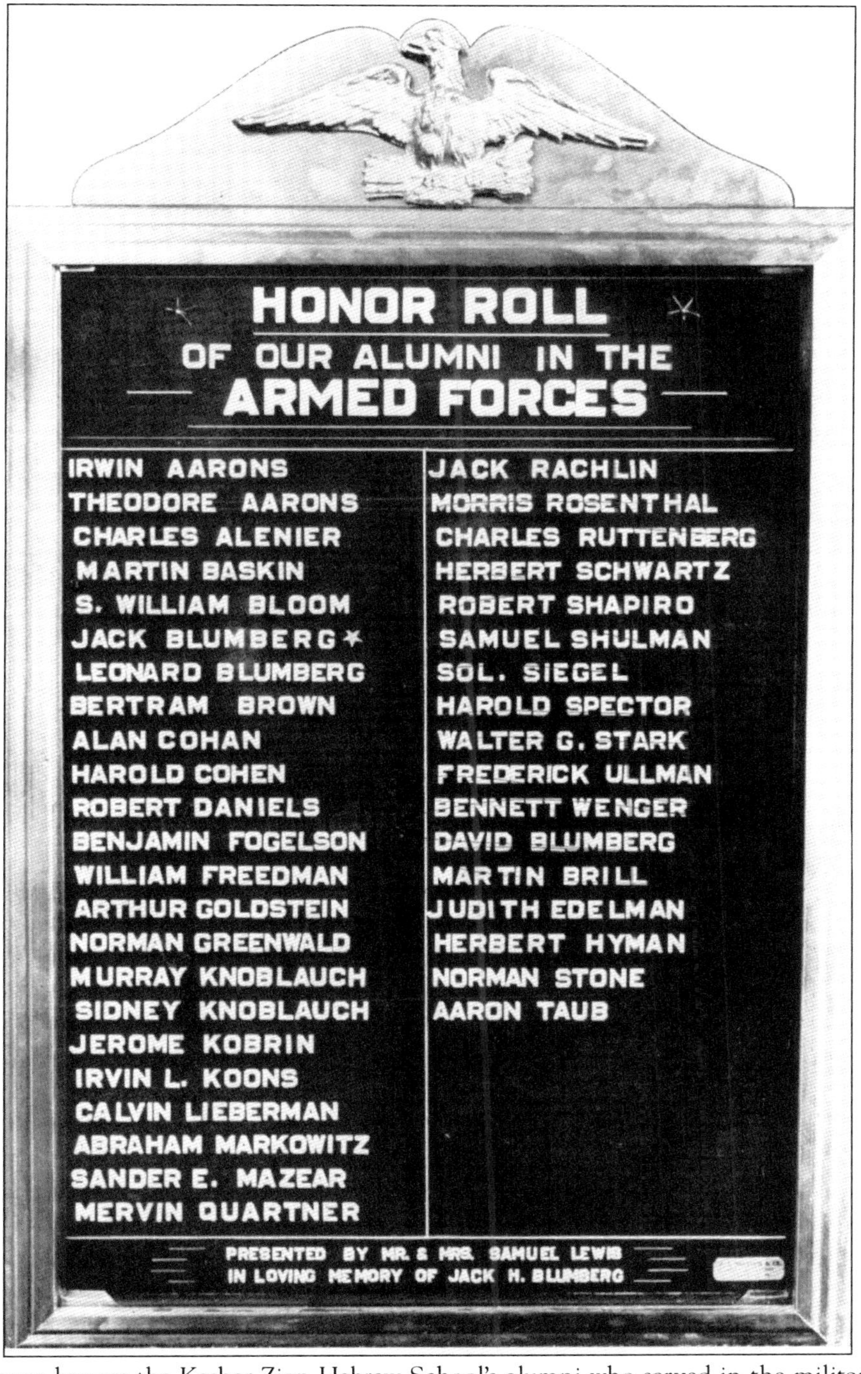

This plaque honors the Kesher Zion Hebrew School's alumni who served in the military. The plaque was presented by Samuel and Lillian Lewis in loving memory of Jack H. Blumberg, who was killed in action in World War II. Lillian Lewis, a member of the Kesher Zion Sisterhood and Hadassah, was also affiliated with the Jewish Welfare League. For many years, the Jack Blumberg Memorial Tournament was held annually at the Berkleigh Country Club. (Courtesy of KZ.)

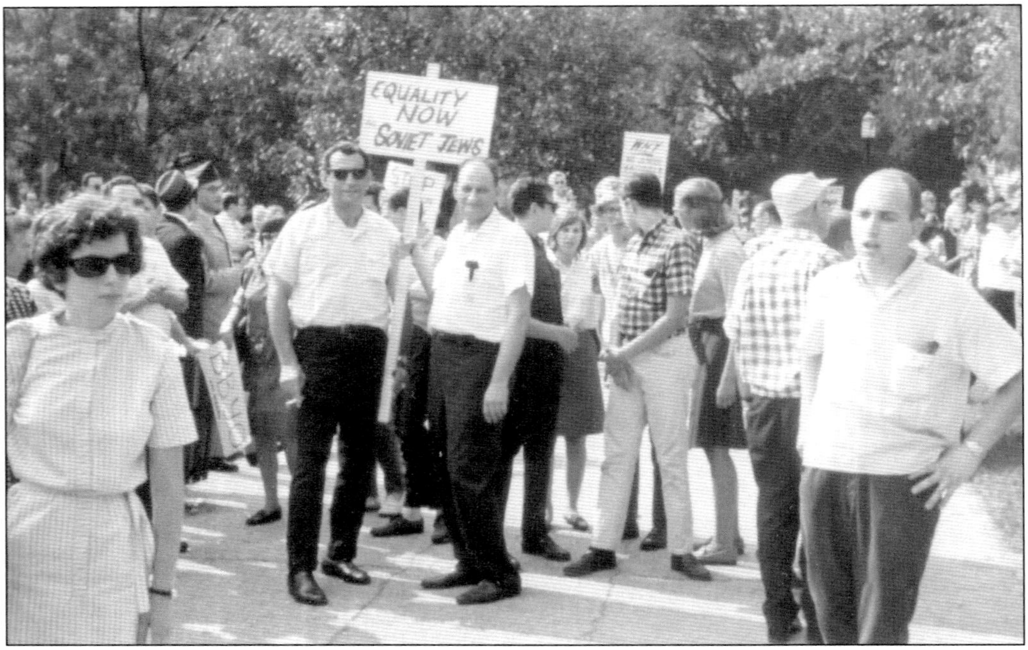

Members of the youth group of Temple Oheb Sholom participated in the September 13, 1965, vigil for Soviet Jewry in Washington, DC. The protest was intended to publicize repressive measures by Soviet Russia against its Jewish citizens. The youth group was comprised of girls and boys from grades 9 through 12. Events such as this would sometimes be coordinated and organized with other local synagogues. (Courtesy of RCOS.)

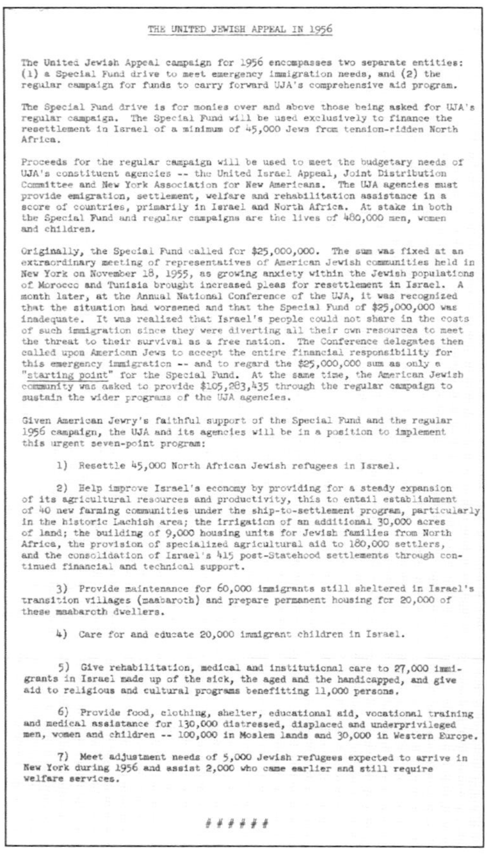

THE UNITED JEWISH APPEAL IN 1956

The United Jewish Appeal campaign for 1956 encompasses two separate entities: (1) a Special Fund drive to meet emergency immigration needs, and (2) the regular campaign for funds to carry forward UJA's comprehensive aid program.

The Special Fund drive is for monies over and above those being asked for UJA's regular campaign. The Special Fund will be used exclusively to finance the resettlement in Israel of a minimum of 45,000 Jews from tension-ridden North Africa.

Proceeds for the regular campaign will be used to meet the budgetary needs of UJA's constituent agencies -- the United Israel Appeal, Joint Distribution Committee and New York Association for New Americans. The UJA agencies must provide emigration, settlement, welfare and rehabilitation assistance in a score of countries, primarily in Israel and North Africa. At stake in both the Special Fund and regular campaigns are the lives of 480,000 men, women and children.

Originally, the Special Fund called for $25,000,000. The sum was fixed at an extraordinary meeting of representatives of American Jewish communities held in New York on November 18, 1955, as growing anxiety within the Jewish populations of Morocco and Tunisia brought increased pleas for resettlement in Israel. A month later, at the Annual National Conference of the UJA, it was recognized that the situation had worsened and that the Special Fund of $25,000,000 was inadequate. It was realized that Israel's people could not share in the costs of such immigration since they were diverting all their own resources to meet the threat to their survival as a free nation. The Conference delegates then called upon American Jews to accept the entire financial responsibility for this emergency immigration -- and to regard the $25,000,000 sum as only a "starting point" for the Special Fund. At the same time, the American Jewish community was asked to provide $105,283,435 through the regular campaign to sustain the wider programs of the UJA agencies.

Given American Jewry's faithful support of the Special Fund and the regular 1956 campaign, the UJA and its agencies will be in a position to implement this urgent seven-point program:

1) Resettle 45,000 North African Jewish refugees in Israel.

2) Help improve Israel's economy by providing for a steady expansion of its agricultural resources and productivity, this to entail establishment of 40 new farming communities under the ship-to-settlement program, particularly in the historic Lachish area; the irrigation of an additional 30,000 acres of land; the building of 9,000 housing units for Jewish families from North Africa, the provision of specialized agricultural aid to 180,000 settlers, and the consolidation of Israel's 415 post-Statehood settlements through continued financial and technical support.

3) Provide maintenance for 60,000 immigrants still sheltered in Israel's transition villages (maabaroth) and prepare permanent housing for 20,000 of these maabaroth dwellers.

4) Care for and educate 20,000 immigrant children in Israel.

5) Give rehabilitation, medical and institutional care to 27,000 immigrants in Israel made up of the sick, the aged and the handicapped, and give aid to religious and cultural programs benefitting 11,000 persons.

6) Provide food, clothing, shelter, educational aid, vocational training and medical assistance for 130,000 distressed, displaced and underprivileged men, women and children -- 100,000 in Moslem lands and 30,000 in Western Europe.

7) Meet adjustment needs of 5,000 Jewish refugees expected to arrive in New York during 1956 and assist 2,000 who came earlier and still require welfare services.

######

Pictured here is a document describing a special fund that was being raised to help resettle Jewish emigrants from around the world. The Reading Jewish Federation and Jewish community supported relocation of Jewish emigrants. This fund helped to resettle 45,000 North African Jewish refugees in Israel, provide maintenance for 60,000 immigrants still sheltered in Israel's villages, and educate 20,000 children in Israel. (Courtesy of JFR.)

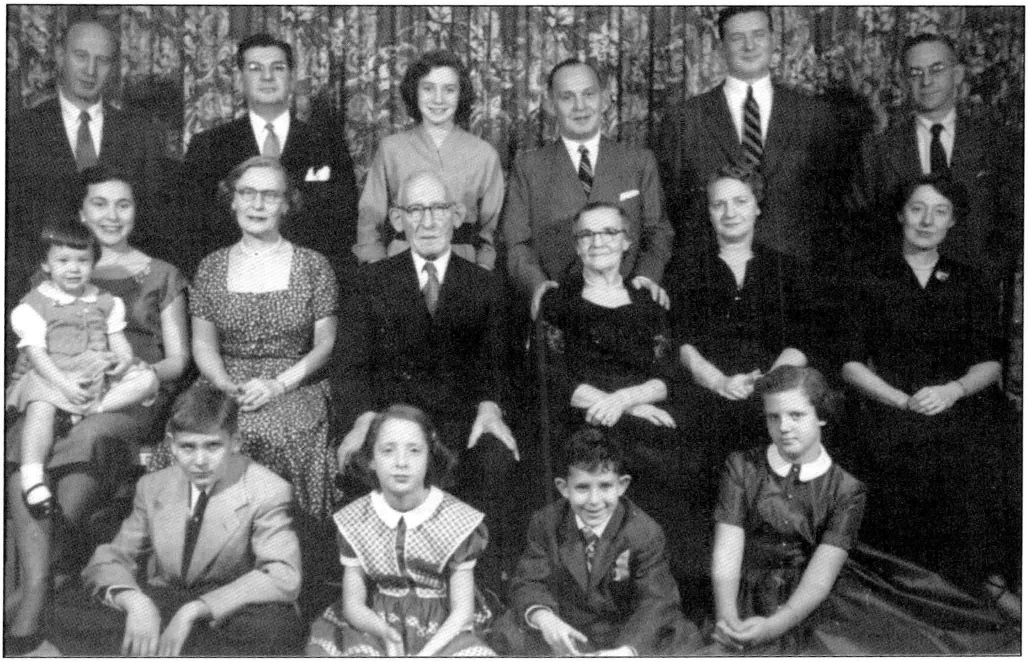

Anna and Isadore Oritsky are pictured with family on their 50th wedding anniversary in 1952. Family members include, from left to right, (first row) Michael Schiffman, Jill Skaist, Allen Rovner, and Sheila Rovner; (second row) Mimi Oritsky, Marcia Sarna Oritsky, Millicent Oritsky, Isadore Oritsky, Anna Oritsky, Pearl Oritsky Rovner, and Gladys Oritsky Skaist; (third row) Herb Oritsky, Phillip Schiffman, Sandy Rovner, Herman Oritsky, Jack Rovner, and Eli Skaist. (Courtesy of Jill Skaist.)

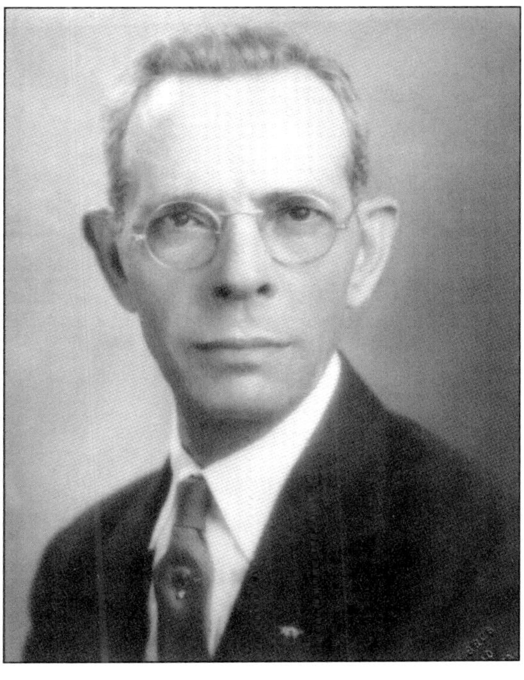

Max J. Skaist (1877–1932), a Zionist leader called "Father of the Jews in Reading," was on the national committee of the Zionist Organization of America (ZOA) and president of the Reading District ZOA. Known for his oratory skill, he was a founder of B'nai Zion and Kesher Zion Synagogue, the Hebrew school, and JCC. Born in Russia, he came to Reading in 1906 after studying law in South Africa. (Courtesy of Jill Skaist.)

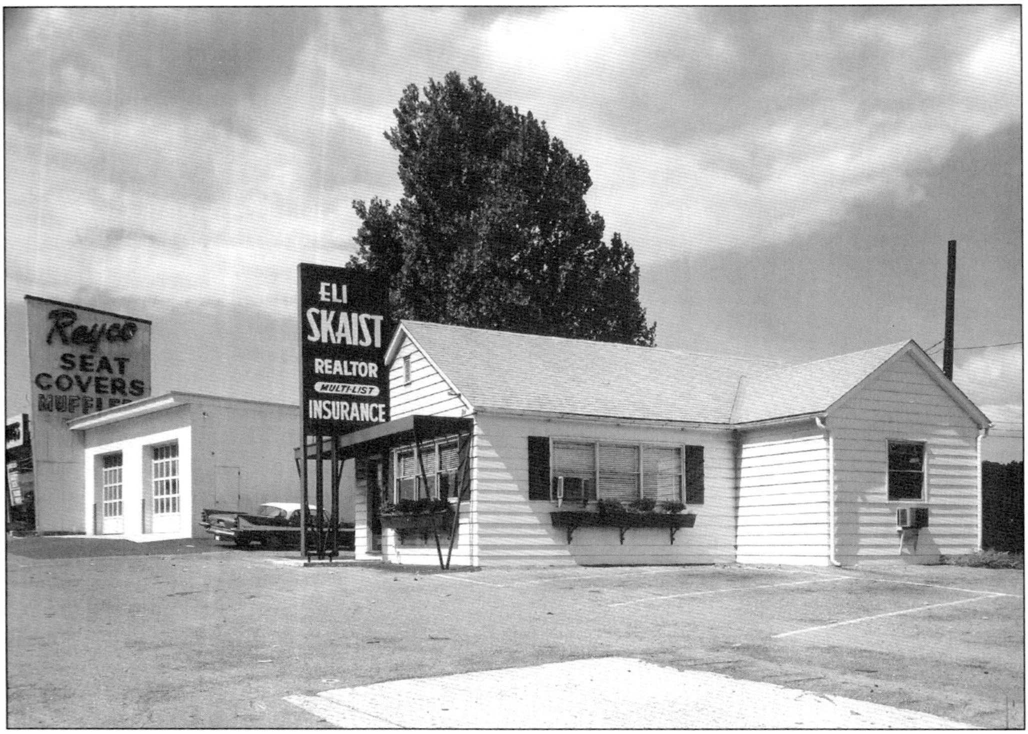

Eli Skaist, Max Skaist's son, moved his real estate and insurance office to 2811 Perkiomen Avenue in 1954. Eli was president of the Reading Board of Realtors in 1957; developed Glen Oley Farms in Exeter Township in 1959; and helped found Reading Multi-List in 1953. He was president of Reading District ZOA in 1947, held leadership roles for the United Jewish Campaign and United Jewish Appeal, and sat on many boards. He was one of Kesher Zion's first Hebrew school teachers. (Courtesy of Jill Skaist.)

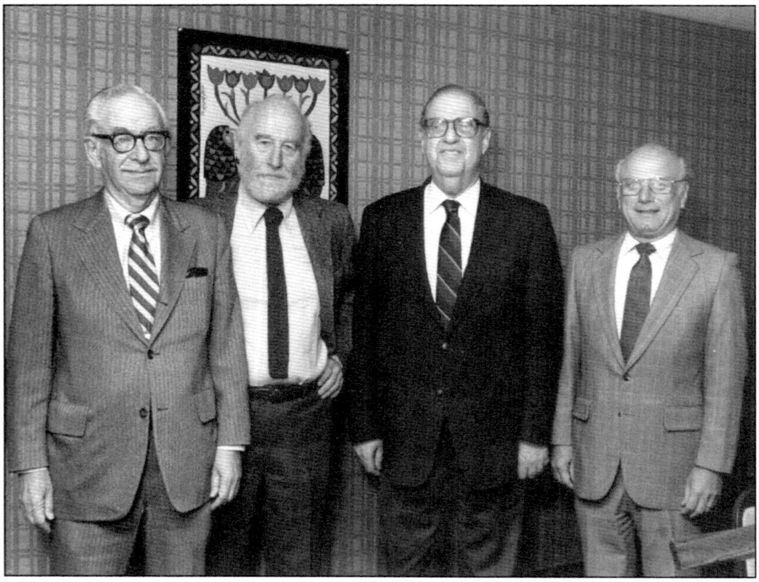

Members of the Reading Jewish community in 1981 are pictured with Abba Eban (second from right), Israeli statesman and diplomat. Eban was in Reading a week after Sadat's assassination to speak at the Leo Camp Memorial Lecture Series about the Middle East situation. From left to right are Eli Skaist, Herb Oritsky, Eban, and Ed Lakin. (Courtesy of Jill Skaist.)

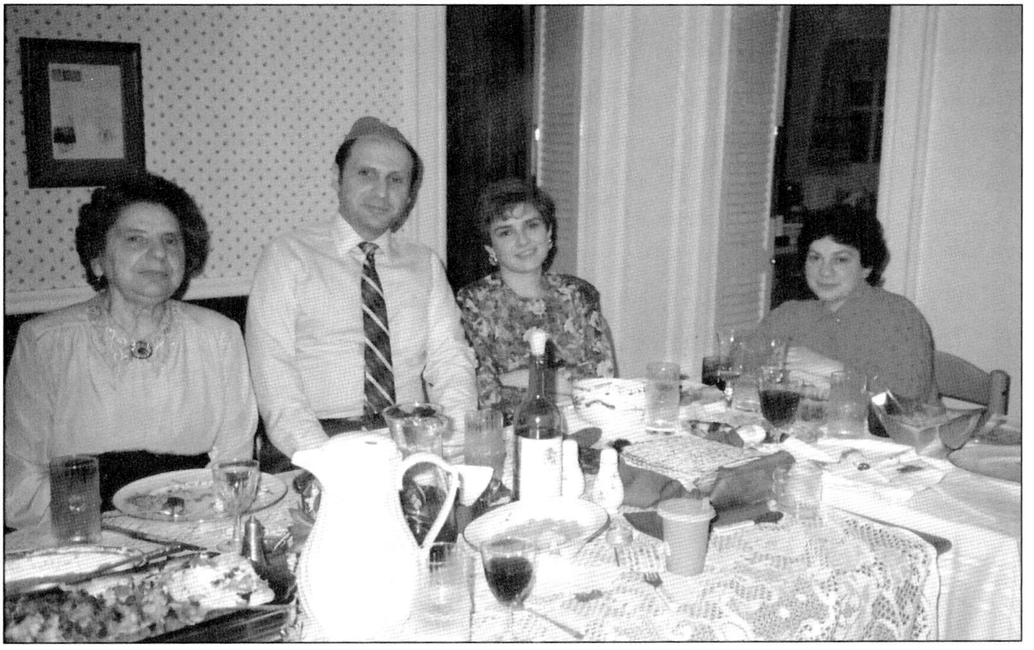

Eve and Mike Pardo conduct a Passover Seder in their home in 1991. They are hosting a recently immigrated Russian family, the Lindermans. Members of the Linderman family are, from left to right, Elena, Alex, and Ann. Eve Pardo is at far right. The Jewish Federation of Reading, Inc., sponsored Soviet Jewish families fleeing the Soviet Union. Eve and Mike Pardo have two children, Sarah and Daniel. (Courtesy of Michael Pardo.)

In November 1954, several women from Reading participated in the national convention for the Women's League of Conservative Judaism in Cleveland, Ohio. From left to right are (first row) Mildred Lyons and Gussie Ruttenberg; (second row) Gertrude Ruttenberg, Edna Kotzen, Ida Kotzen, and Sadie Wurman. (Courtesy of JFR.)

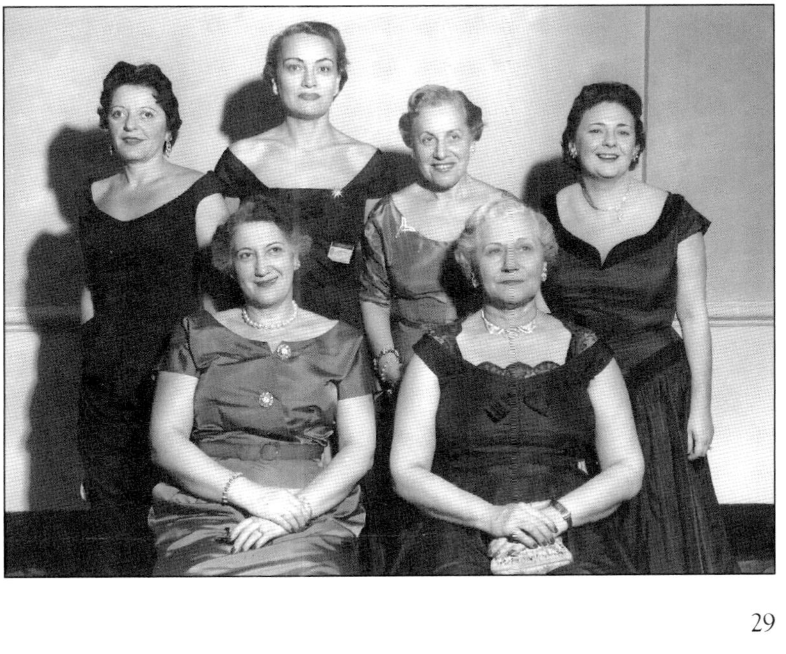

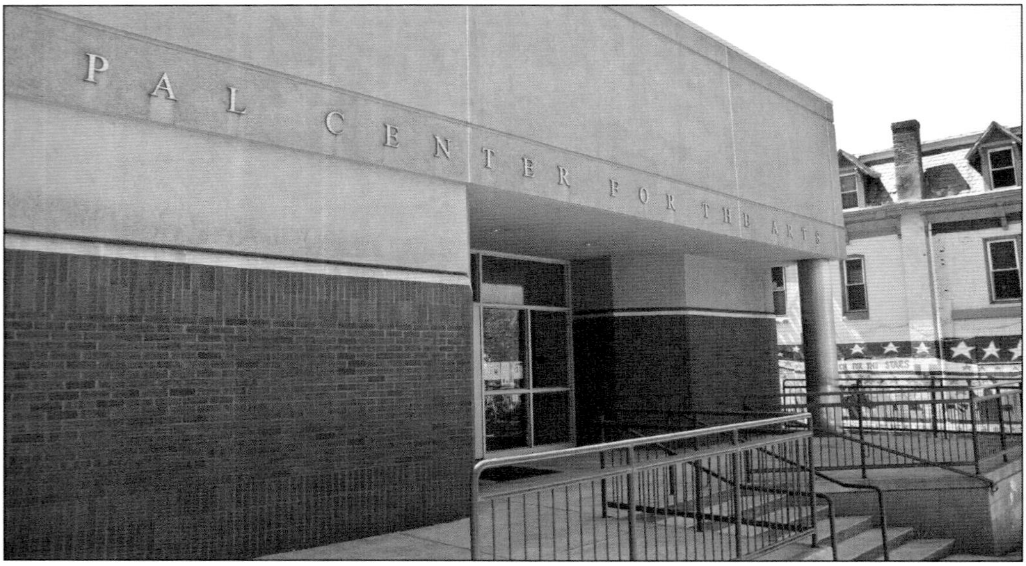

Pictured here is the Police Athletic League (PAL) Center for the Arts, which opened in 2000. The Police Athletic League of Reading and Berks County is now the Olivet Boys & Girls Club's PAL club. The clubs provide activities and opportunities for disadvantaged children in Reading and Berks. The PAL Center for the Arts has expanded the offerings into the world of creative expression. Children get involved in mural painting around the city, visual and performing arts, digital music, photography, cooking, art history, and other arts. As the image below demonstrates, local philanthropists Irvin and Lois Cohen donated a significant amount of money for the center. The Cohens' philanthropy is extensive. The Opportunity House Donor of the Year Award was presented to them on Monday, May 2, 2011. (Both photographs by Jeffrey Watts, courtesy of Jeffrey Watts.)

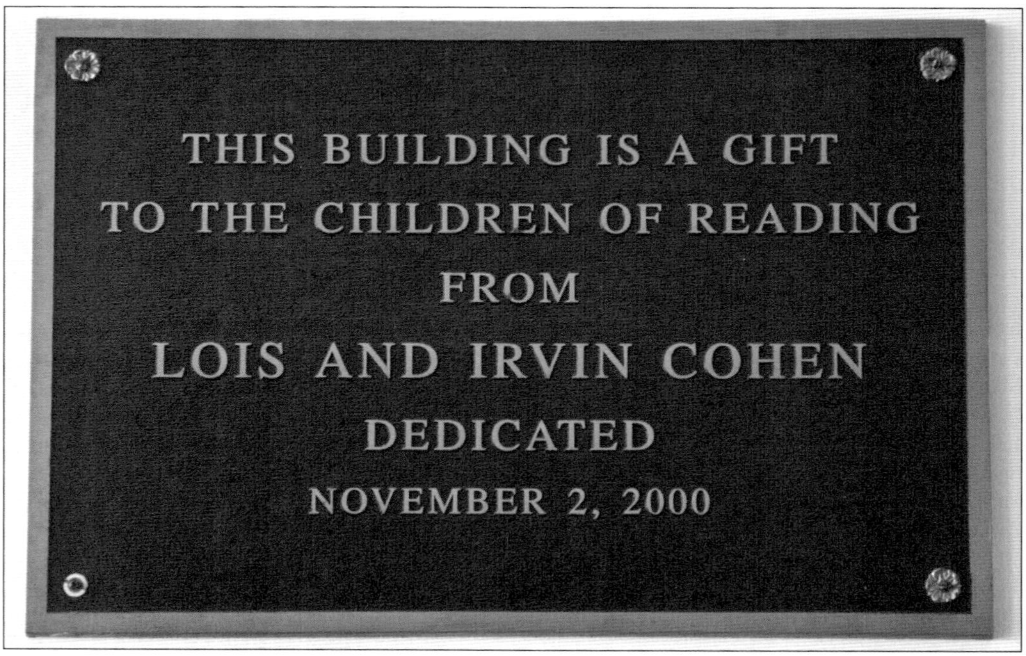

Albert Boscov is the chairman of Our City Reading, a 501(c) nonprofit corporation whose mission is to improve the quality of commercial and residential life in the city of Reading. On April 30, 2009, a bronze statue was unveiled and a city parking garage was renamed in his honor. At the time, the Our City Reading nonprofit development group had refurbished more than 300 rundown city homes for first-time home buyers. In his hand is the traditional Flair pen he's known to always carry. Pictured below is the Boscov-Lakin Information Commons at the Thun Library at Penn State Berks, a college of the Pennsylvania State University. The addition to the library is named in honor of Shirley P. Boscov Holzman and Reba Boscov Lakin. Among the features are electronic classrooms, a multimedia studio, an instructional design laboratory, and a cyber café. (Both photographs by Jeffrey Watts; courtesy of Jeffrey Watts.)

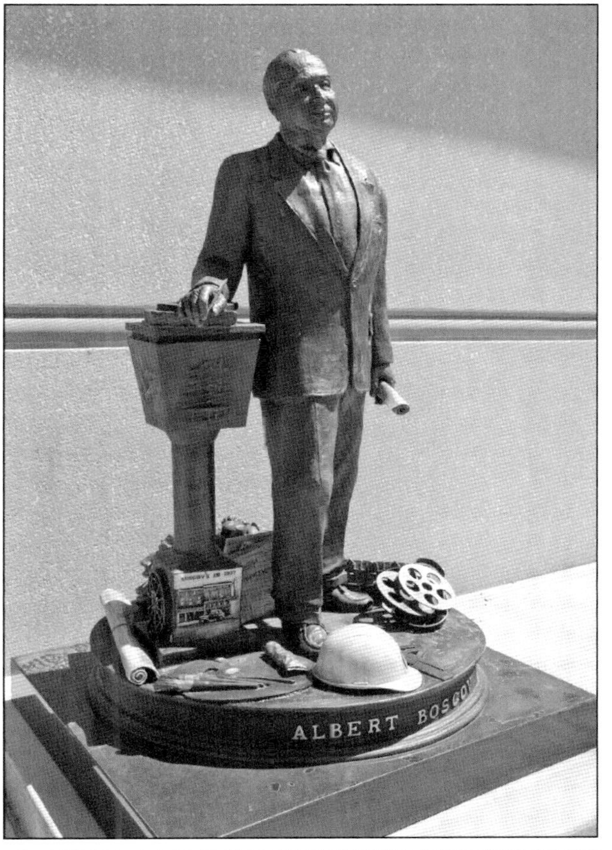

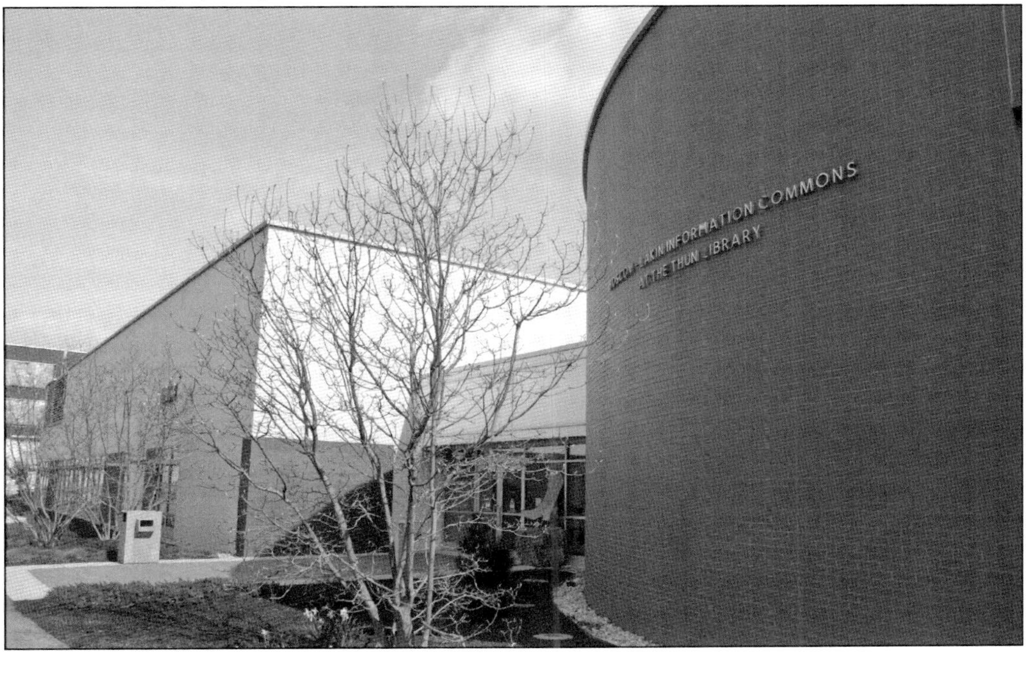

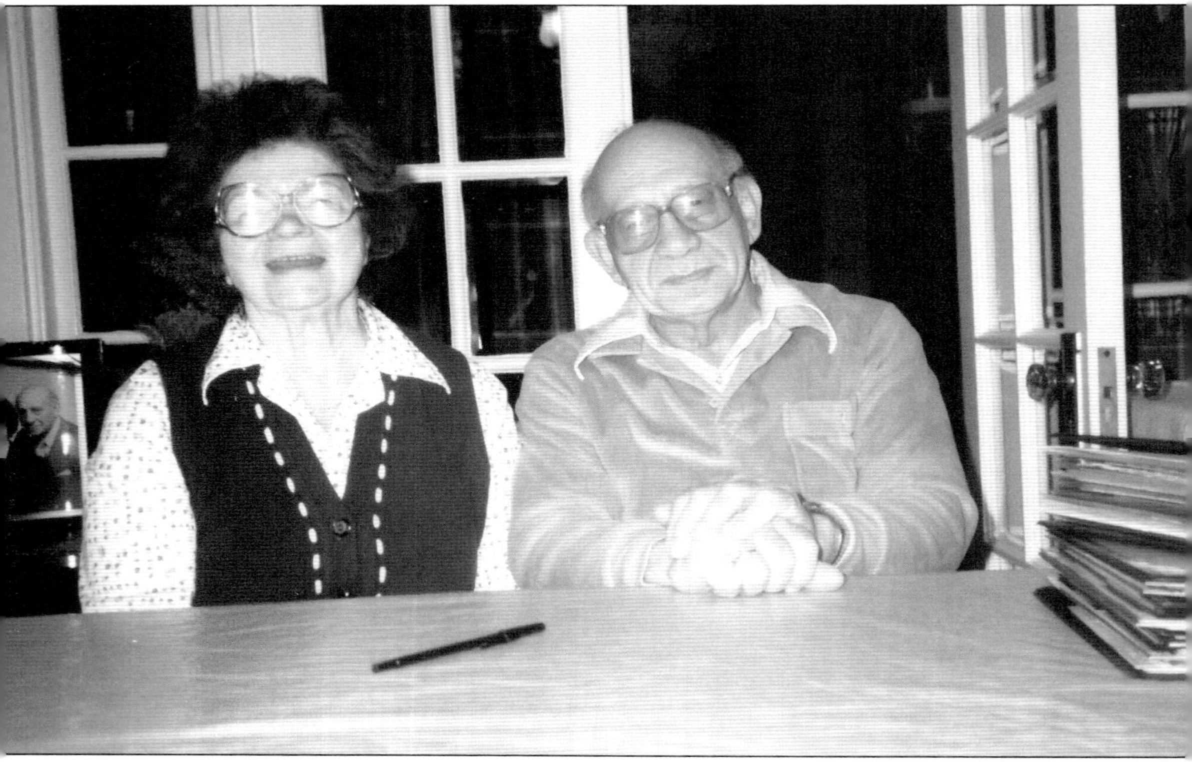

Twenty-six-year-old Hilde Flehinger came to the United States in 1939. Her father had a cousin in Baltimore, a man that he didn't even know existed, but with whom he shared the same last name. This cousin helped Hilde escape Nazi Germany. She traveled by herself and struggled through the Depression. Her sister arrived in America, and Hilde helped pay for her sister to complete nursing school. Hilde married Herman Bodenheimer in 1941 and had one son. On her wedding day, Hilde Bodenheimer got the news that her parents' bodies were found in a concentration camp in Germany. After her voyage to America, her parents were taken by Nazi soldiers. Her mother died in the gas chambers, and her father worked himself to death in the camps. Bodenheimer opened the Fashion and Sewing Studio in Reading, teaching young girls the knowledge she found and refined using all her experiences in America. Bodenheimer's videotaped testimony is archived in the Albright College Holocaust Resource Center. (Courtesy of Albright College Holocaust Resource Center.)

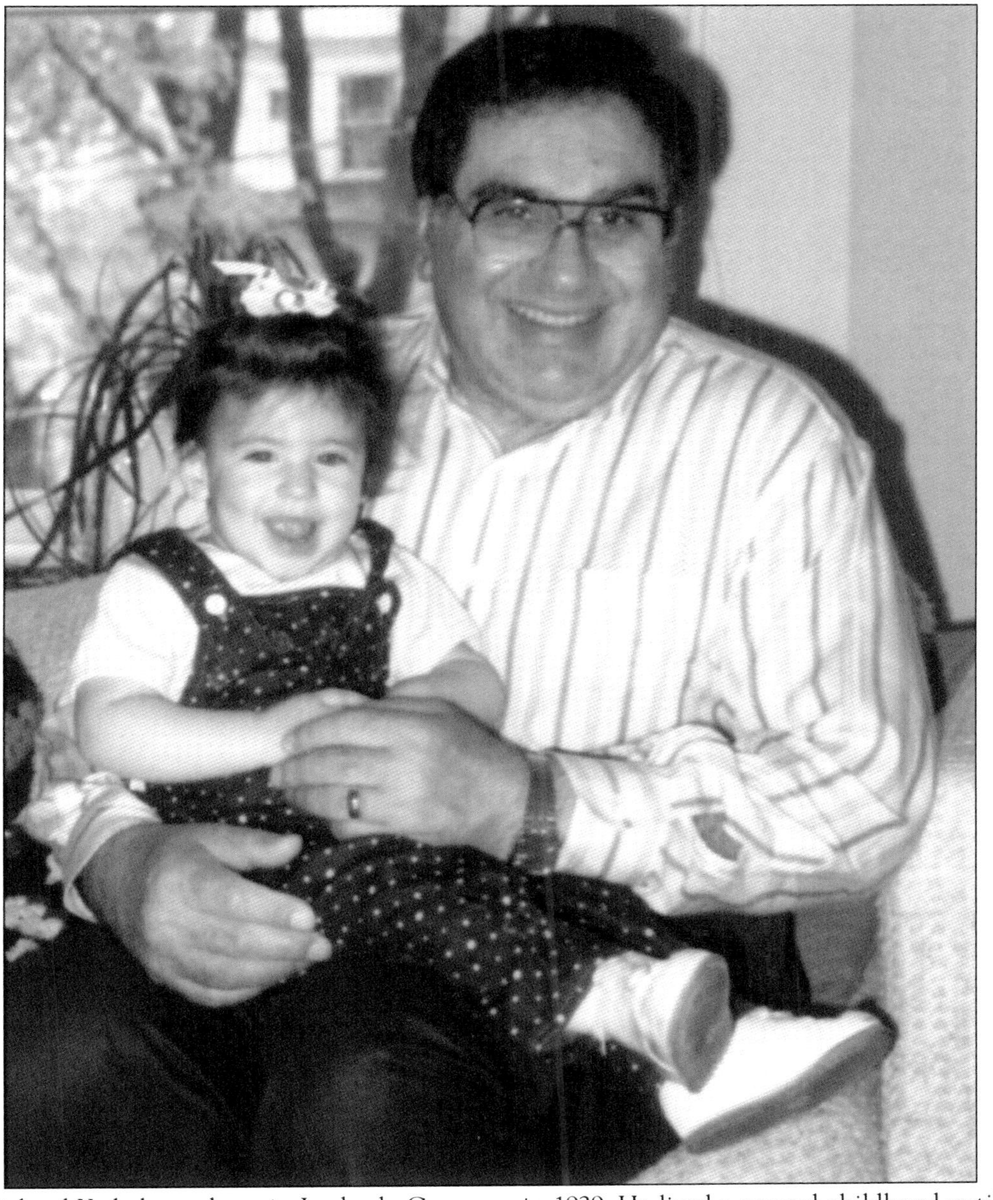

Richard Yashek was born in Luebeck, Germany, in 1929. He lived a normal childhood until Hitler's rise to power. In 1941, Yashek was deported the Riga Ghetto in Latvia and then to the small camp of Jungfernhof in Latvia, along with his parents and younger brother, Jochen. The family was separated in March 1942. Yashek and his father remained together during subsequent deportations to locations such as Kaiserwald (near Riga). Yashek was separated from his father in October 1944. After being sent to Stuthoff, Yashek was sent on a death march and eventually ended up in Burgrabben. He was liberated there in 1945. Yashek survived the Holocaust but never again saw his mother, father, or brother. He served in the US Army from 1951 to 1953. Yashek was also an executive vice president and co-owner of the J.C. Ehrlich Co., Inc., in Reading. He died in 2005 and is survived by his wife, Rosalye, and their daughters, Kim and Linda. (Courtesy of Albright College Holocaust Resource Center.)

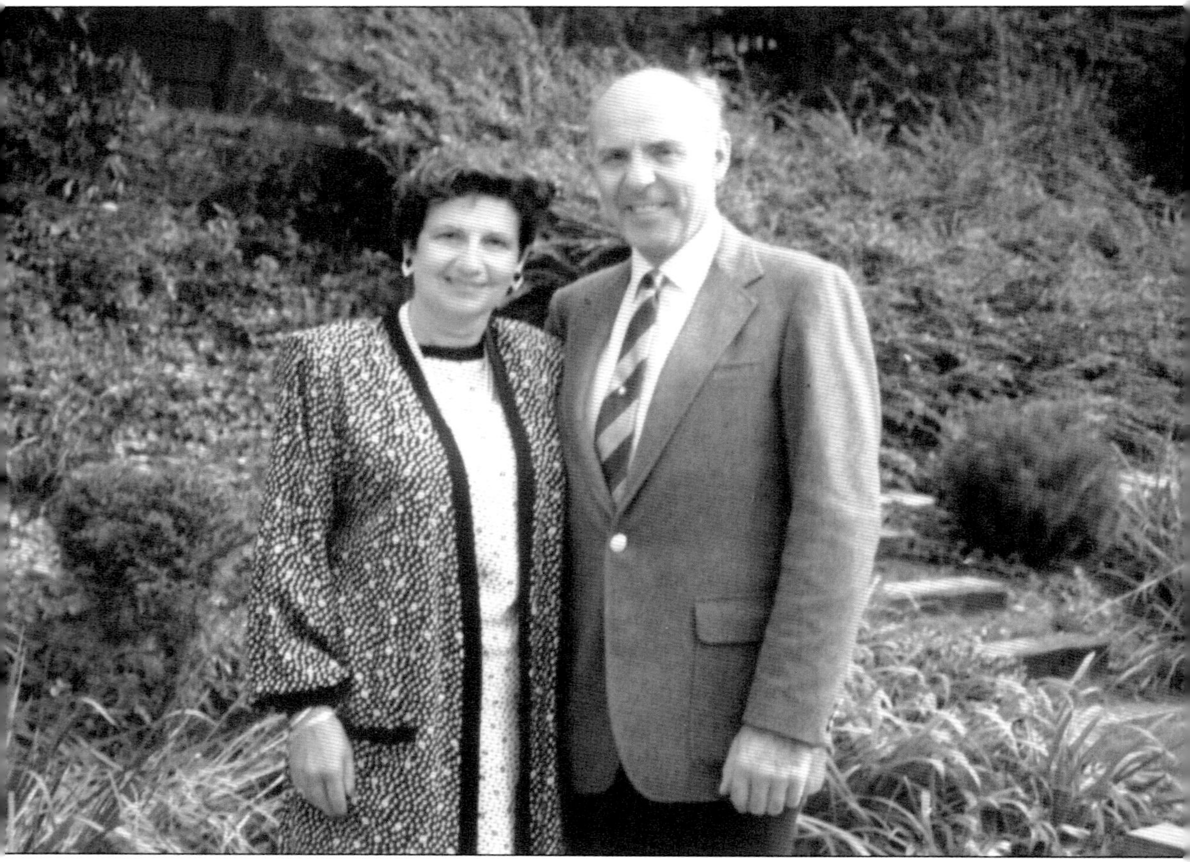

Sid and Esther Bratt are both Holocaust survivors. Sidney Bratt, born on August 28, 1928, in Guttstadt, Germany, to Alfred and Else Bratt, survived by escaping to England on the Kindertransport on June 30, 1939, when his father was already in a concentration camp. Esther Izraelit Bratt, born on March 3, 1930, in Wilno, Poland, to Samuel and Marcia Izraelit (Elson), lived in a Jewish ghetto from 1941 until 1943, when she was moved to a concentration camp with her parents. They remained there until July 1944, when they were liberated by the Russian Army. (Courtesy of Albright College Holocaust Resource Center.)

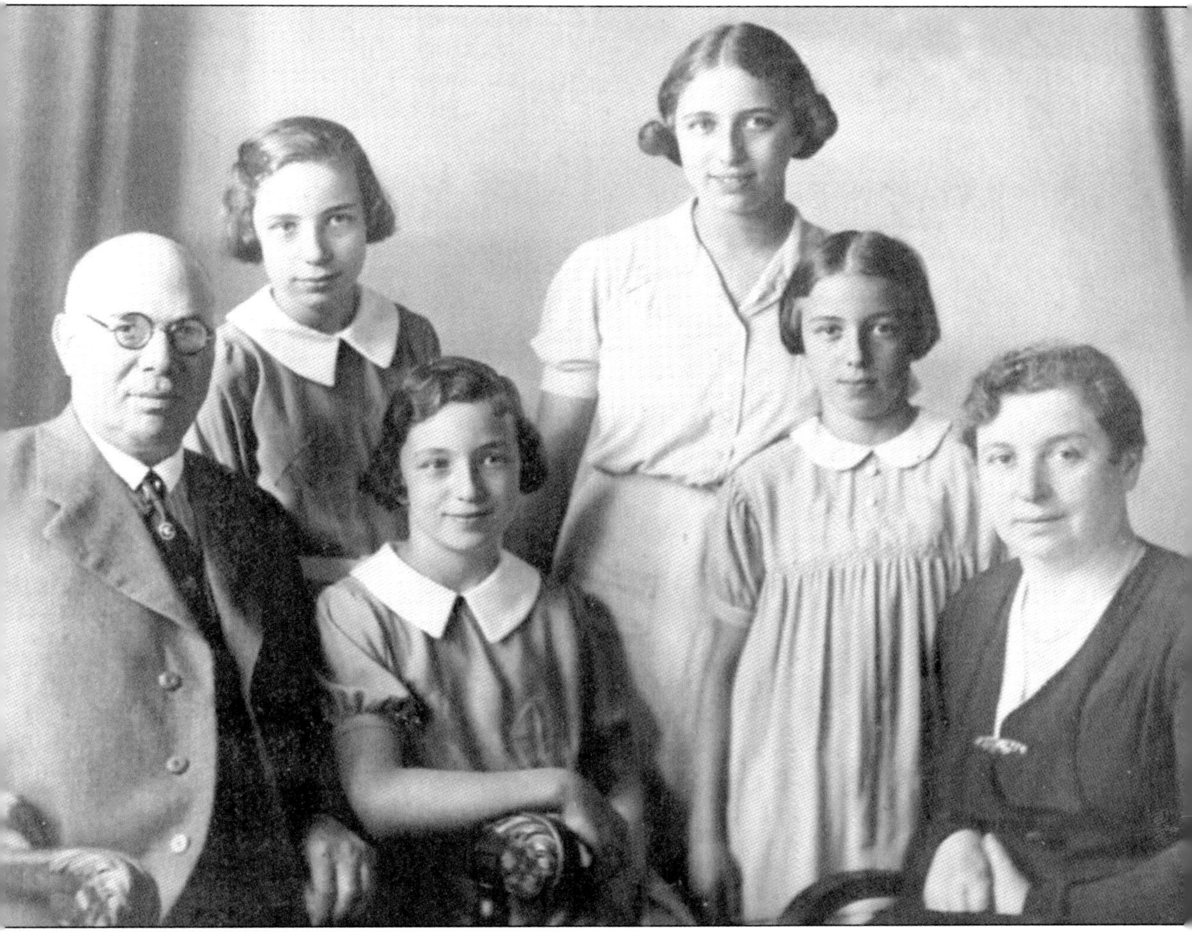

Pictured here from left to right are Karl; Hildegard, or "Hilde;" Ruth; Edith; Ilse; and Selma Simon in Germany around 1935. On December 2, 1938, Hilde and Ruth, 12 and 13 years old respectively, left their family on the first Kindertransport to England. They boarded a train from Hamburg to Rotterdam, where a ship that took them across the English Channel. They were placed in a summer camp until they were relocated. The children were assigned to cabins with no heat or warm water. They were introduced to porridge. Ten days later, they went to an orthodox boardinghouse for young girls being set up in Harrogate. Ruth and Hilde sailed on a Canadian Red Cross ship on December 28, 1944. There was a severe blizzard when the convoy of ships landed in Halifax, Nova Scotia. German U-boats had sunk two of the ships during the voyage. Hilde and Ruth had no warm clothes, but several days later, they managed to get on a train to New York. Hilde later settled in Berks County. (Courtesy of Jeff Gernsheimer.)

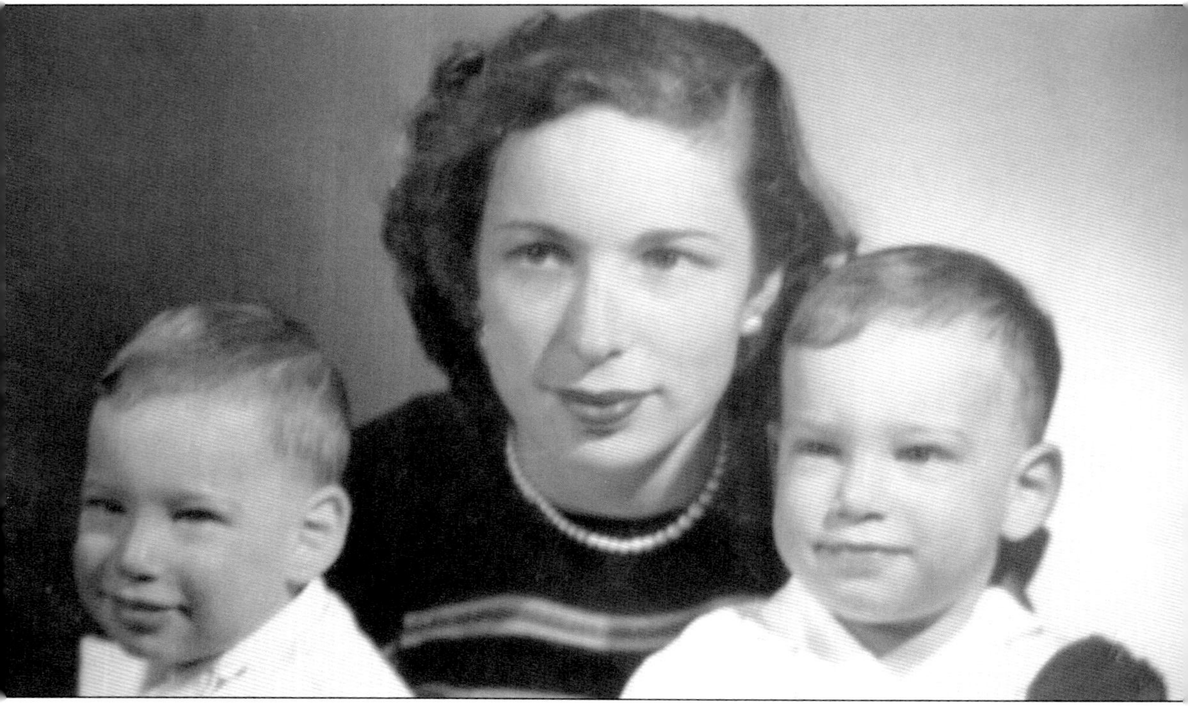

Solly and Hilde Gernsheimer were married on March 31, 1946. Twins Jeff (left) and Jack Gernsheimer (right), pictured here, were born in December 1946, and their sister, Sharon Gernsheimer, who lives in New Jersey, was born in August 1951. Solly Gernsheimer died in 1987. Hilde's sister, Edith, died in Florida in 2005. Hilde's parents, Karl and Selma Simon, and sister, Ilse Simon, after being turned away from Cuba and the United States on the SS *St. Louis*, went to Holland. After the Nazi invasion, they were sent to the Westerbork labor camp and then to Sobibor Concentration Camp in Poland, where they were murdered in a gas chamber on May 21, 1943. Ilse was 15 years old. In 2010, Hilde, Jack, Jeff, and Sharon Gernsheimer, as well as Sharon's daughters, Carly and Julia Levine, visited Cloppenburg, Germany, Hilde's childhood home, to dedicate the stumble stones placed on the site where her house had been. (Courtesy of Jeff Gernsheimer.)

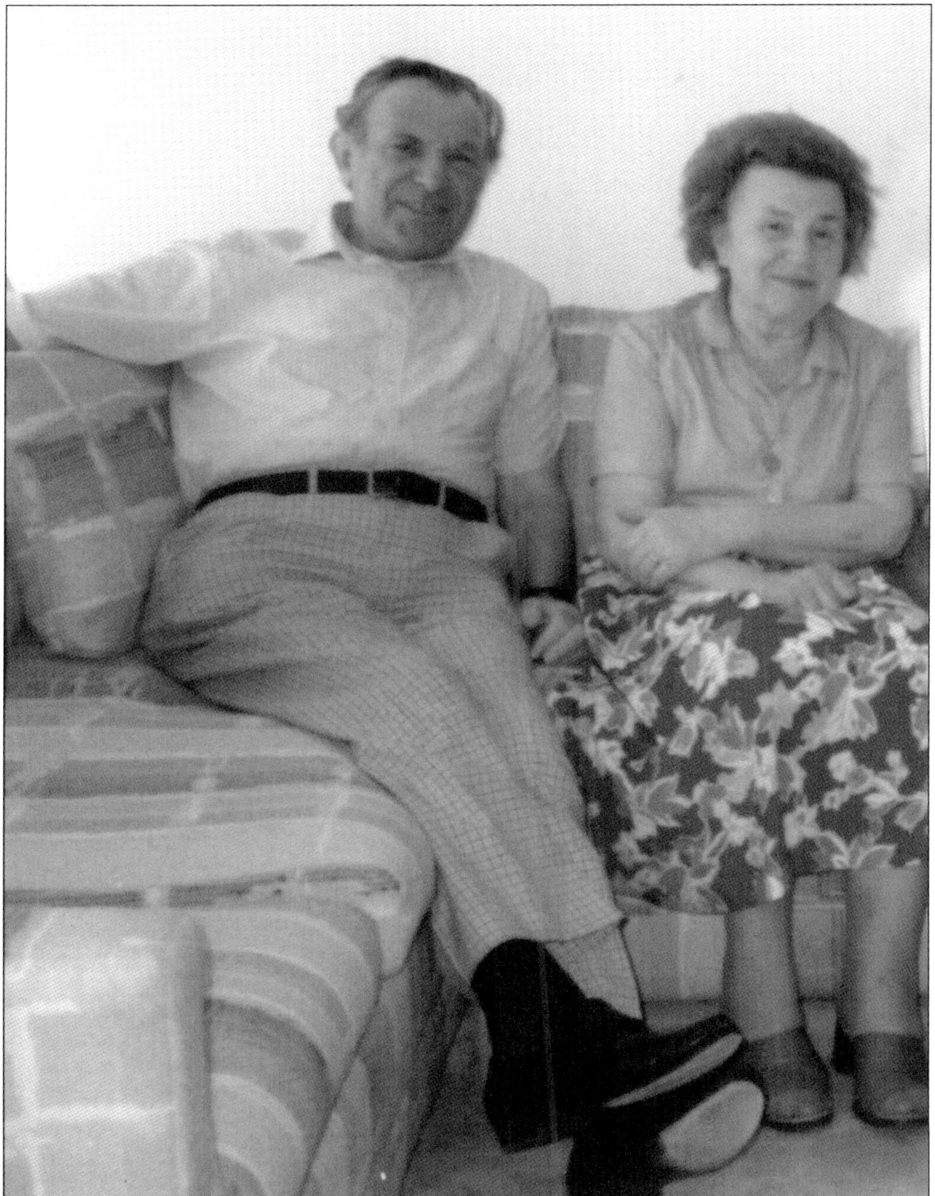

Maurice and Celia (Schwartz) Kornblit were Holocaust survivors who relocated to Reading after World War II. Celia Kornblit was the daughter of Moshe and Esther (Mandel) Schwartz. The Kornblits met as teenagers at Auschwitz. Celia Kornblit was originally from Czechoslovakia and was taken to Auschwitz with her sisters, Mimi and Ruza. Maurice Kornblit worked in the crematoria at Auschwitz. They owned the Community Kosher Meat Market in Reading and were members of Shomrei Habrith Synagogue. The Kornblits had three children: Susan (Kornblit) Strom; Eva (Kornblit) Brown; and Arthur Kornblit, a doctor. Celia died at the age of 87 of natural causes in 2007; Maurice passed away in 1994 in a car accident. Celia Kornblit's sisters, Mimi (Schwartz) Hen and Ruza (Schwartz) Pretter, relocated to Israel, and Celia lived with Ruza at the time of her death. (Courtesy of Albright College Holocaust Resource Center.)

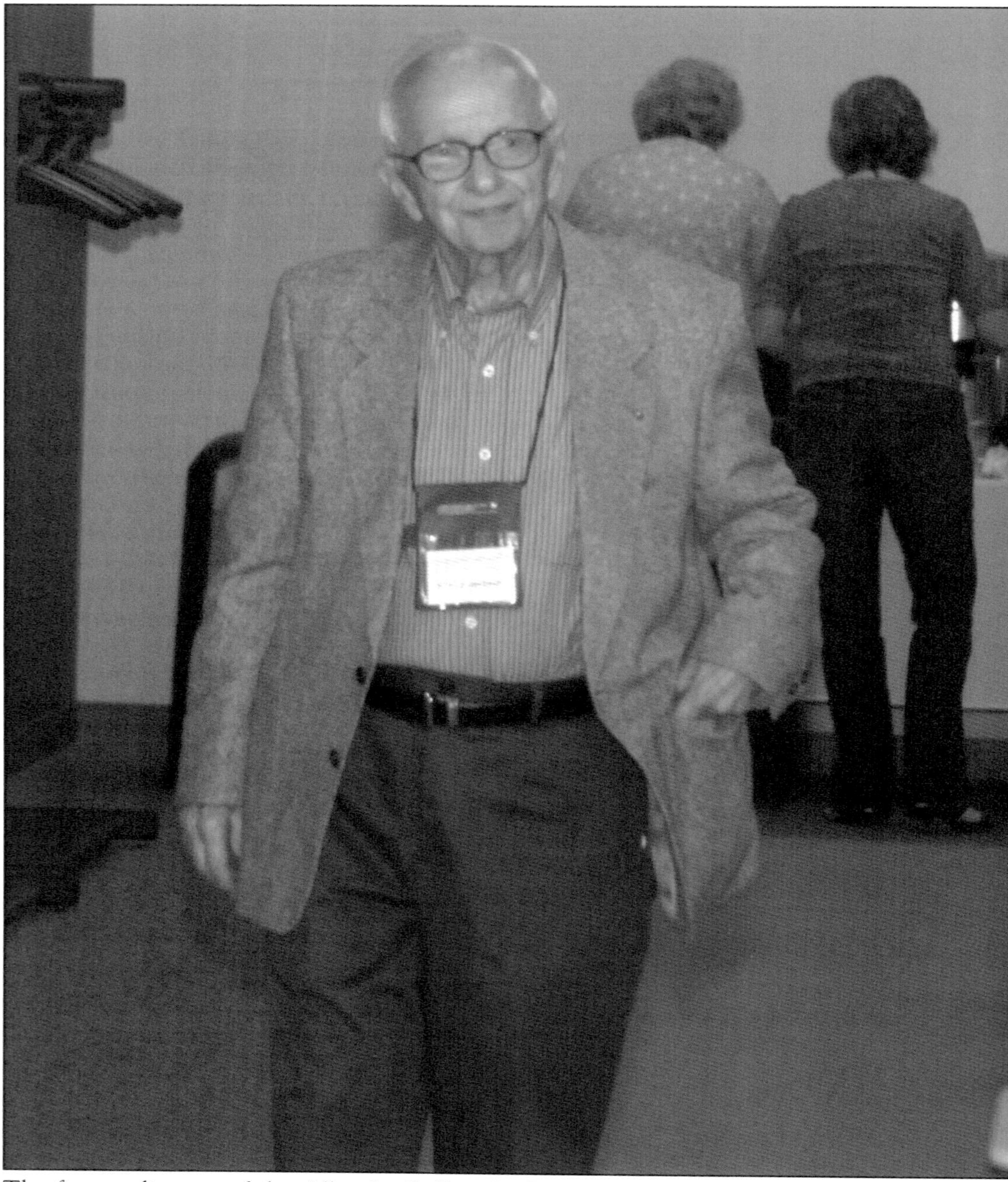

The former director of the Albright College Holocaust Library and Resource Center, Daniel Tannenbaum was dedicated to Holocaust education. During his tenure as the executive director of the Jewish Federation of Reading, Tannenbaum was instrumental in helping to found the center. He would later assist with the creation of a Holocaust studies program at Albright and the many programs that support it, including the annual Richard J. Yashek lecture. Tannenbaum arrived in Reading after a long career serving Jewish federations and community centers throughout the United States. A former social worker with an MA in social work from the Ohio State University, Tannenbaum served in the Navy in the Pacific theater during World War II. He was married to Shoshana Harrision for over 50 years, and they had two children, Marc and Miriam. Tannenbaum died in December 2010, leaving behind an important legacy for the Holocaust education community. (Photograph by Matthew Goss, courtesy of Matthew Goss.)

Two

Synagogues and Religious Activities

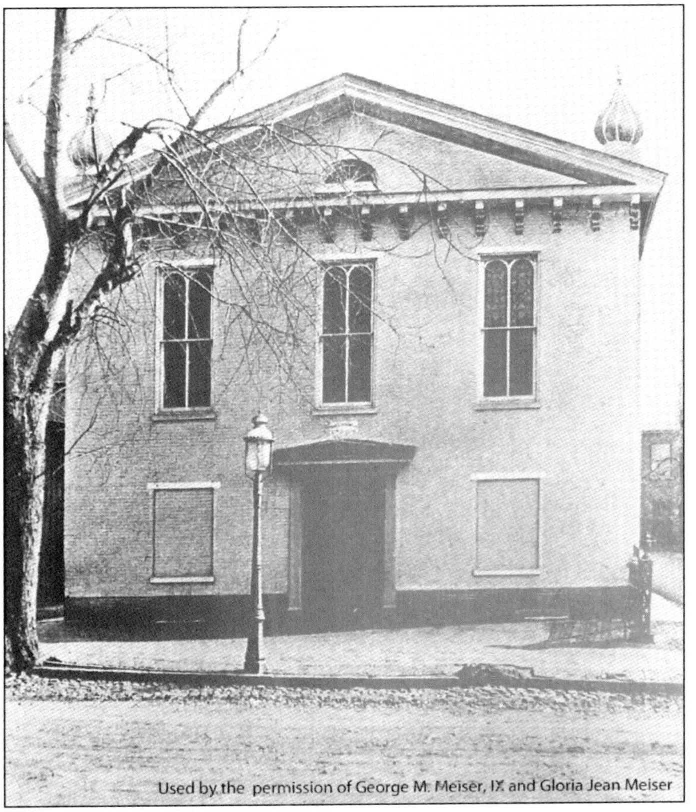

The first synagogue in this area, founded in May 1864 by a small number of German Jews (16 families), was Reform Congregation Oheb Sholom. The congregants has worshipped in different buildings over the years. In July 1885, the congregation bought the building pictured here at 525 Chestnut Street in Reading. This synagogue was used by Oheb Sholom from 1885 to 1919. (Courtesy of George M. Meiser IX and Gloria Jean Meiser.)

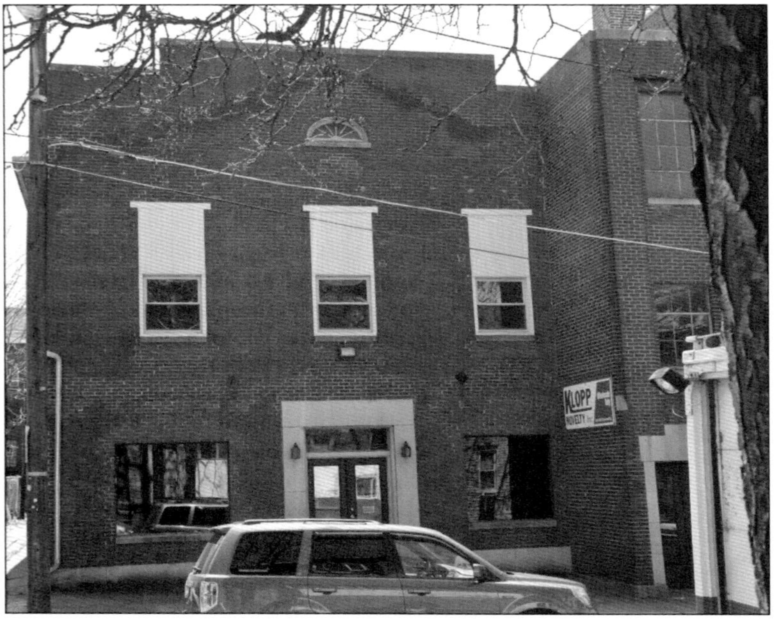

Pictured here in 2011 is the former Oheb Sholom building at 525 Chestnut Street, built in 1884. The building has since been refaced and attached to a neighboring warehouse for Klopp Novelty of Reading. (Photograph by Jeffrey Watts, courtesy of Jeffrey Watts.)

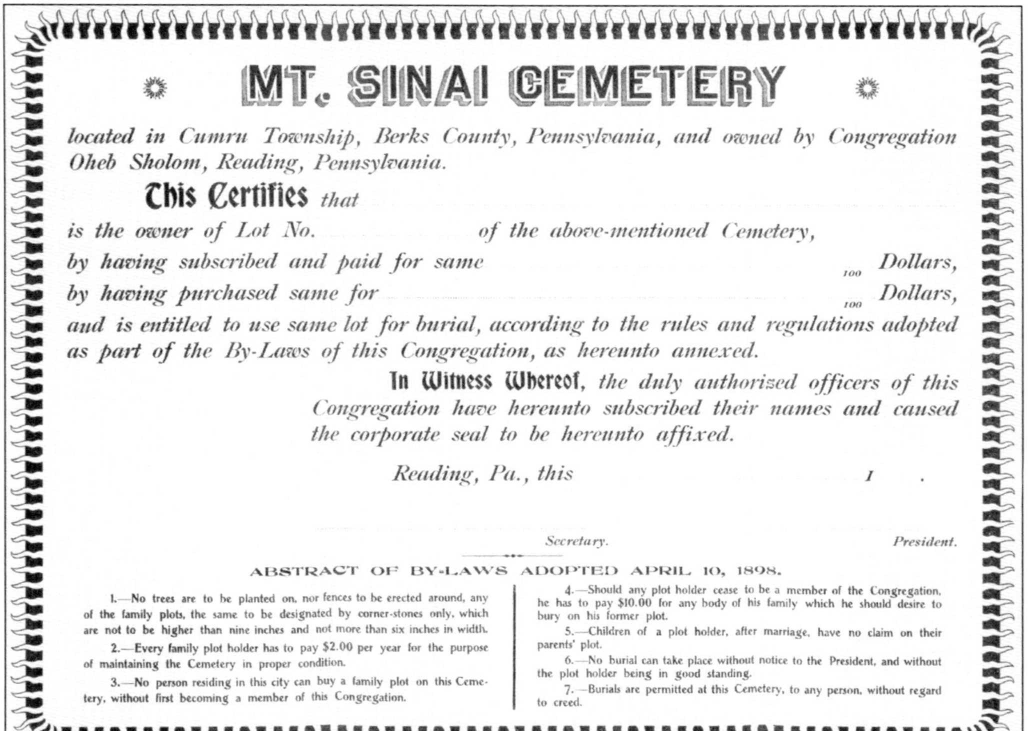

MT. SINAI CEMETERY

located in Cumru Township, Berks County, Pennsylvania, and owned by Congregation Oheb Sholom, Reading, Pennsylvania.

This Certifies *that*

is the owner of Lot No. of the above-mentioned Cemetery,

by having subscribed and paid for same $\frac{\ }{100}$ *Dollars,*

by having purchased same for $\frac{\ }{100}$ *Dollars,*

and is entitled to use same lot for burial, according to the rules and regulations adopted as part of the By-Laws of this Congregation, as hereunto annexed.

In Witness Whereof, *the duly authorized officers of this Congregation have hereunto subscribed their names and caused the corporate seal to be hereunto affixed.*

Reading, Pa., this 1 .

Secretary. *President.*

ABSTRACT OF BY-LAWS ADOPTED APRIL 10, 1898.

1.—No trees are to be planted on, nor fences to be erected around, any of the family plots, the same to be designated by corner-stones only, which are not to be higher than nine inches and not more than six inches in width.

2.—Every family plot holder has to pay $2.00 per year for the purpose of maintaining the Cemetery in proper condition.

3.—No person residing in this city can buy a family plot on this Cemetery, without first becoming a member of this Congregation.

4.—Should any plot holder cease to be a member of the Congregation, he has to pay $10.00 for any body of his family which he should desire to bury on his former plot.

5.—Children of a plot holder, after marriage, have no claim on their parents' plot.

6.—No burial can take place without notice to the President, and without the plot holder being in good standing.

7.—Burials are permitted at this Cemetery, to any person, without regard to creed.

This is a sample deed from the first year of the Mount Sinai Cemetery, which was founded in 1898. Mount Sinai Cemetery is located in Shillington, Cumru Township, along New Holland Avenue. The cemetery, owned and operated by Reform Congregation Oheb Sholom, was the first official Jewish cemetery in Reading, Pennsylvania. (Courtesy of RCOS.)

In 1919, after Reform Congregation Oheb Sholom had grown to more than 40 families, the congregation decided to build a new synagogue. Pictured at right is Sigmund S. Schweriner speaking at the 1921 cornerstone dedication of the new Oheb Sholom synagogue on Perkiomen Avenue at the top of Chestnut Street. The photograph below features Herman Hammel at the same dedication, and behind him is Leo Sondheim. A *Reading Eagle* reporter described the new building as "iconic architecture," since it was constructed entirely of white stone. The new temple was designed by architect Edward Z. Scholl. Henry Loeb, the oldest member of the congregation at 82 years old, removed the first shovelful of earth at the ground-breaking. Loeb helped to organize the congregation 55 years earlier. (Both, courtesy of RCOS.)

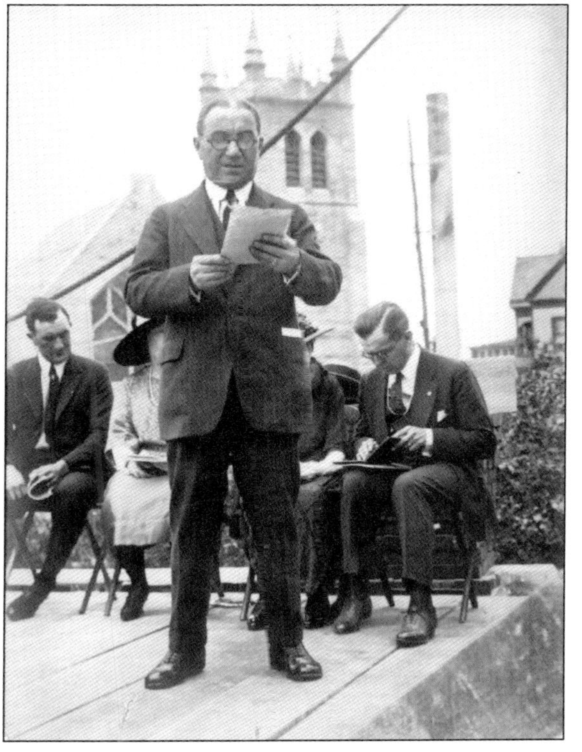

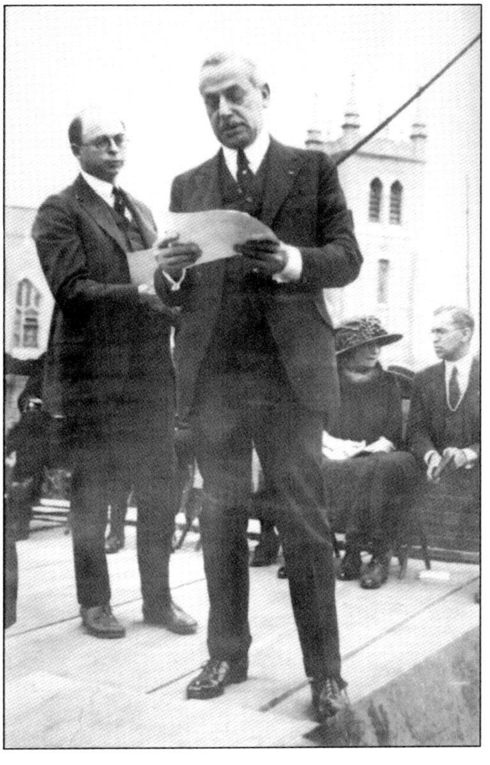

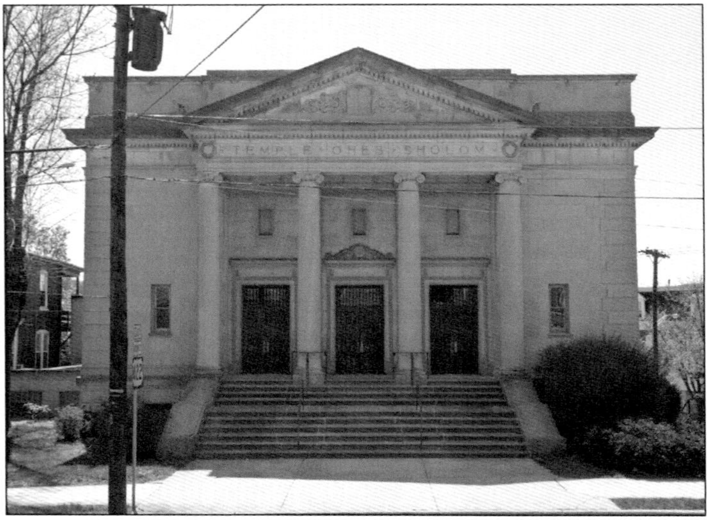

Pictured here is a 2011 photograph of the former Reform Congregation Oheb Sholom on Perkiomen Avenue. This building was dedicated by Stephen S. Wise in 1923. Today, the building is home to one of the Olivet Boys and Girls Club locations in Reading. (Photograph by Jeffrey Watts, courtesy of Jeffrey Watts.)

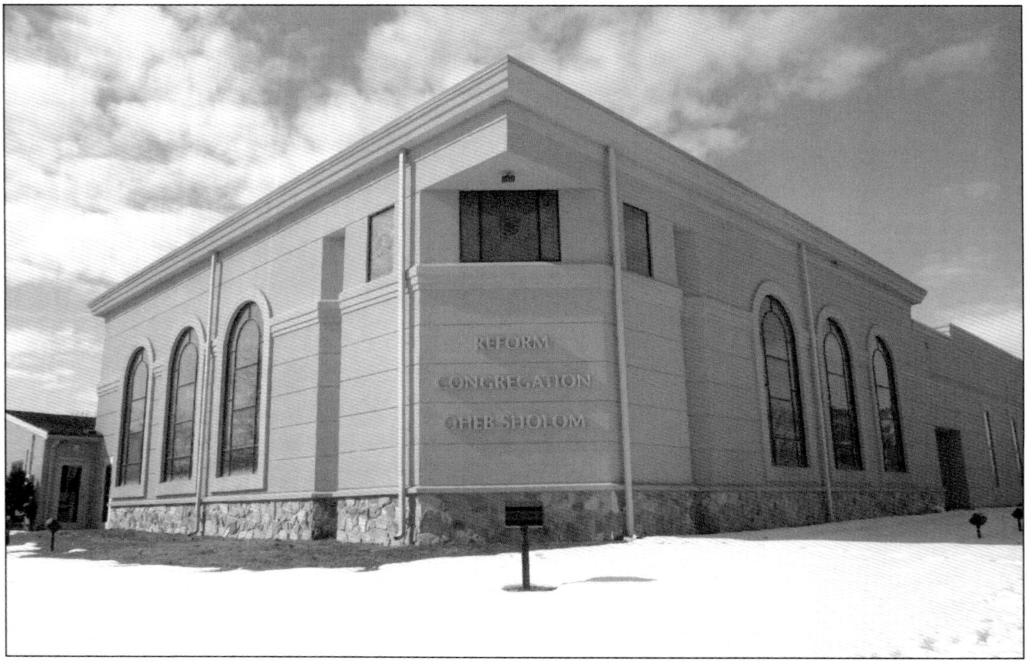

In 1983, Reform Congregation Oheb Sholom had its peak membership of 320 families. Current membership is approximately 260 families and is on the rise. The temple supports several affiliate clubs, the sisterhood, and the brotherhood. The temple has had 40 presidents; the first female president was Barbara G. Stein from 1987 to 1990. Rabbi Brian I. Michelson is a graduate of Franklin & Marshall College in Lancaster, Pennsylvania. He has led the congregation since 1998. The mission statement reads as follows: "The purpose of the Congregation shall be to promote Reform Judaism in all aspects of life, by means of public and private worship, by proper instruction in the religious school and from the pulpit, and by such other means and methods as may be appropriate, and to advance the cause of liberal Judaism, as generally interpreted by the Central Conference of American Rabbis and the Union of American Hebrew Congregations." (Photograph by Jeffrey Watts, courtesy of Jeffrey Watts.)

In the photograph at right, taken on May 15, 1999, a group of children from Reform Congregation Oheb Sholom participate in the ground-breaking of the new Oheb Sholom in Wyomissing Hills, pictured on the previous page. Although construction had already begun, the cold winter postponed the ground-breaking until the spring. Pictured below are the ground-breaking tools for Reform Congregation Oheb Sholom's second location on Perkiomen Avenue, dedicated in 1923 by Rabbi Stephen S. Wise. The tools were used again in 1999 for Oheb Sholom's new location. This reuse of tools represents the importance of continuity throughout the synagogue's relocations, while a new rabbi and cantor show change in prayer leaders and congregants. (Right, courtesy of RCOS; below, photograph by Jeffrey Watts, courtesy of Jeffrey Watts.)

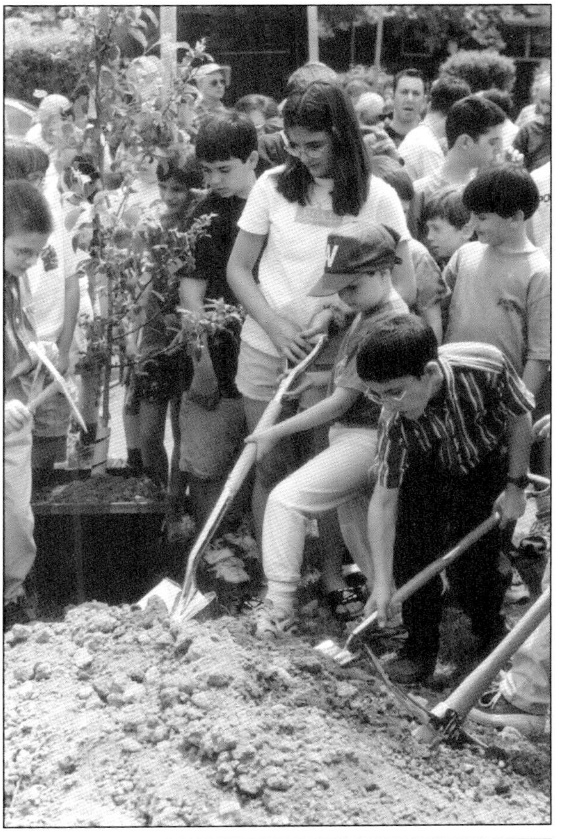

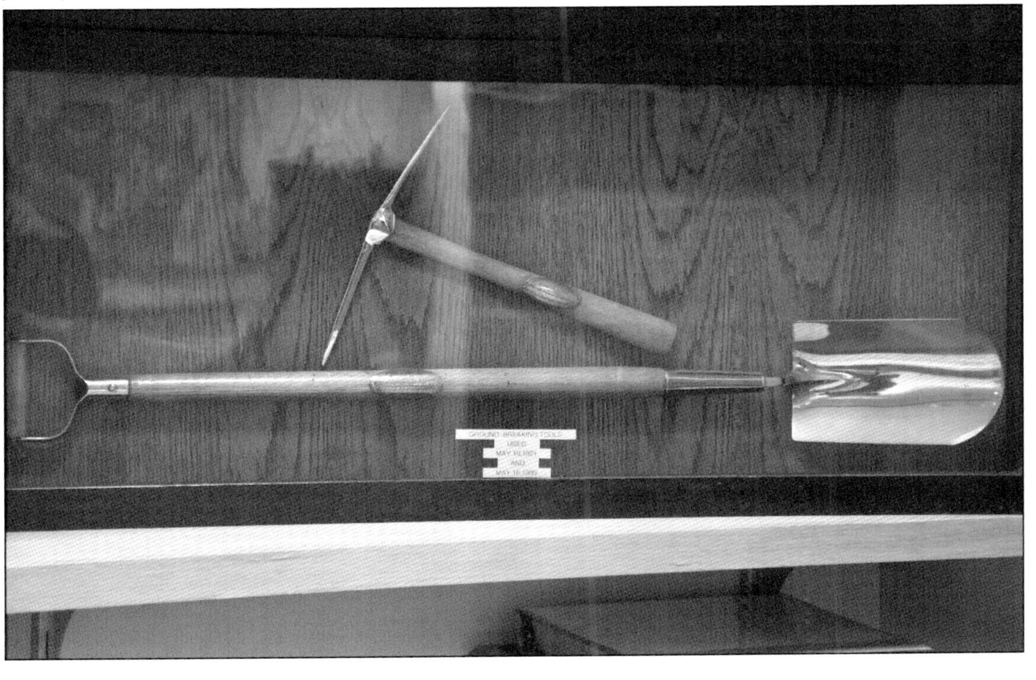

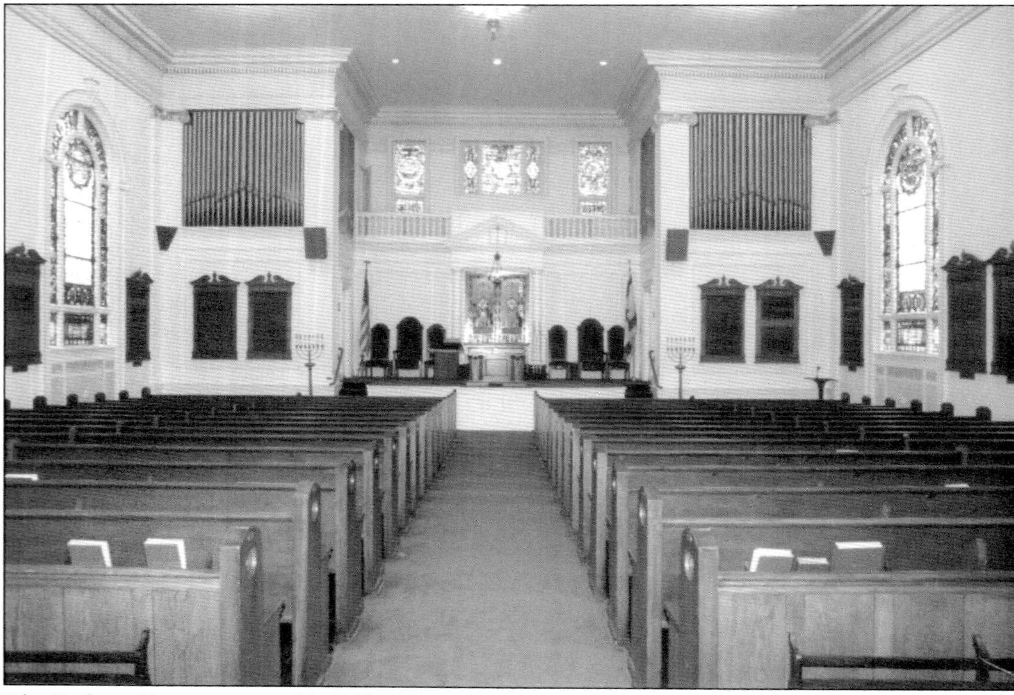

The Reform Congregation Oheb Sholom in Wyomissing Hills contains many important pieces of the synagogue's former location on Perkiomen Avenue in Reading. Pictured above is the bimah from the Perkiomen Avenue synagogue. The bimah of the new Oheb Sholom is a reconstruction of this one and closely resembles it. However, as pictured below, the stained-glass windows were moved piece by piece to the new building and reconstructed in 1999. In this picture taken on September 7, 1999, the stained-glass windows are being installed. Again, it was important for congregant members to hold on to their history throughout the synagogue's relocations. (Both, courtesy of RCOS.)

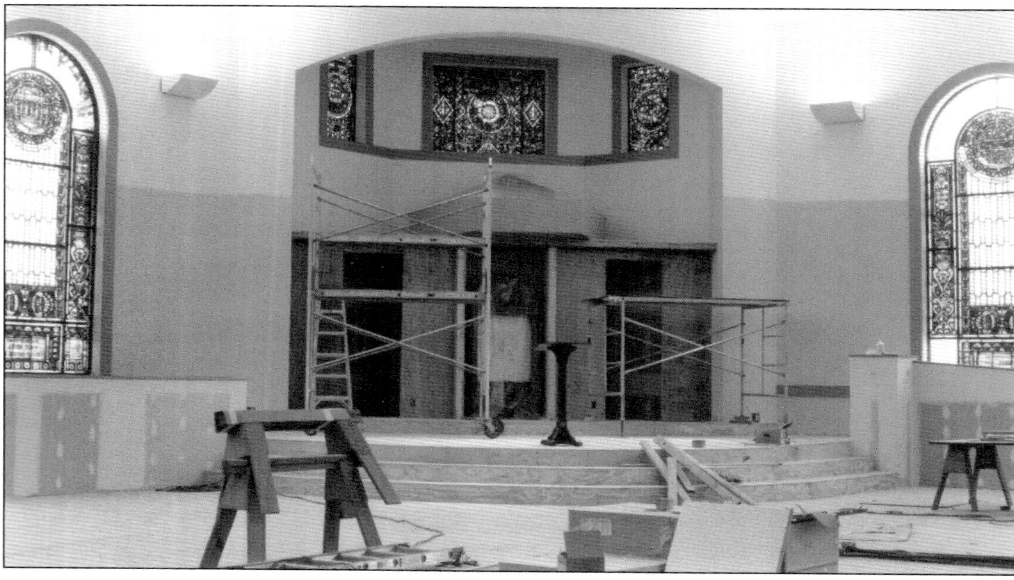

During the relocation of the old Oheb Sholom synagogue from the Perkiomen Avenue building to the new residence, the congregation was able to preserve some of the decorations and bring them to the new synagogue, including this beautiful chandelier. Many plaques and Judaica were also moved. (Courtesy of Michael Pardo.)

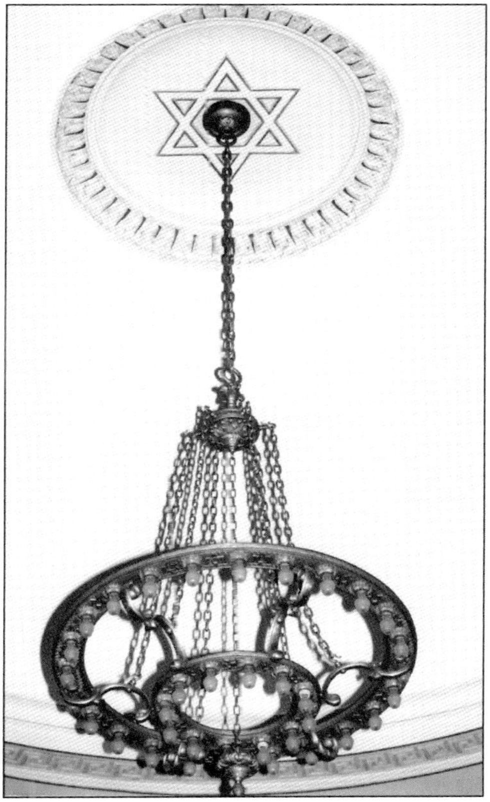

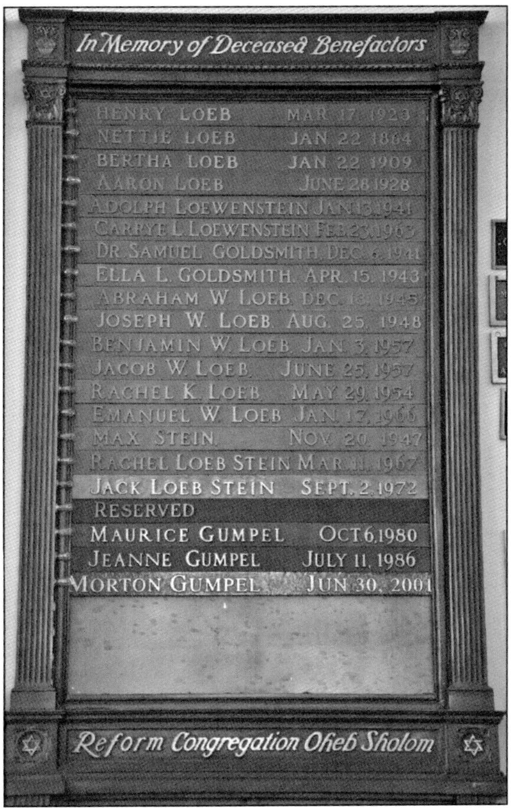

The memorial plaque pictured here honors deceased benefactors from Reform Congregation Oheb Sholom's long history, as far back as 1864, when the Emanuel Congregation of the Evangelical Association church building was officially dedicated as Reform Congregation Oheb Sholom. The plaque hangs in the current Oheb Sholom on Warwick Drive in Wyomissing Hills. The oldest date on the plaque, January 22, 1864, is held in remembrance of Nettie Loeb. (Photograph by Jeffrey Watts, courtesy of Jeffrey Watts.)

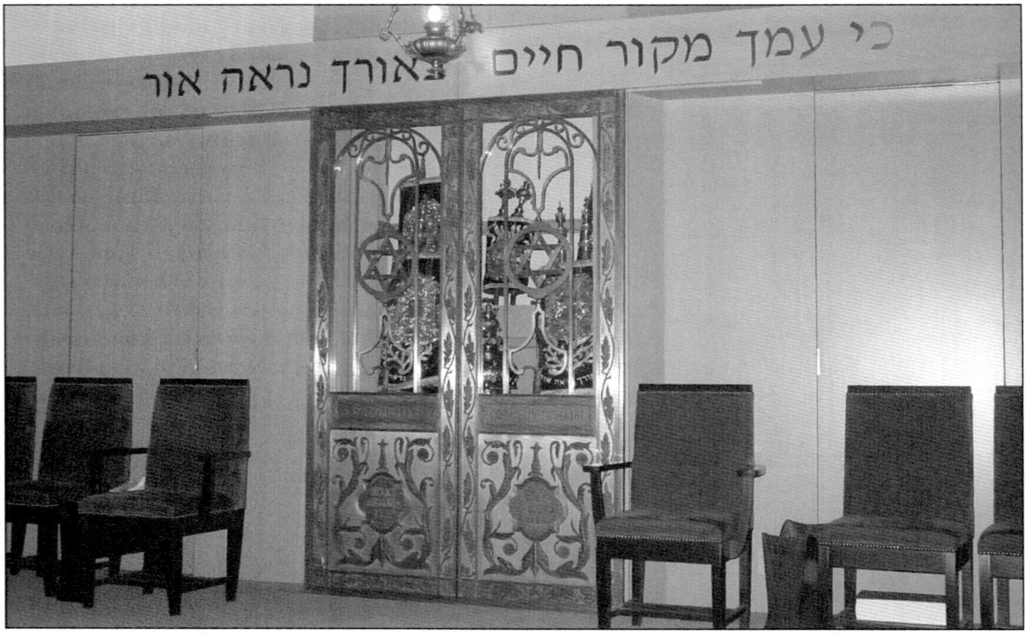

Located in the back of the sanctuary of Reform Congregation Oheb Sholom is this picture of the Aron Kodesh, also known as Holy Ark or the Holy of Holies. Within this cabinet, ornamentally decorated with the Star of David, are the Torah scrolls used to perform Jewish religious services for the congregation. The Torah is the holiest book within Judaism. (Photograph by Jeffrey Watts, courtesy of Jeffrey Watts.)

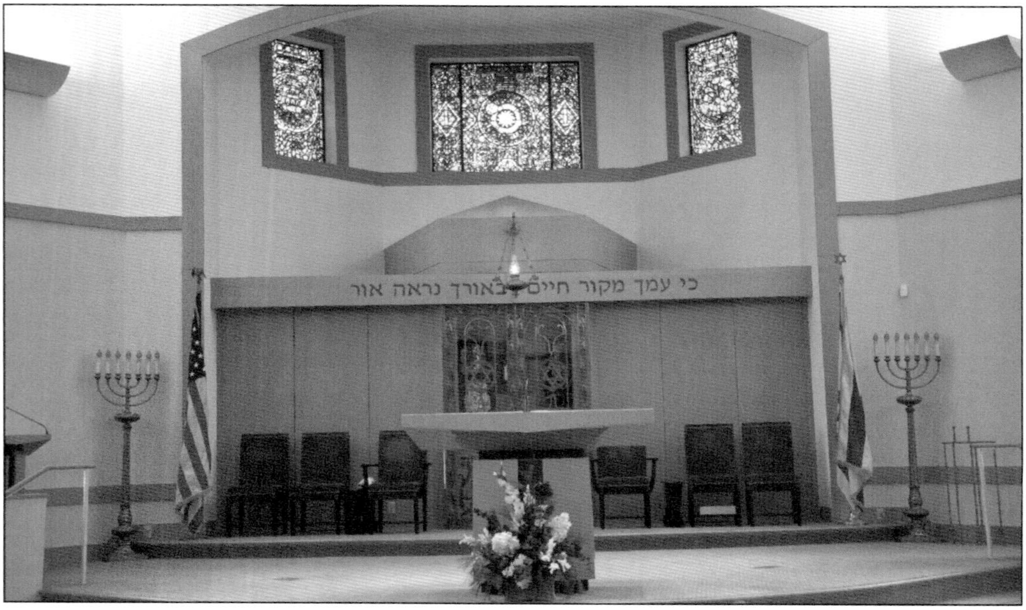

In the main sanctuary in Reform Congregation Oheb Sholom, there are six floor-to-ceiling stained-glass windows, and there are three above the bimah. Each window contains spiritual images intricately cut from colored glass. The bimah in Reform Congregation Oheb Sholom is adorned with stained glass portraying celestial images. (Photograph by Jeffrey Watts, courtesy of Jeffrey Watts.)

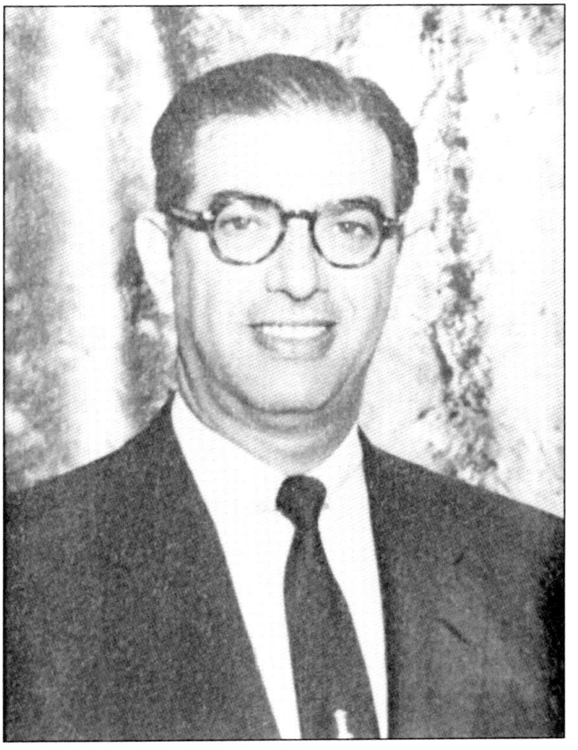

Leo J. Sondheim served as president of the Financial Committee of Reform Congregation Oheb Sholom; he served as president of the synagogue from 1917 through 1924. Leo was instrumental in the construction of the new Oheb Sholom on Perkiomen Avenue in 1921. He also worked to improve the greater Berks community, serving on the Reading-Berks Conservation Committee in the 1940s. Sondheim owned a clothing store in Reading. (Courtesy RCOS.)

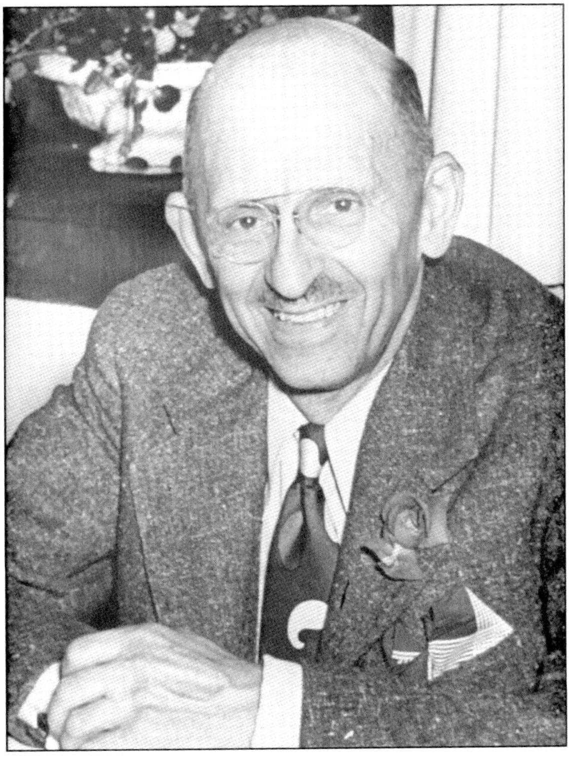

This 1923 photograph pictures Irwin Kins, Esq., who served as the chairman of the legal committee at Reform Congregation Oheb Sholom. Nearly 30 years later, in 1953, Kins was elected as president of Oheb Sholom. He was admitted to the Pennsylvania Bar in 1932. Kins was a World War II veteran and achieved the rank of captain. His father, Abraham Kins, was manager of Kins, a clothing store. (Courtesy of RCOS.)

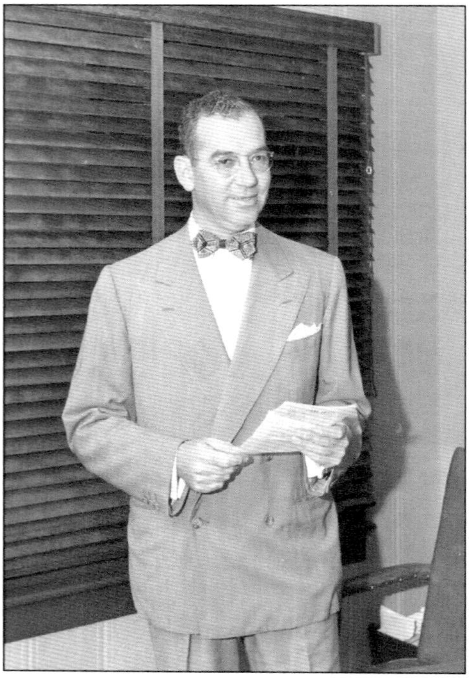

In 1923, Joseph Scherer was serving on the financial committee of Reform Congregation Oheb Sholom. Twenty-seven years later, in 1950, Scherer was elected president of the synagogue, and he served until 1953. On October 15, 1950, as president, Scherer participated in the ground-breaking ceremonies for the addition to the Oheb Sholom building. His wife, Mary, served as president of the Sisterhood of Oheb Sholom. (Courtesy of RCOS.)

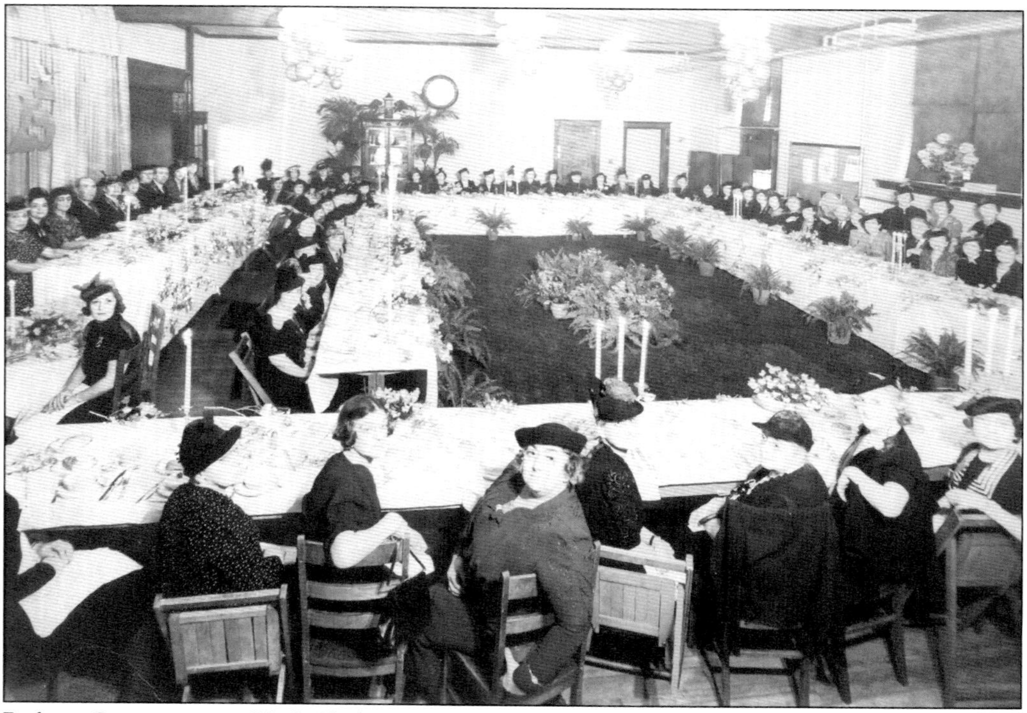

Reform Congregation Oheb Sholom's sisterhood celebrates its 25th anniversary in 1939. Dora Greenberg was the president of the sisterhood. The Sisterhood of Oheb Sholom was active in the community and held monthly meetings to plan events such as choir shows and theatrical productions. Further, the sisterhood raised funds for the local community. (Courtesy of RCOS.)

This letter from Congregation Oheb Shalom secretary Herman Folkman thanks the sisterhood for their willingness to provide electric lights, equipment, and other furnishings for the new synagogue on Perkiomen Avenue in Reading. The letter is dated April 9; because the synagogue was completed in 1923, the letter was presumably written in 1923. The letter exhibits the significant work done by the Oheb Sholom Sisterhood. (Courtesy of RCOS.)

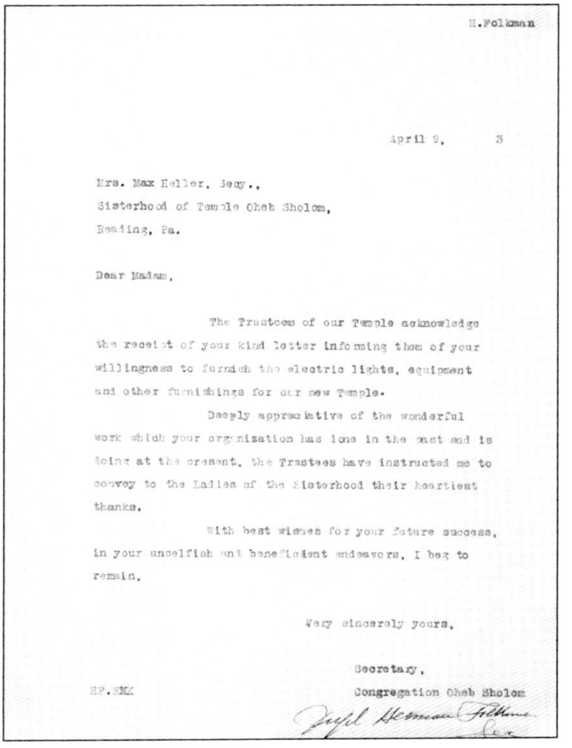

H.Folkman

April 9, 3

Mrs. Max Keller, Secy.,
Sisterhood of Temple Oheb Sholom,
Reading, Pa.

Dear Madam,

The Trustees of our Temple acknowledge the receipt of your kind letter informing them of your willingness to furnish the electric lights, equipment and other furnishings for our new Temple.

Deeply appreciative of the wonderful work which your organization has done in the past and is doing at the present, the Trustees have instructed me to convey to the Ladies of the Sisterhood their heartiest thanks.

With best wishes for your future success, in your unselfish and beneficient endeavors, I beg to remain,

Very sincerely yours,

Secretary,
Congregation Oheb Sholom

HF.EMK

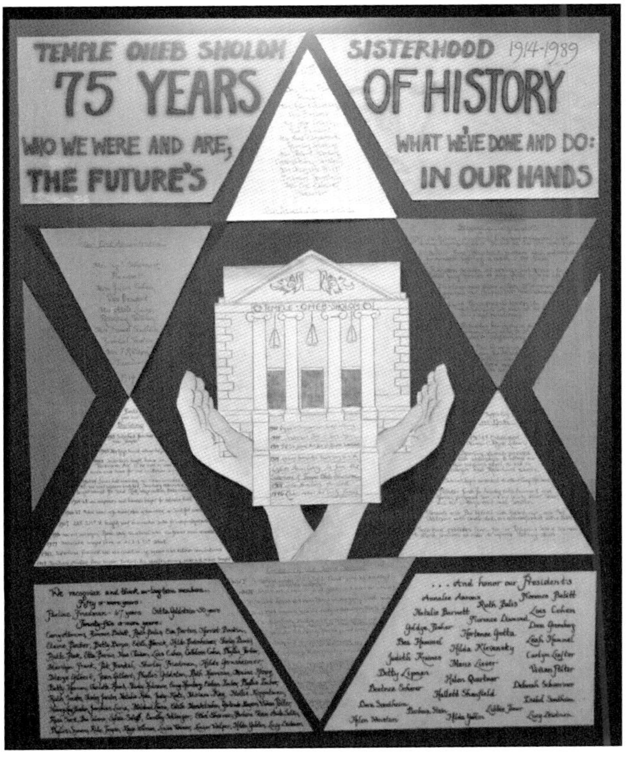

This Reform Congregation Oheb Sholom Sisterhood commemoration plaque was produced by local artist Eve Pardo of Pennside in 1989. The plaque commemorates 75 years of the Oheb Sholom Sisterhood, begun in 1914. Pardo, who also makes *ketuvim*, is a Wyomissing High School special education aid. The plaque, which is rich in color, hangs on the wall of the synagogue. (Photograph by Jeffrey Watts, courtesy of Jeffrey Watts.)

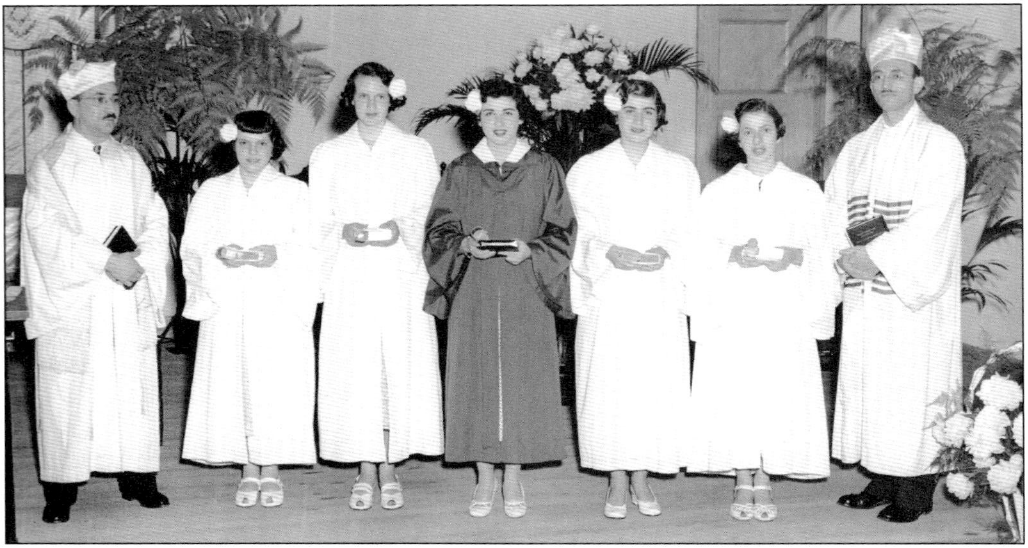

This photograph, taken in June 1950, marks the transitional period between Kesher Zion's old and new buildings. The Bat Mitzvah of Rose Wagman, standing in the center of the photograph, took place six months before the dedication of the new building. The celebration was held in vestry rooms used as the synagogue. (Courtesy of KZ.)

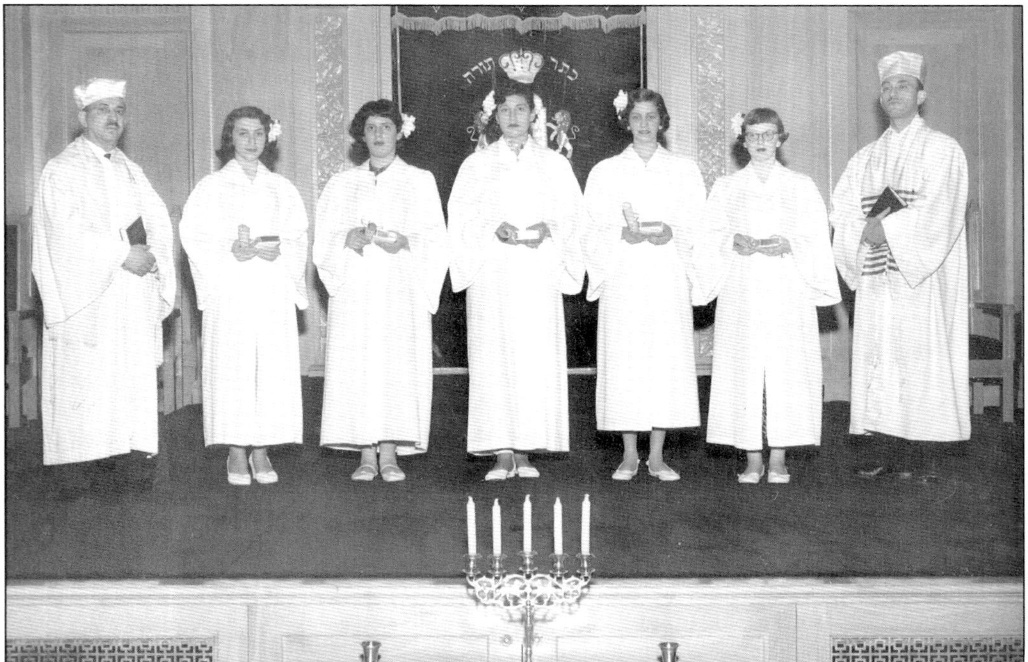

These five 13-year-old girls became Bat Mitvah at Kesher Zion in 1951. From left to right are Rabbi Abraham Simon, Deborah Klonsky, Janet Weil, Kathy Gilman, Eleanor Daniels, Harolyn Lustig, and Cantor Ben Klonsky. Until 1950, the Hebrew school was situated on the second floor of a three-story house at the corner of Eckert and Perkiomen Avenues. Since 1950, that has been referred to as the old building. (Courtesy of KZ.)

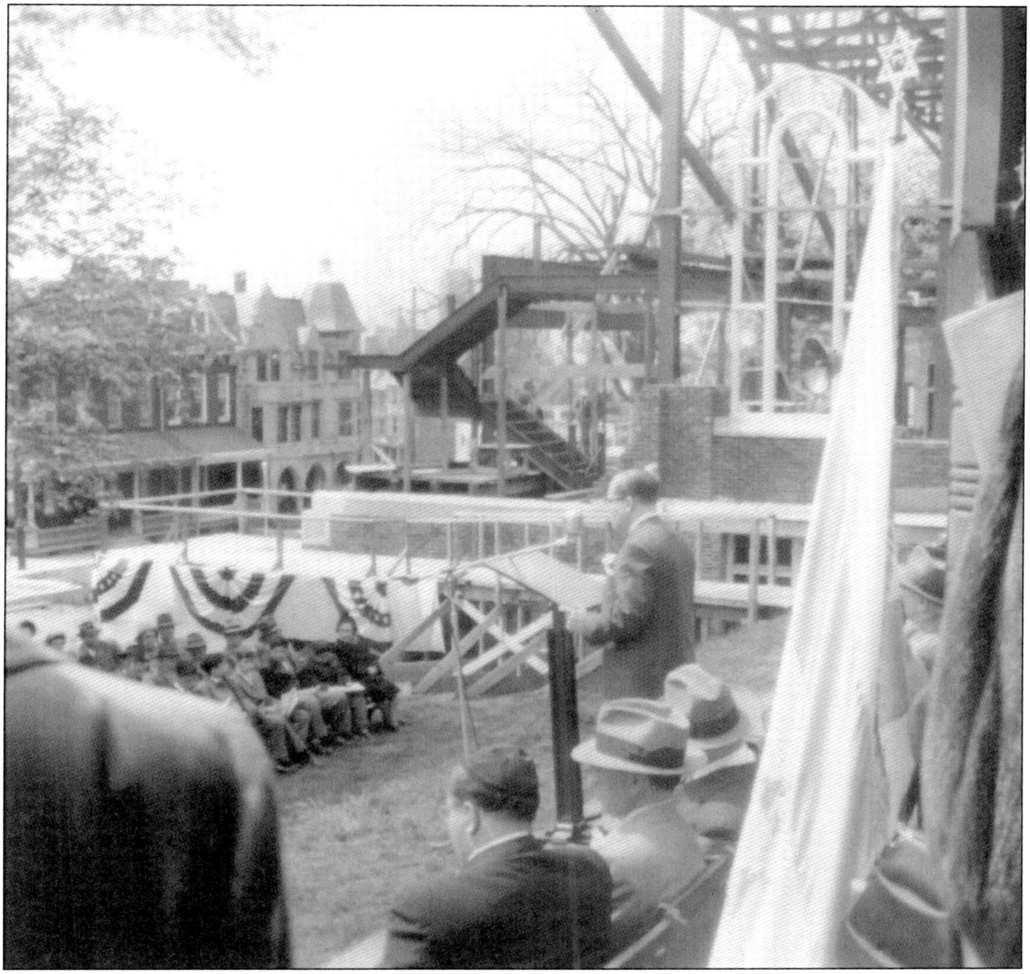

This is a photograph of Kesher Zion's current building at 1245 Perkiomen Avenue under construction. The building was dedicated in December 1950, and many congregants came to celebrate and honor the dedication and consecration of the synagogue's new home. Kesher Zion is an affiliate of the United Synagogue of Conservative Judaism. It has an active sisterhood, men's club, and Hebrew school. In 1911, a charter was granted to B'nai Zion, and in 1920, the congregation purchased the old Chestnut Street Synagogue that had been dedicated by Oheb Sholem in 1885. In 1913, a charter was granted to Kesher Israel, which bought a church at Eighth and Court Street, and in 1929, the merger of B'nai Zion and Kesher Israel produced the Kesher Zion Synagogue. (Courtesy of KZ.)

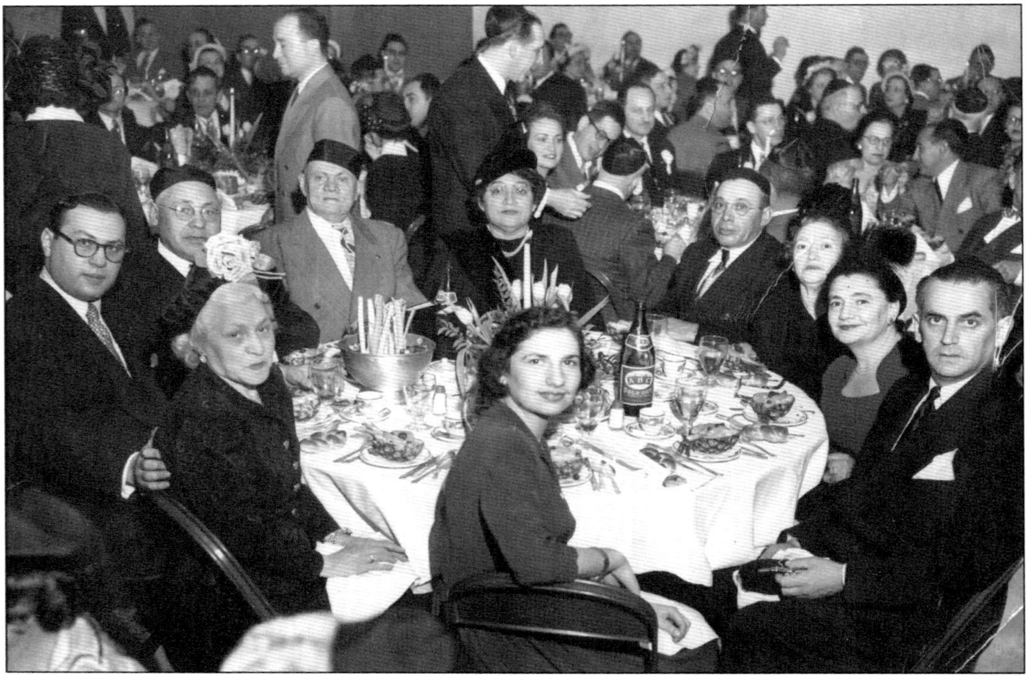

Shown here is a photograph taken of a celebratory dinner at Kesher Zion in the 1950s or 1960s. The synagogue held many dinners and celebrations, often organized by Kesher Zion Sisterhood. In its long history, the sisterhood has supported the synagogue and Hebrew school, the libraries, and donations to many charities. Shown on the tables is ABC Pale Ale, which was produced by ABC Beverage Company in Reading. Robert Lyons and Maurice Goldberg were partners in the company; Lyons died in 1957. (Courtesy of Bernie Gerber.)

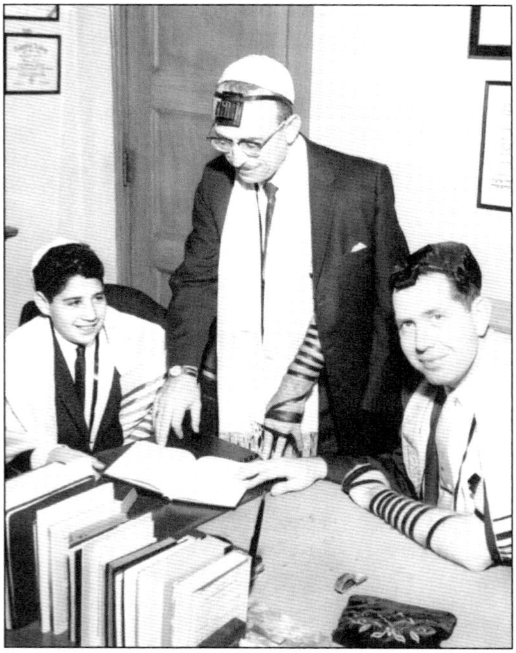

Taken on Thanksgiving Day in 1962, this picture shows Rabbi Melvin Glatt (sitting at right) and Cantor Ben Klonsky with Bar Mitzvah Raymond Kahn. On their arms and heads are the tefillin, which are shown as black boxes that contain passages from the Torah inside. These boxes are attached to the leather straps wrapped around their arms and heads, called *retzuot*. (Courtesy of KZ.)

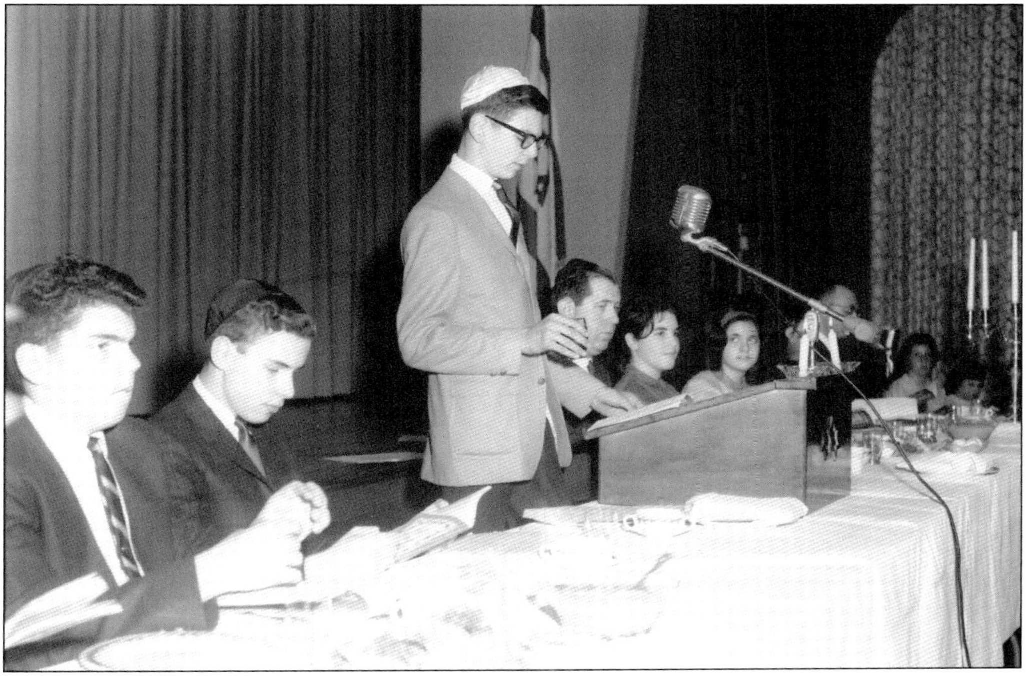

The photograph above is from Kesher Zion's 1963 Pesach Model Seder. The Kiddush is being made by Fred Goldberg. The Kiddush for Passover is read from the Haggadah, which tells the story of the Exodus from Egypt. In 1966, Goldberg played on the All-American basketball team in a competition held in Israel. Goldberg was also an excellent golfer. Below, Barbara Cutler, a student of the Hebrew school, lights the Passover candles before saying the blessings. The oldest female member of the household would traditionally perform this. A year earlier, Cutler and her mother attended the mother-daughter dinner of Kesher Zion Sisterhood. Cutler attended the University of Pittsburgh. (Both, courtesy of KZ.)

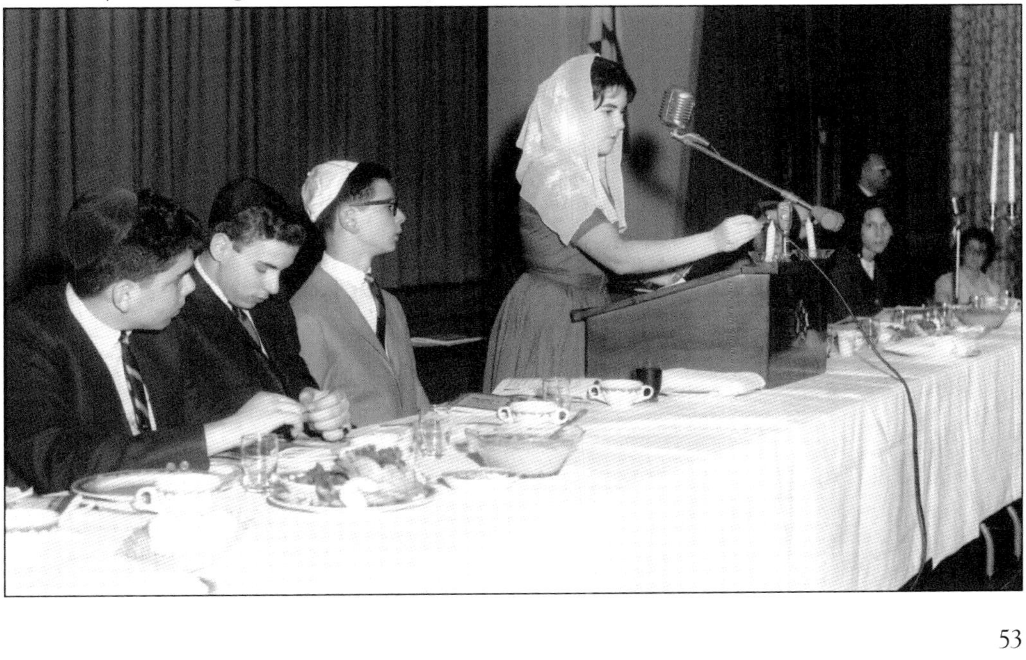

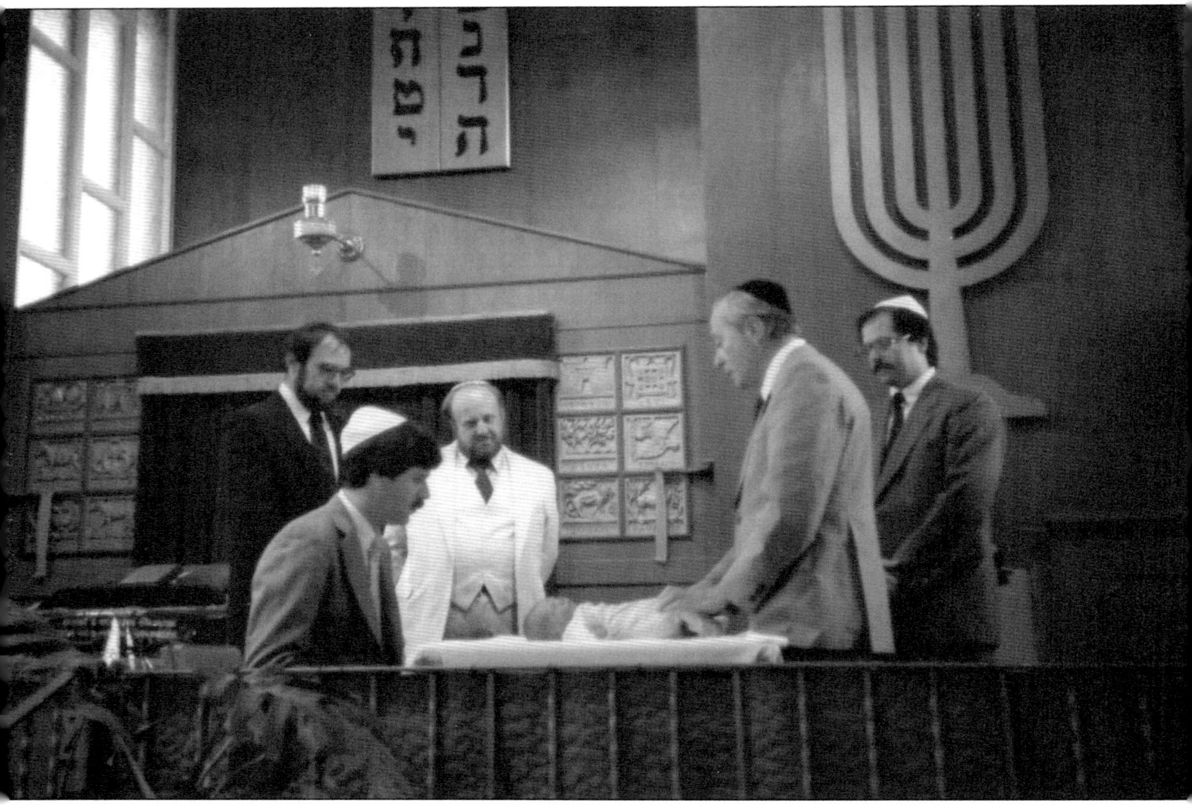

Pictured here is a bris at Shomrei Habrith Synagogue for Allen Heisler's infant son. Heisler is front left. A bris is a ceremony during which an infant is circumcised and given his Hebrew name. It is typically done by a *moile*. Because this is an Orthodox congregation, the mother, Laurie Heisler, is not allowed on the bimah during the bris. As a boy, Allen Heisler lived at 932 Union Street. Allen Heisler was awarded the B'nai B'rith Label Katz Young Leadership Award. He spent many Christmases volunteering at local hospitals so employees could spend the day with families, and he served as president of Shomrei Habrith. Heisler also served in the US Navy. (Courtesy of Jenny Satt.)

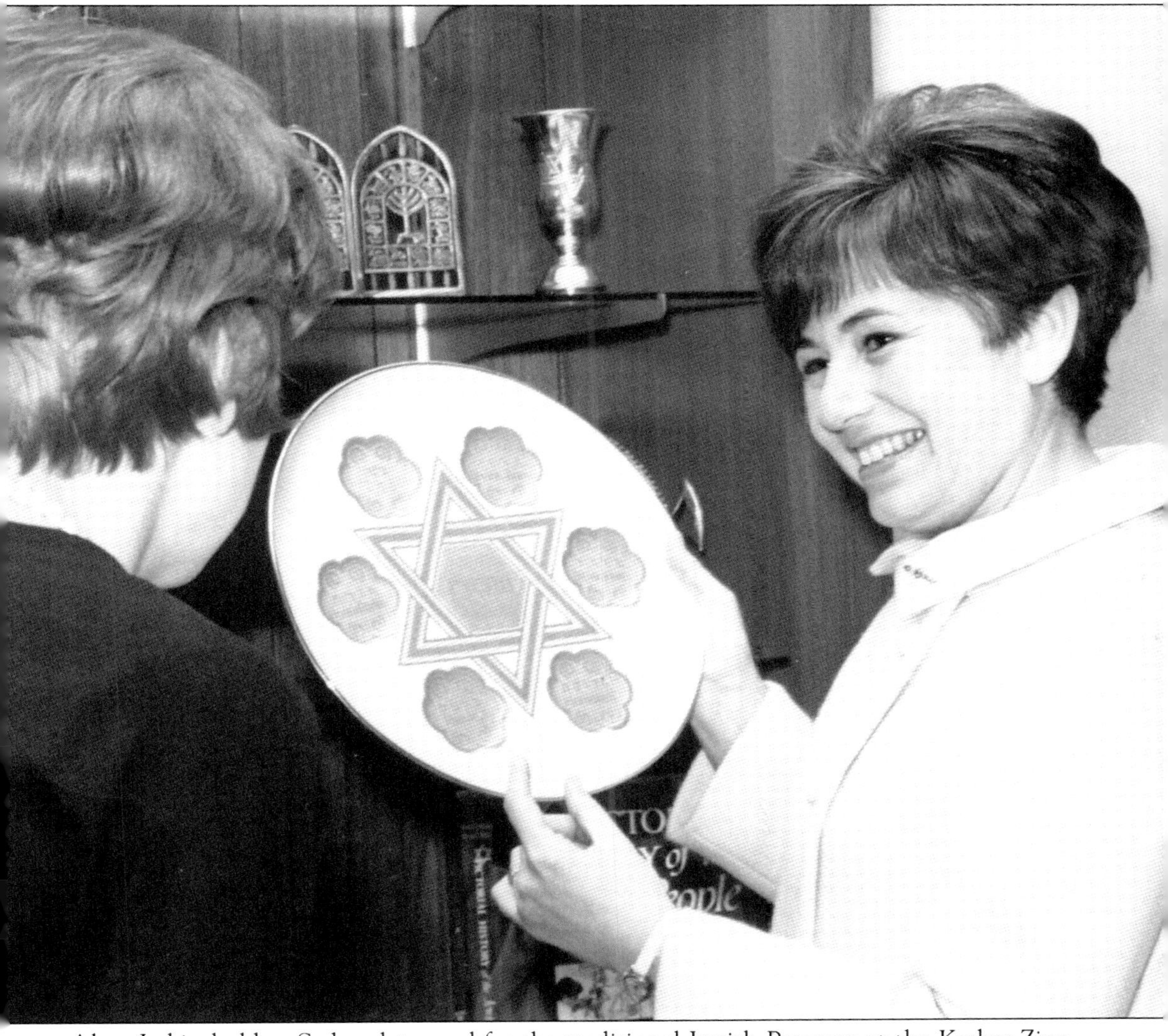

Alma Lakin holds a Seder plate used for the traditional Jewish Passover at the Kesher Zion Synagogue's Helen Rudolph Memorial Display. Lakin, wife of Edwin Lakin, is a highly respected woman in Berks. She was a board member of Fellowship House and an honorary board member of Rainbow Home. In 1996, Lakin received a Lifetime Achievement Award from the Reading Chapter of Hadassah. She has served as president of Kesher Zion Sisterhood and the Jewish Federation of Reading. In 2000, Alma and Edwin Lakin won the National Society of Fundraising Executives Outstanding Volunteer Fundraisers Award. She serves on the board of trustees of Albright College, her alma mater; she received her baccalaureate degree in 1951. In 2010, the Jewish Federation of Reading recognized Ed and Alma Lakin for their lifelong commitment to Holocaust education. (Courtesy of KZ.)

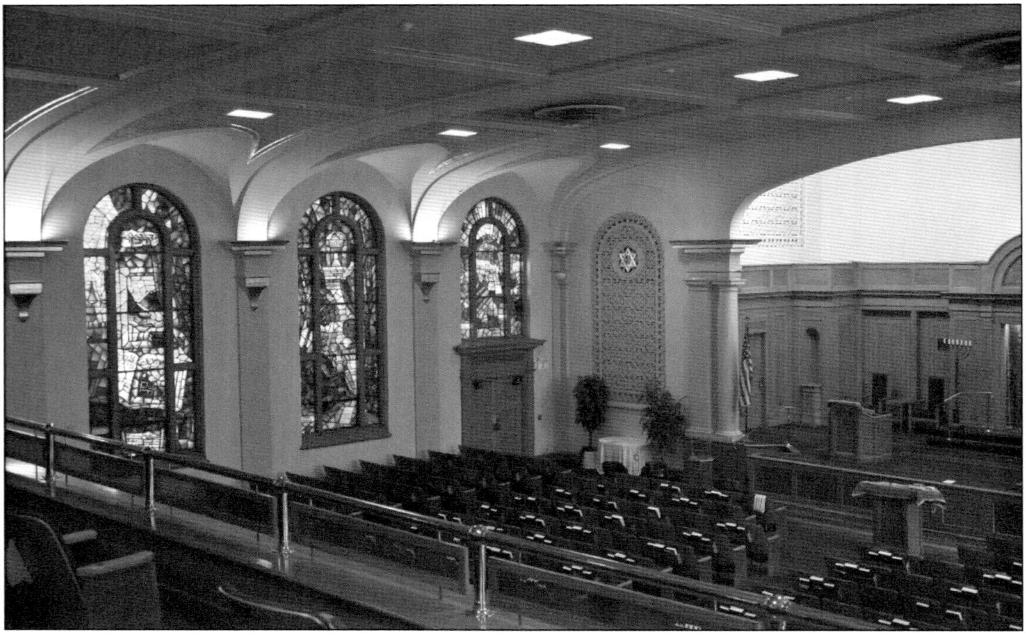

In the above photograph, the view from the balcony in the sanctuary of the Kesher Zion Synagogue provides a beautiful vista of the stained-glass windows. The windows lining the sanctuary's walls are two stories high and reach from floor to ceiling. Each of the impressive works in stained glass portrays a different Jewish ideal. Below is the sanctuary's ark with a tapestry covering the Torahs. There are also plaques commemorating the Hassel family for the donations they made for this synagogue. This is the current location of Kesher Zion, where the congregation has resided for 63 years. (Both photographs by Jeffrey Watts, courtesy of Jeffrey Watts.)

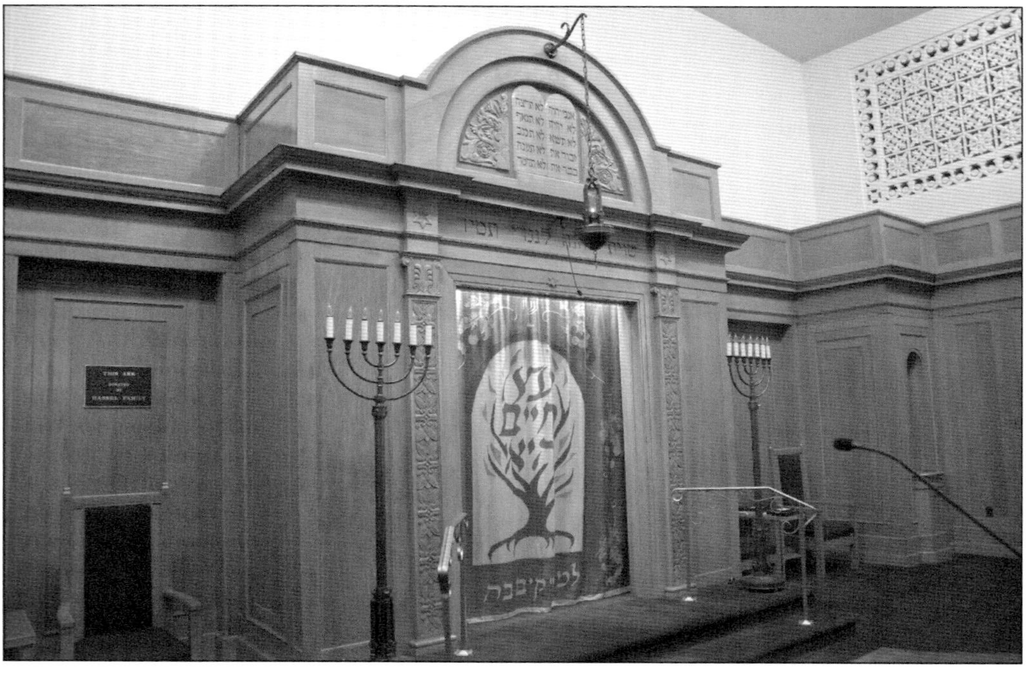

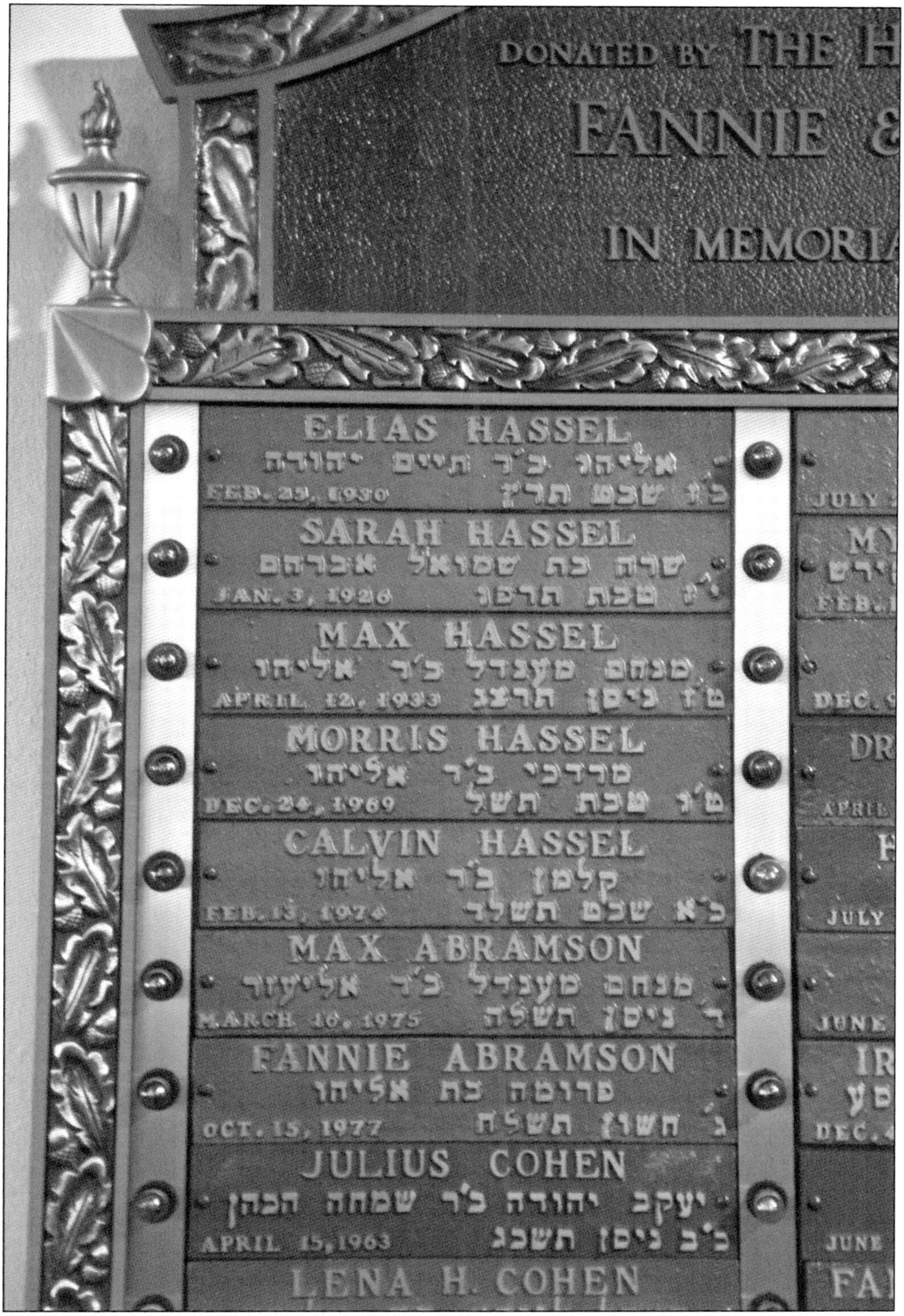

This plaque is a tribute to members of the Kesher Zion Synagogue whose generosity and dedication to the congregation has been commendable. The panels on this plaque show a detailed commemoration for members of the Hassel family for their generosity. Max Hassel's legacy in the Reading community is ambivalent. However, several other members of the Hassel family are on the plaque. (Photograph by Jeffrey Watts, courtesy of Jeffrey Watts.)

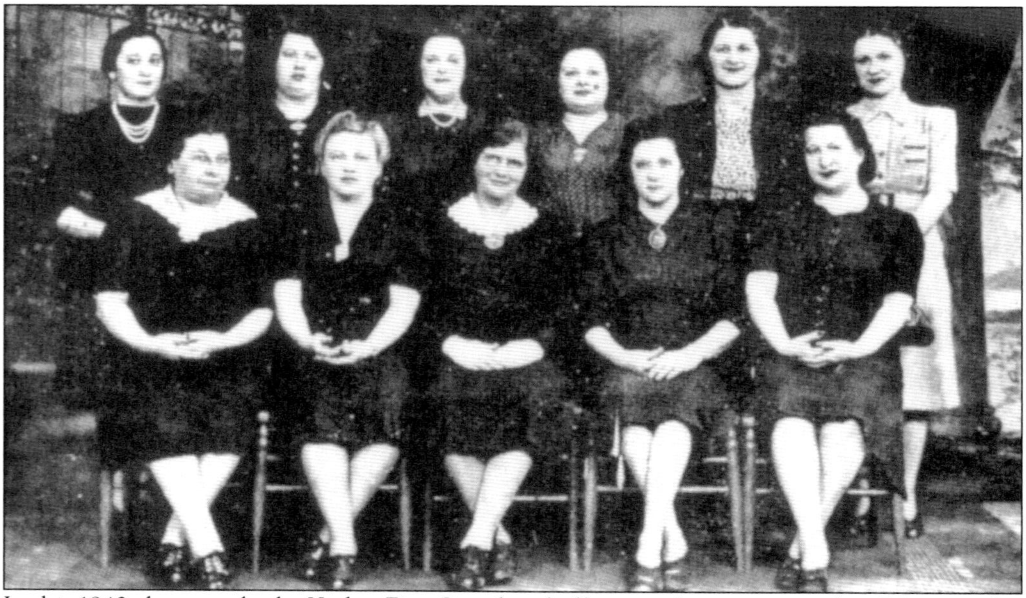

In this 1940 photograph, the Kesher Zion Sisterhood officers are honorary president Rhena Miller and president Esther Kauffman. The sisterhood had many members at this time, including the 11 women pictured here. In 1966, Rhena Miller was a national office of the Ladies Auxiliary of the Veterans of Foreign Wars. From left to right are (first row) Laura Ruttenberg, Sarah Rosenberg, Rhena Miller, Lean LeVin, and Celia Cooper; (second row) Anna Blecker, Loretta Yaffee, Ella Heller, Esther Kauffman, Esther Brown, and Reba Porter. (Courtesy of Fogelman family.)

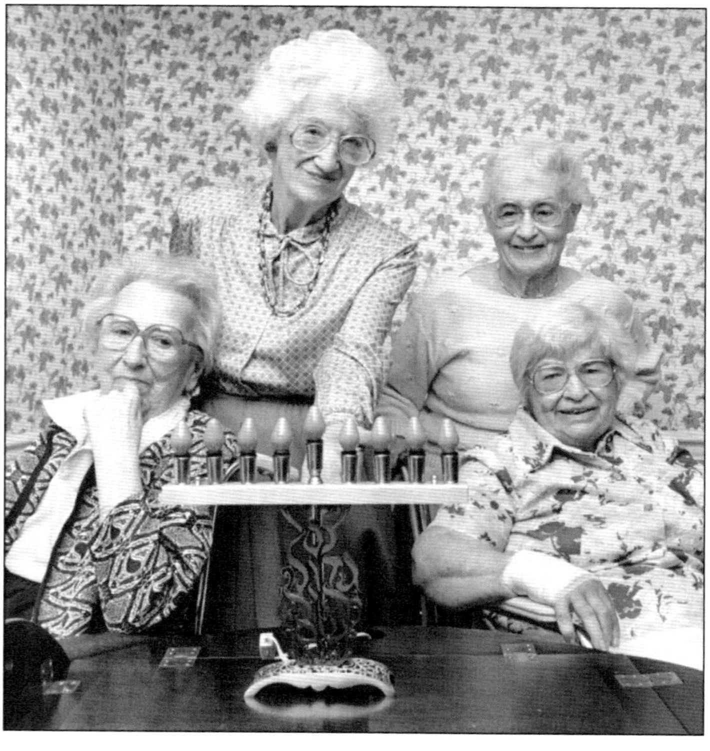

In early December 1985, members of the Sisterhood of Kesher Zion donated a Chanukah menorah to the Jewish wing of the Leader Nursing Center. Pictured at left with the menorah are, from left to right, Martha Sherman, former president of Kesher Zion's sisterhood; Mildred Lyons, Blanche Gross, and Deenie Evelev, who was a resident at the center at the time. (Courtesy of KZ.)

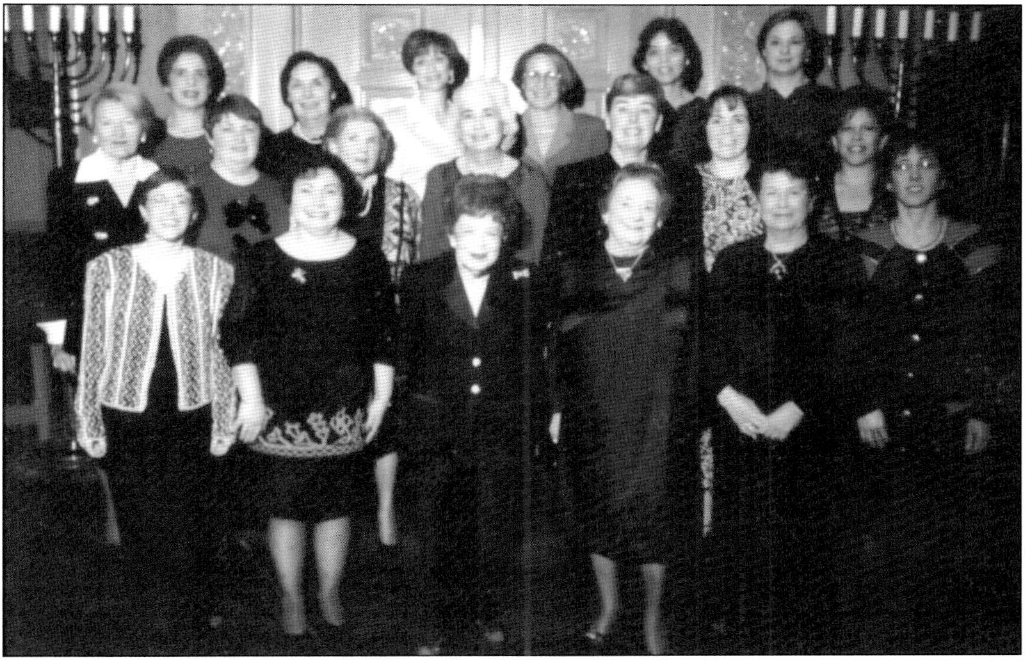

Pictured here is a 1999 group photograph of Kesher Zion Sisterhood presidents. The Sisterhood of Kesher Zion encourages cultural and communal participation among their members and continually hold banquets in honor of the community, religion, and learning. In the photograph, from left to right, are (first row) Lisa Levine, Pam Weisberg, Hanna Goldsmith, Sadie Wurman, Alma Lakin, and Elaine Pleet; (second row) Mickie VanTosh, Esther Strauss, Sheila Lidman, Shirley Kauffman, Carol Perlmutter, Beth Heyman, and Robin Drezner; (third row) Janet Kaplan, Sylvia Wenger, Mara Winn, Gayle Kastenbaum, Carole Robinson, and Carol Greenberg. (Courtesy of KZ.)

The Senior Ladies Society provided activities for retired women, such as cooking and raising money for the synagogues through hosting rummage sales. At the friendship circle, gossiping was said to be another favorite pastime of the society. Standing on the left is the previous program director of the Jewish Community Center, Hilda Yablin, and standing on the right is Ann Popkin. (Courtesy of JFR.)

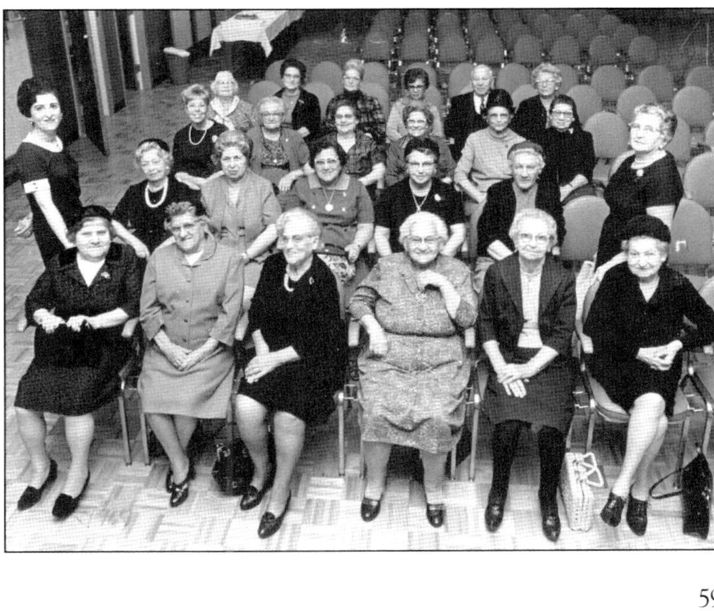

Dedication of Congregation Beth Jacob

955 NORTH 10th STREET, READING, PENNA.

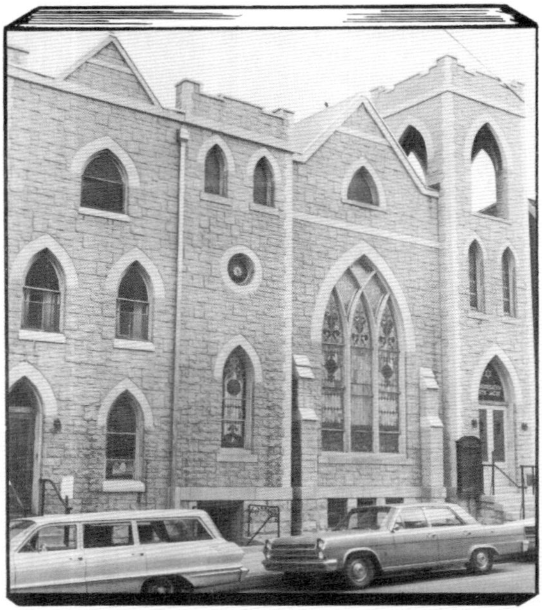

" I will dwell therein,
among the Children of Israel,
and will not forsake my
People Israel..."

King 1; 6 : 13

Dedication Sunday December 18, 1966

The dedication of Congregation Beth Jacob, located at 955 North Tenth Street in Reading, took place on December 18, 1966. Approximately 75 members of Shomrei Habrith Synagogue purchased a former Evangelical United Brethren church building in 1965 to form the Beth Jacob Traditional Orthodox Synagogue. Beth Jacob received its charter for practicing Traditional Orthodoxy in June 1965 and became affiliated with the Union of Orthodox Organizations of America. Those who formed Beth Jacob decided to form a new synagogue after Shomrei Habrith members voted to adopt the practices of Modern Orthodoxy. For example, Beth Jacob separates men and women when worshipping in the synagogue sanctuary. The first Beth Jacob officers were president Max Hindin of Hindin's Bakery, religious leaders Hessel Levin and Samuel A. Siegel, and sisterhood president Lillian Levin. A rabbi had not yet been named. (Courtesy of SH.)

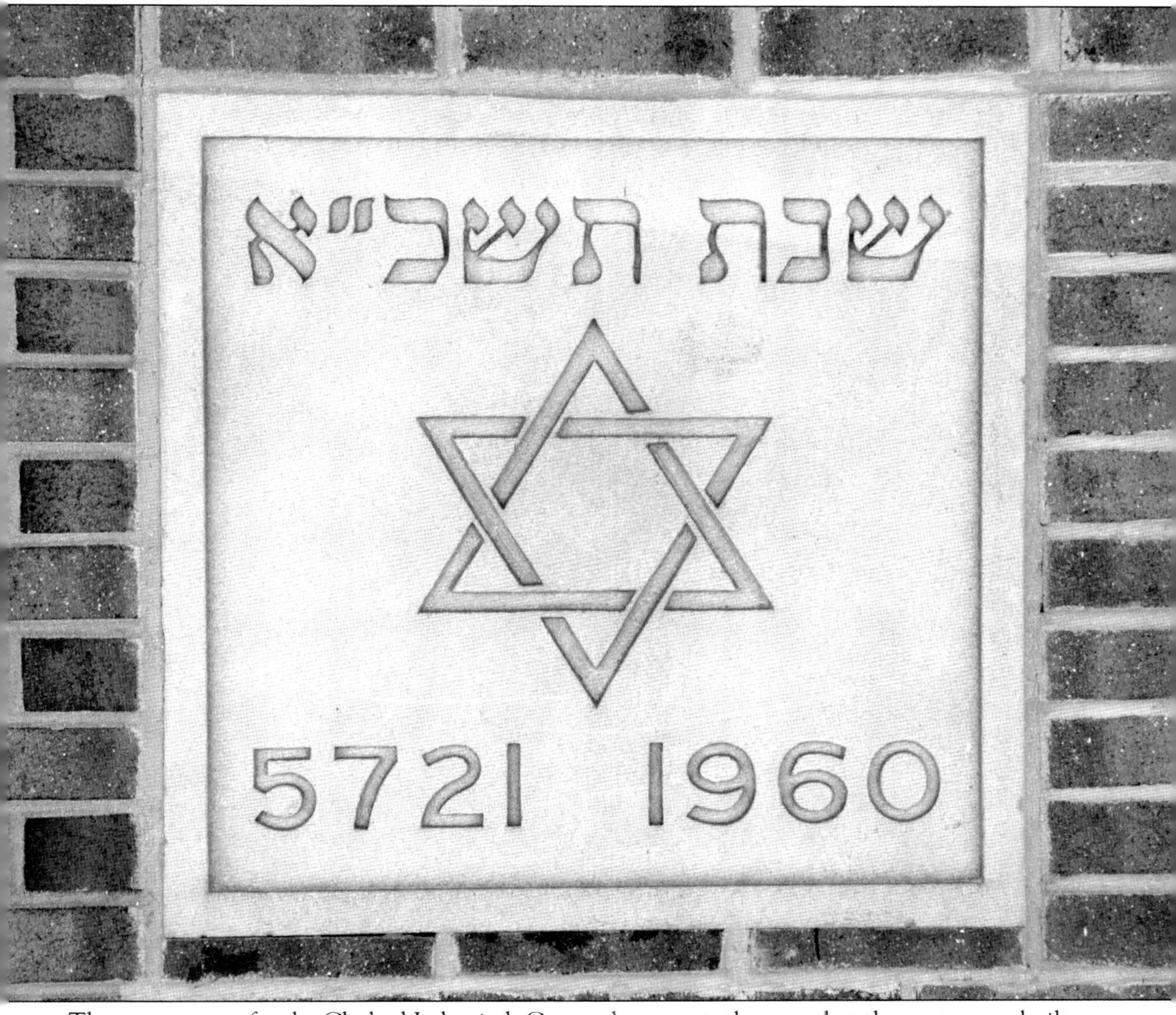

The cornerstone for the Chabad-Lubavitch Center documents the year that the center was built. The date is recorded as 1960 in Common Era on the bottom right and 5721 by the Jewish calendar on the bottom left. In 1880, Jewish immigrants began their travels to Reading, Pennsylvania, and through the decade, they began worshipping in a room at Eleventh and Elm Streets and, later, at 750 Penn Street and Eighth and Elm Streets. It was not until October 20, 1888, that a charter was established for Shomrei Habrith. In 1893, Shomrei Habrith synagogue was built at 533 North Eighth Street, and in 1902, property at 415 Moss Street was purchased as a social hall. In 1913, a new Shomrei building was erected at 533 North Eighth Street for $25,000, and in 1929, a vestry room, auditorium, and kitchen were added. In 1960, Shomrei Habrith moved to 2320 Hampden Boulevard. In 2009, Shomrei Habrith sold the building to the Chabad-Lubavitch Center of Berks County. (Photograph by Jeffrey Watts, courtesy of Jeffrey Watts.)

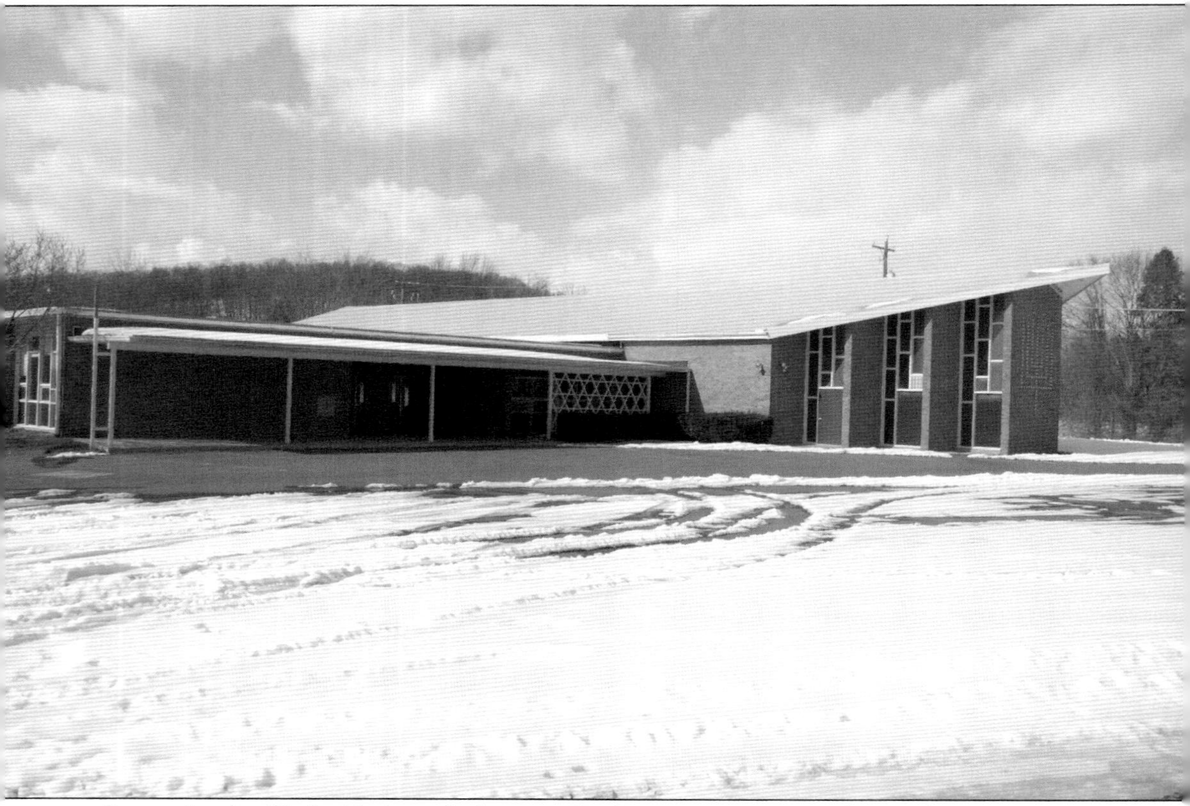

Pictured is the Chabad-Lubavitch Center of Berks County on Hampden Boulevard in Reading, led by Rabbi Yosef Lipsker ,who serves on the Board of Directors of the Reading Jewish Federation. Chabad-Lubavitch is a Brooklyn-based Jewish movement that sends its followers around the world on the mission of building Jewish community. The building was purchased from Congregation Shomrei Habrith in 2009. Congregation Shomrei Habrith continues without a building. (Photograph by Jeffrey Watts, courtesy of Jeffrey Watts.)

This letter from Allen Heisler, centennial chairman for Congregation Shomrei Habrith, was written to congregants on December 8, 1988, to seek funds for the anniversary book, one of the components of the centennial anniversary. Proceeds were used toward capital improvements. In 1986, Heisler was named recipient of the B'nai B'rith Label Katz Young Leadership Award. He joined B'nai B'rith in 1975 after his service to the US Navy. (Courtesy of SH.)

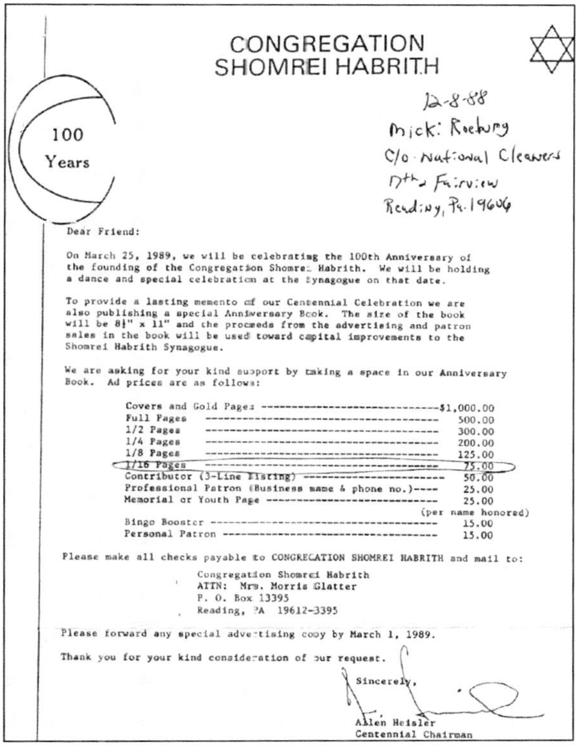

CONGREGATION
SHOMREI HABRITH

100 Years

12-8-88
C/o National Cleaners
17th & Fairview
Reading, Pa. 19606

Dear Friend:

On March 25, 1989, we will be celebrating the 100th Anniversary of the founding of the Congregation Shomrei Habrith. We will be holding a dance and special celebration at the Synagogue on that date.

To provide a lasting memento of our Centennial Celebration we are also publishing a special Anniversary Book. The size of the book will be 8½" x 11" and the proceeds from the advertising and patron sales in the book will be used toward capital improvements to the Shomrei Habrith Synagogue.

We are asking for your kind support by taking a space in our Anniversary Book. Ad prices are as follows:

Covers and Gold Pages	$1,000.00
Full Pages	500.00
1/2 Pages	300.00
1/4 Pages	200.00
1/8 Pages	125.00
1/16 Pages	75.00
Contributor (3-Line listing)	50.00
Professional Patron (Business name & phone no.)	25.00
Memorial or Youth Page	25.00 (per name honored)
Bingo Booster	15.00
Personal Patron	15.00

Please make all checks payable to CONGREGATION SHOMREI HABRITH and mail to:

Congregation Shomrei Habrith
ATTN: Mrs. Morris Glatter
P. O. Box 13395
Reading, PA 19612-3395

Please forward any special advertising copy by March 1, 1989.

Thank you for your kind consideration of our request.

Sincerely,

Allen Heisler
Centennial Chairman

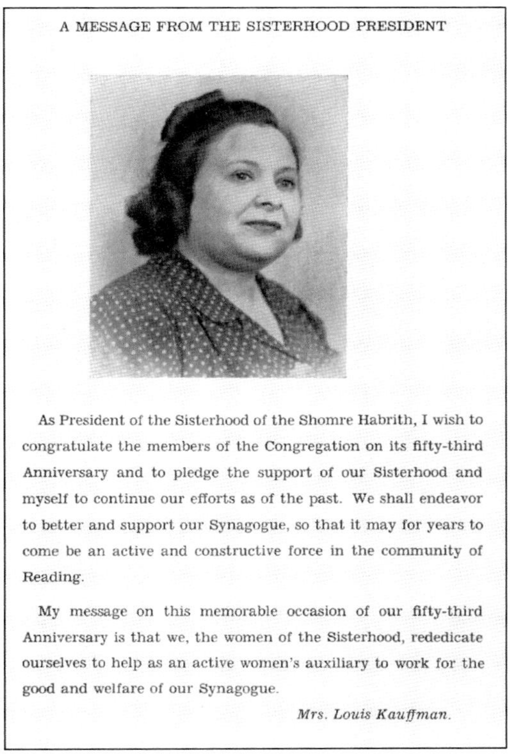

A MESSAGE FROM THE SISTERHOOD PRESIDENT

As President of the Sisterhood of the Shomre Habrith, I wish to congratulate the members of the Congregation on its fifty-third Anniversary and to pledge the support of our Sisterhood and myself to continue our efforts as of the past. We shall endeavor to better and support our Synagogue, so that it may for years to come be an active and constructive force in the community of Reading.

My message on this memorable occasion of our fifty-third Anniversary is that we, the women of the Sisterhood, rededicate ourselves to help as an active women's auxiliary to work for the good and welfare of our Synagogue.

Mrs. Louis Kauffman.

A message from sisterhood president Esther Kauffman on Congregation Shomrei Habrith's 53rd anniversary recommends that the women of the sisterhood rededicate themselves to work for the good of the synagogue. She was also a member of the Senior Hadassah. Her husband, Louis Kauffman, owned a wholesale fruits and vegetables business in Reading. The Kauffmans have two children, Robert Kauffman and Joan Moscowitz. (Courtesy of SH.)

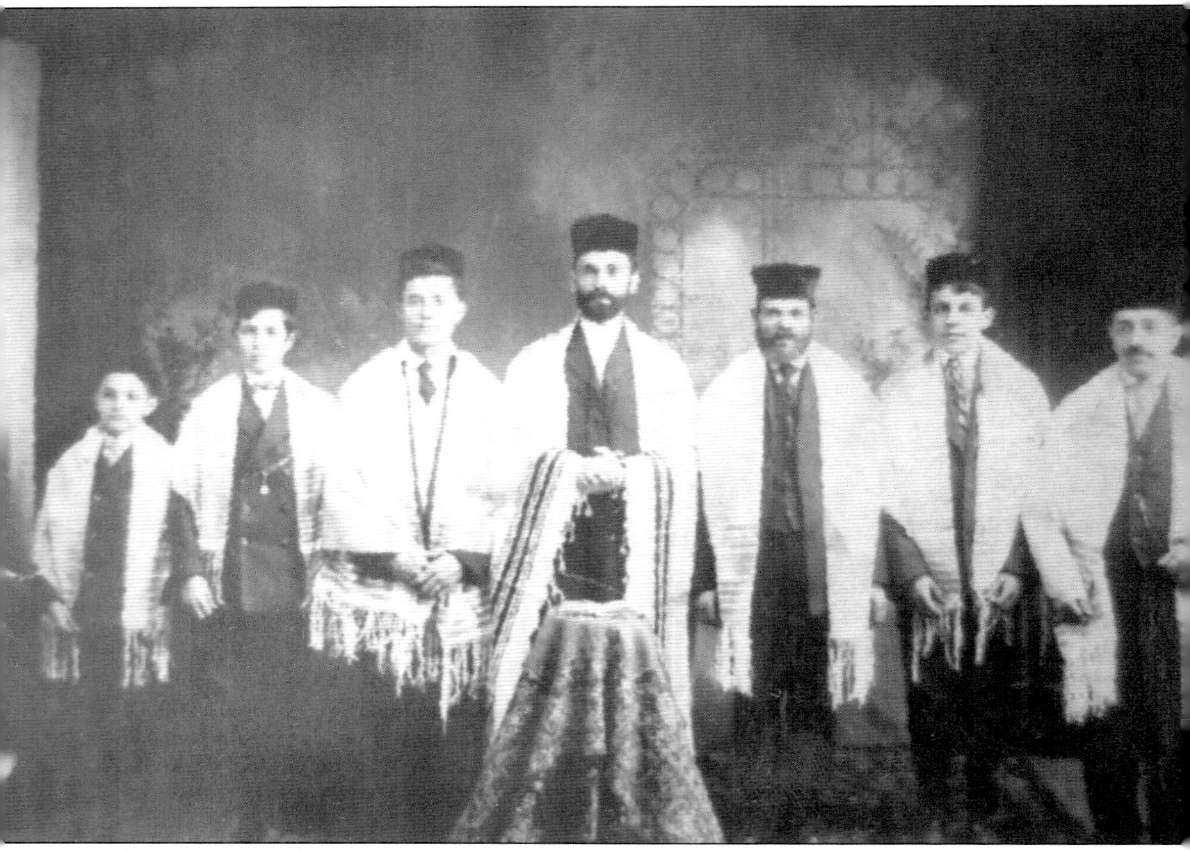

The centennial of Congregation Shomrei Habrith was celebrated in 1988 with several special events. A rededication service was led by Rabbi Sidney A. Green. This centennial picture, entitled *Keepers of the Covenant*, displays the historical leadership of the synagogue. Moses (Morris) Aaronsohn was the first rabbi in 1888. On October 20, 1888, Judge James Ermentrout issued a charter for establishment of a place of worship and a burial ground. A *Reading Eagle* article in 1918 notes that an unusually high percentage of Shomrei Habrith congregants were US service members. The Charter of Honor awarded to Congregation Shomrei Habrith by the Union of Orthodox Jewish Congregations in tribute to 73 years of service was presented to the synagogue on November 9, 1960. From left to right in the photograph are Meyer Sher, brother of Mrs. Mahlon Shapiro; unidentified; Benjamin Goldberg; Rev. Elias Kaplan, cantor and father of Dr. Bernard and Norman Kaplan; Berely Woods; unidentified; and Israel Goodman, father of Pauline Goldberg and Morris Goodman. (Courtesy of SH.)

Three

Religious Education

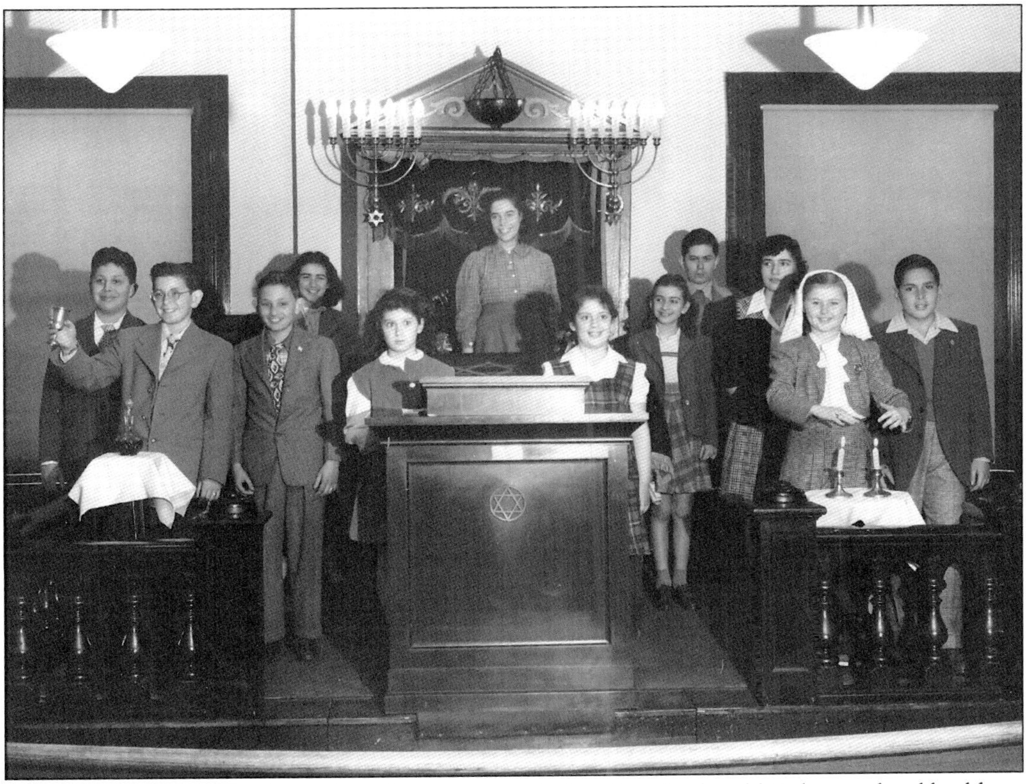

This is a 1940s photograph of a Shabbat service at Kesher Zion in the old Hebrew school building. Pictured from left to right are Sidney Fogelman, Bernard Mendelsohn, George Mason, Rose Wagman, Eleanor Abrams, Lenore Lonker, Janet Weil Kaplan, Jackie Wagman, Gene Goodwin, Ethel Ravitz, Evelyn Furman, and Alan Gibstein. Furman lights the Shabbat candles before saying the ritual blessings. (Courtesy of KZ.)

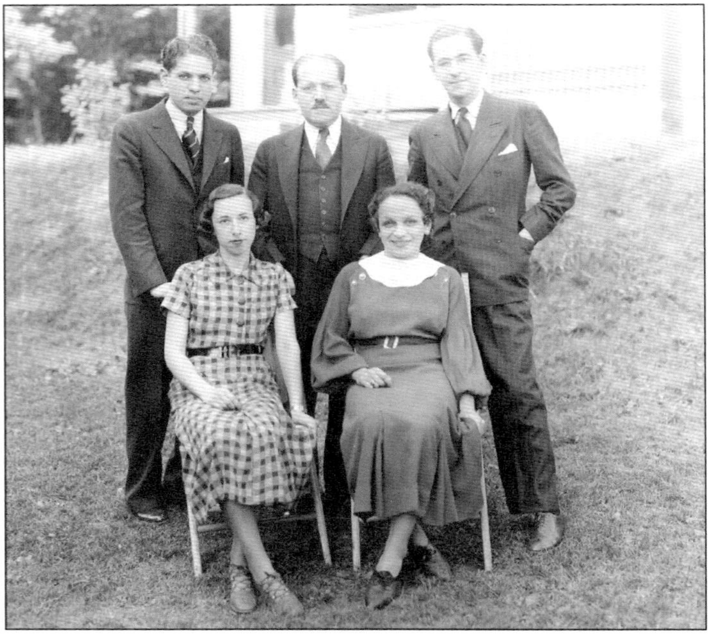

The 1934 Hebrew school faculty of Kesher Zion includes, from left to right, (first row) Renee Levi and Betty Harrison; (second row) Samuel Grand, Rabbi Max J. Routtenberg, and Eli Skaist. These men and women provided leadership for the growing Jewish community. Morris N. Blumberg was the school's founder and president for 12 years. The Hebrew school was founded in 1933 at Eckert and Perkiomen Avenues; the services continued to be held at Eighth and Court Streets for years. (Courtesy of KZ.)

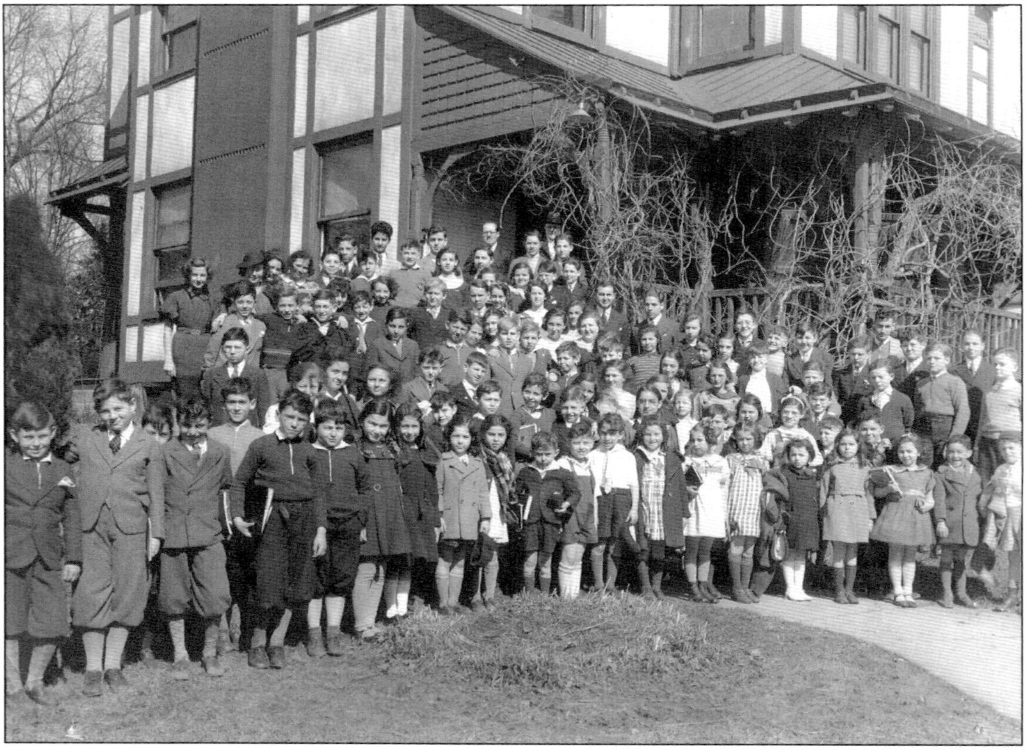

Taken in 1944 or 1945, this is a view of the exterior of the Kesher Zion Hebrew School. The well-dressed Hebrew school students stand at the entrance. This building remained after the new building was opened in 1950 and continued to be an active place in the Jewish community. Adjoining plots were purchased between 1936 and 1945. (Courtesy of KZ.)

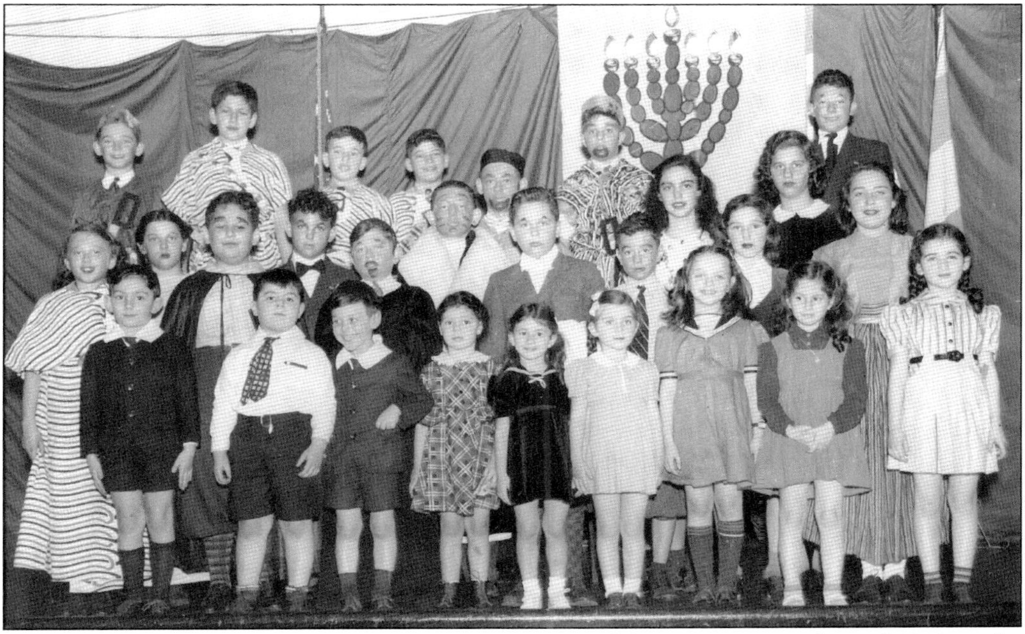

This is a photograph of the Kesher Zion Hebrew School celebrating Purim in the mid-1940s at the old Hebrew school location. Some of the children are dressed in costumes and makeup to reenact Megillat Esther. Girls emulate the beautiful Queen Esther, while the boys are likely representing the evil advisor, Haman, who temporarily convinced the ancient Persian king Ahasuerus to kill all of the Jews in Persia. (Courtesy of Bernie Gerber.)

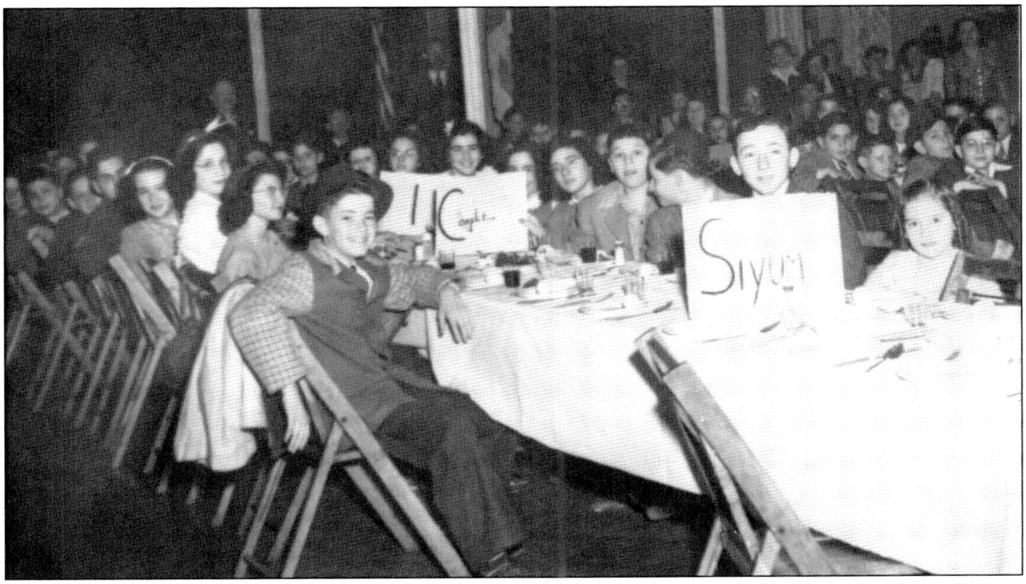

This photograph of a Kesher Zion Hebrew School celebratory dinner, or *seudat mitzvah*, was taken in 1944 or 1945. The student table in the foreground reads "Siyum," which is a celebratory meal that honors students who completed a section of Torah study. Larger celebratory occasions such as this would have been held at the old Jewish Community Center location at 134 North Fifth Street. (Courtesy of Bernie Gerber.)

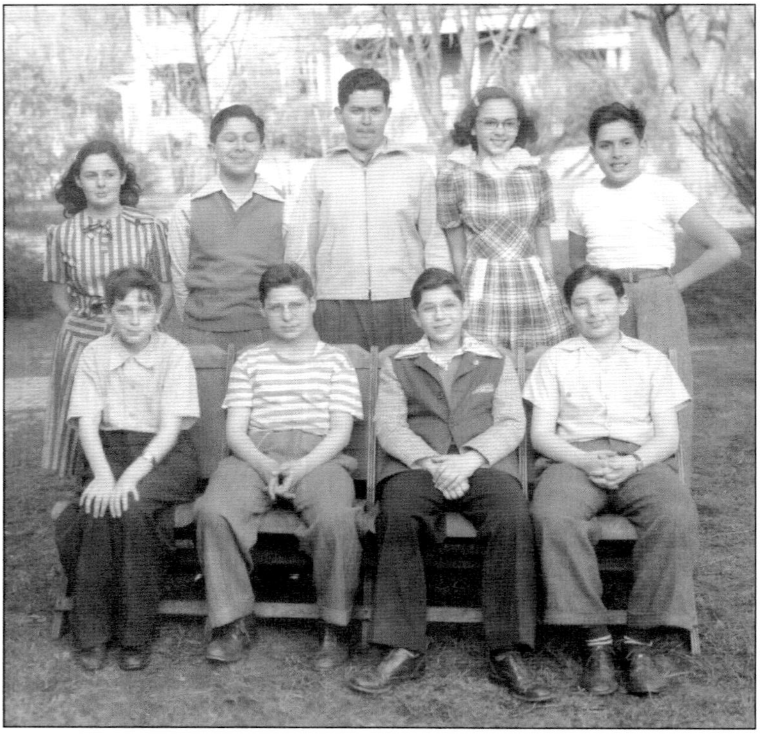

This photograph of the older Hebrew school classes at the former Kesher Zion in the 1940s was taken while the new building was under construction. Although here they are seated and wearing nice clothing, students frequently took bricks and placed them in the construction area to contribute to the building. This was done without encouragement from adults, but the children liked to feel involved in the construction. (Courtesy of Bernie Gerber.)

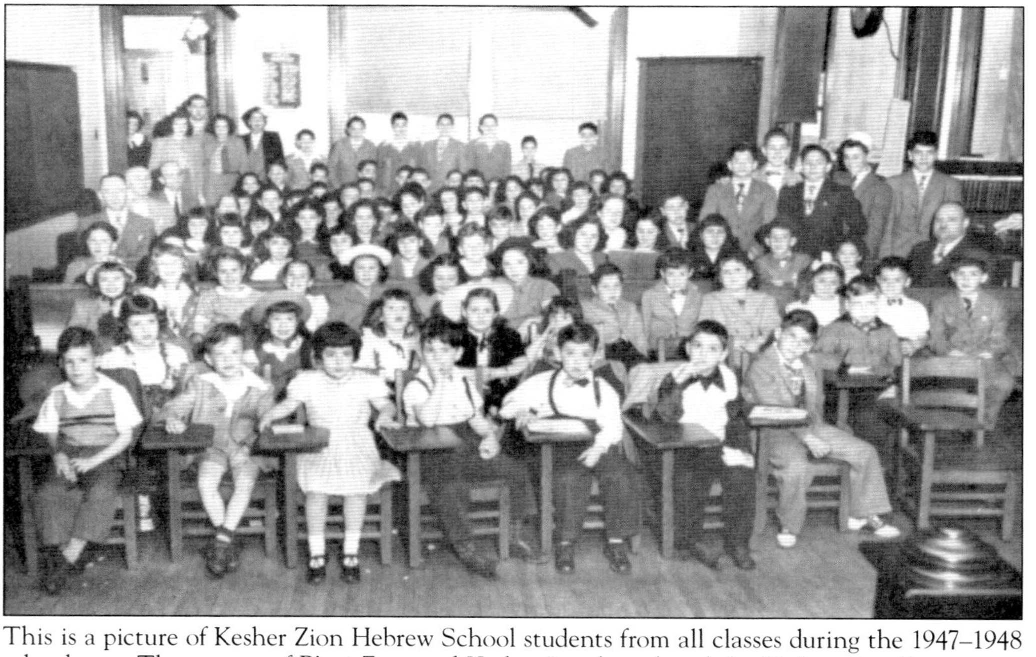

This is a picture of Kesher Zion Hebrew School students from all classes during the 1947–1948 school year. The merger of B'nai Zion and Kesher Israel produced the Kesher Zion Synagogue. Construction of the present home for Kesher Zion began in 1947, and the building was dedicated on December 9, 1950, during the festival of Chanukah, which in itself means "celebration." School principal Joseph M. Ravitz and Cantor Bernard Matlin are pictured. (Courtesy of JFR.)

This image features Kesher Zion Hebrew School's honor society during the school year of 1948–1949. The students whose high marks are being honored are, from left to right, Ivan Botvinick, Sylvia Wagman, Elaine Hinden, Janet Weil Kaplan, Arthur Sager, Mona Reidenberg, and George Mason. Botvinick holds the American flag, and Mason holds the Israeli flag. The service was performed once a year, and winners received a certificate and a mention in the Kesher Zion bulletin. (Courtesy of KZ.)

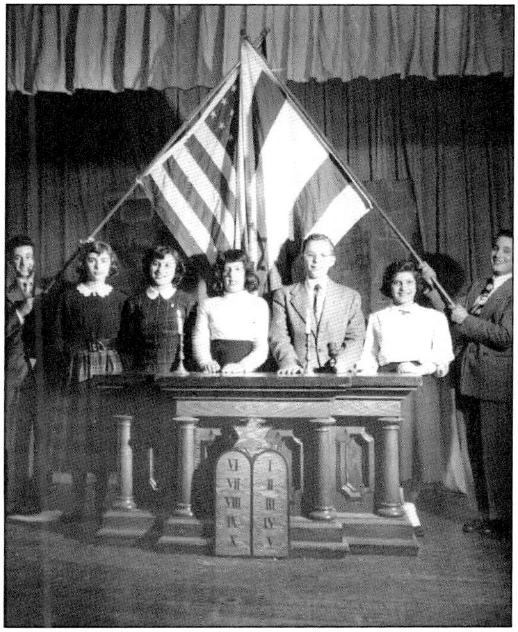

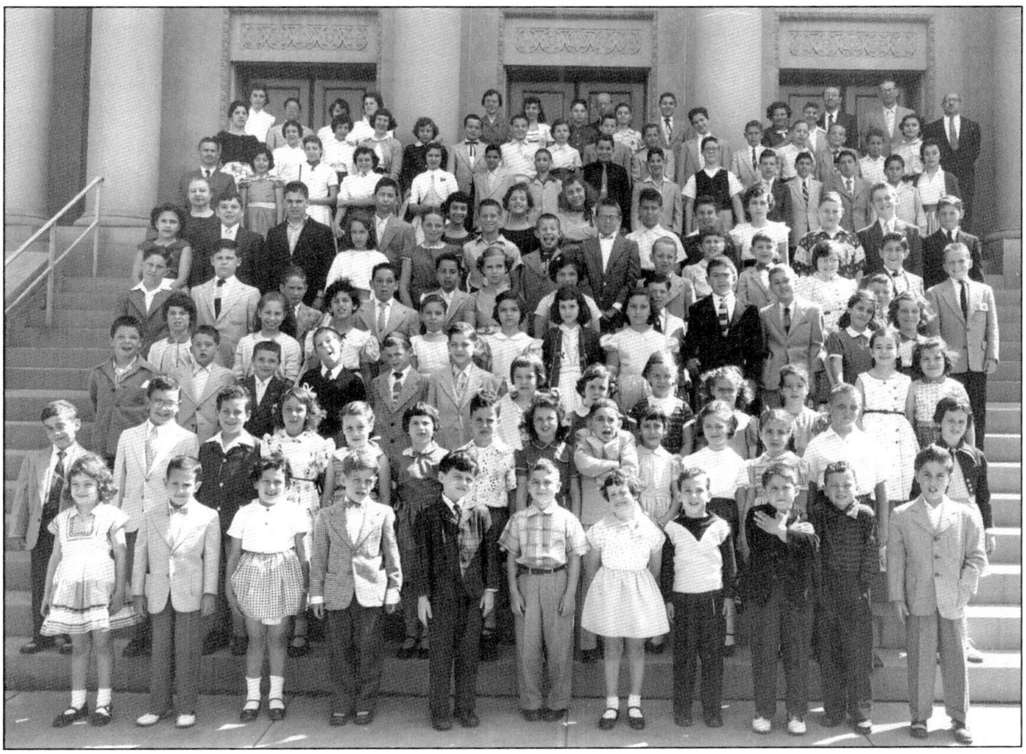

The children and faculty of the Hebrew school are standing on the steps of Kesher Zion's new building on Perkiomen Avenue in the early 1950s, marking a tradition that lasted for several years. People identified in this photograph are Rabbi Abraham Simon (top row, far right) and Cantor Ben Klonsky (top row, third from right). (Courtesy of KZ.)

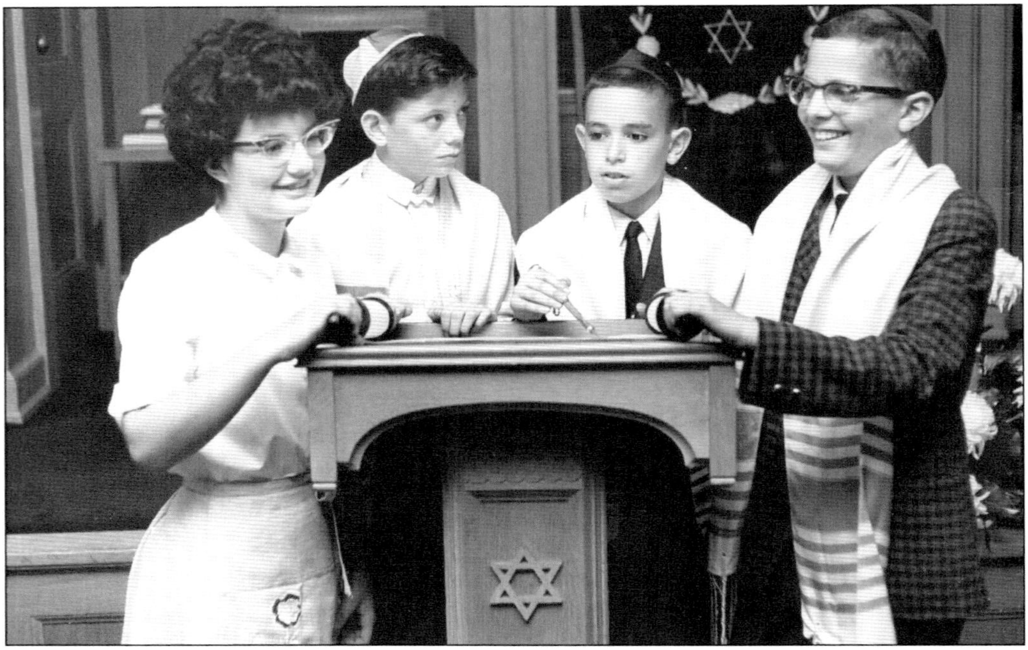

Pictured above is the Kesher Zion Junior Congregation in June 1963. These four students were members of the Kesher Zion Hebrew School and youth congregation, which was held separately from the adults. Lisa Brown, Jody Joseph, David Kuperstock, and Mark Perloe are shown together, from left to right. Pictured below is the graduation ceremony at the Kesher Zion Hebrew School in 1963 commemorating the students' religious-scholarly achievements. A graduation was important to the congregation, and students are shown wearing caps and gowns to honor their achievement. In the back row, standing at far right, is the school's principal, Joseph M. Ravitz, and Cantor Ben Klonsky is third from the right. (Both, courtesy of KZ.)

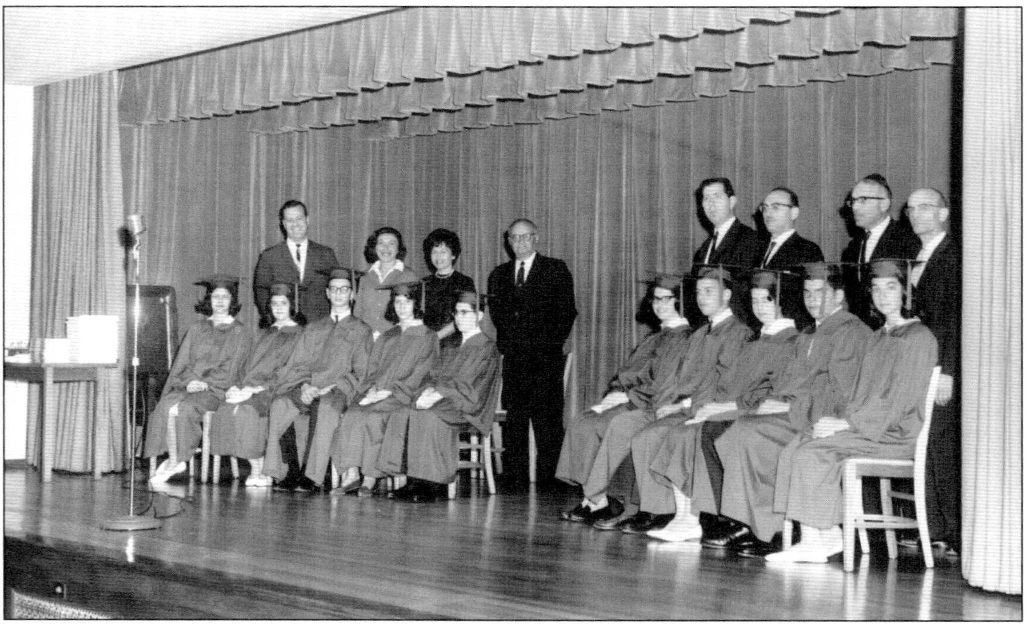

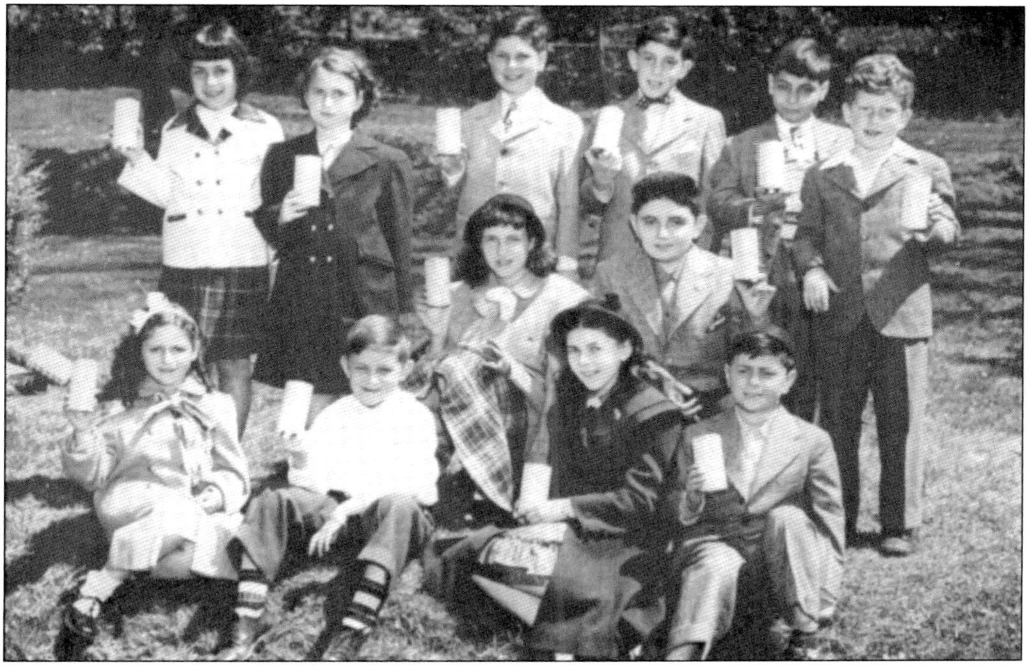

Pupils in Hebrew schools collect money for the Jewish National Fund, a common occurrence in Hebrew schools across the country. These students collected $118.07. The National Fund was affiliated with the Jewish Federation and raised money for Israel by doing such activities as planting trees. Each child received a savings box in order to raise money. (Courtesy of KZ.)

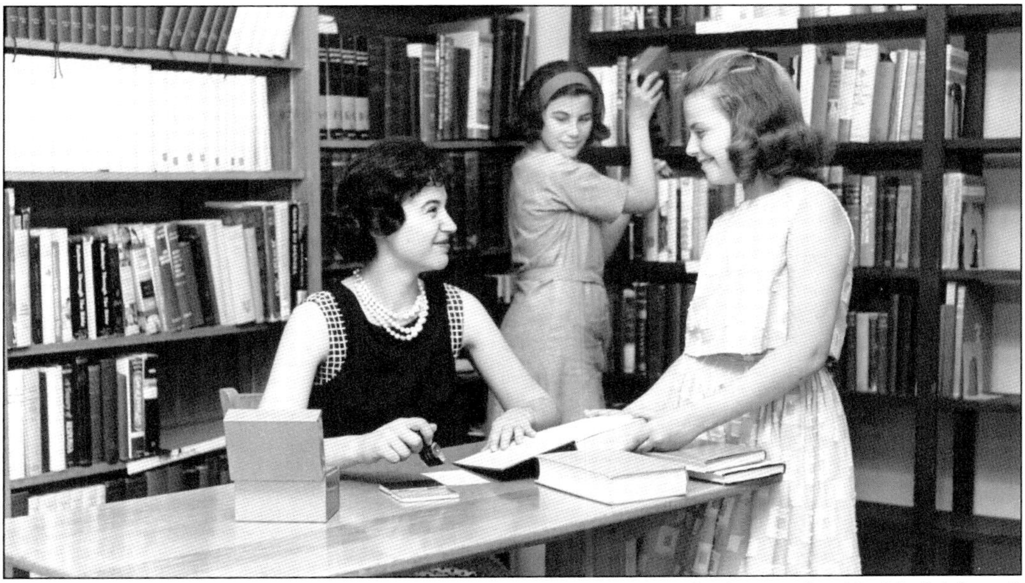

This 1963 picture of Kesher Zion's library features librarian Carol Glatt, wife of Rabbi Melvin J. Glatt, sitting at the table and checking out books to the students. The two girls standing around her are Laurie Silverman (in the back near the bookshelf) and Deborah Daniels Cieplinski (standing near the table). Kesher Zion's library is currently subsidized by the Joseph M. Ravitz Library Fund in memory of the former Hebrew school teacher and principal. (Courtesy of KZ.)

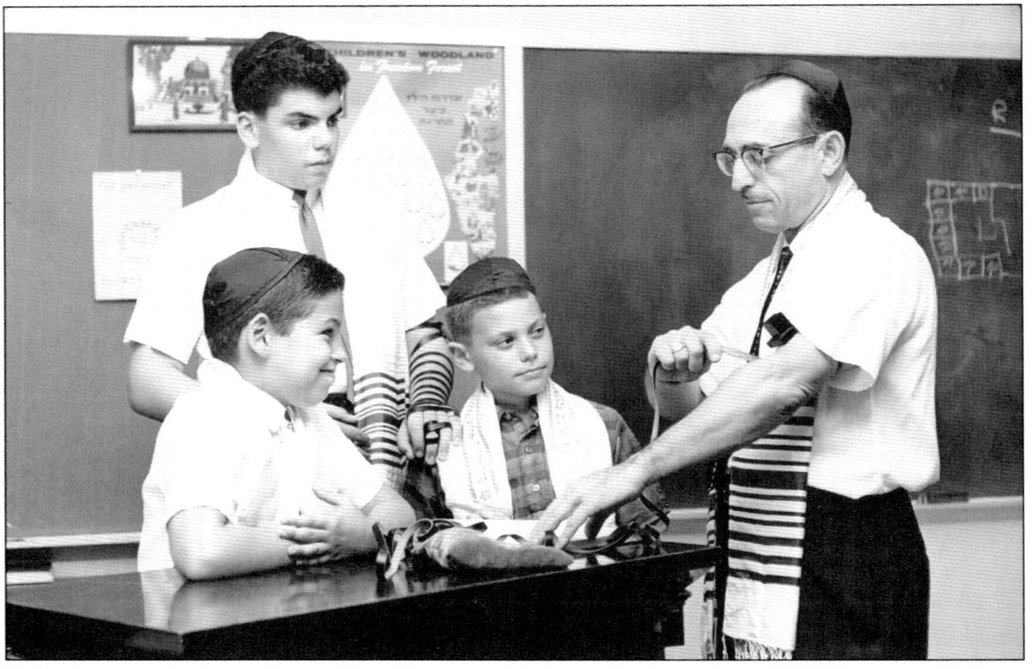

This photograph shows Cantor Ben Klonsky with Bruce Seidman, Ronald Williams, and Glenn Horowitz in June 1963. They are laying tefillin. These rituals are practiced prior to the boys' Bar Mitzvahs. Each boy will give a Devar Torah, or explanation of the reading, after the Torah and Haftarah readings. (Courtesy of KZ.)

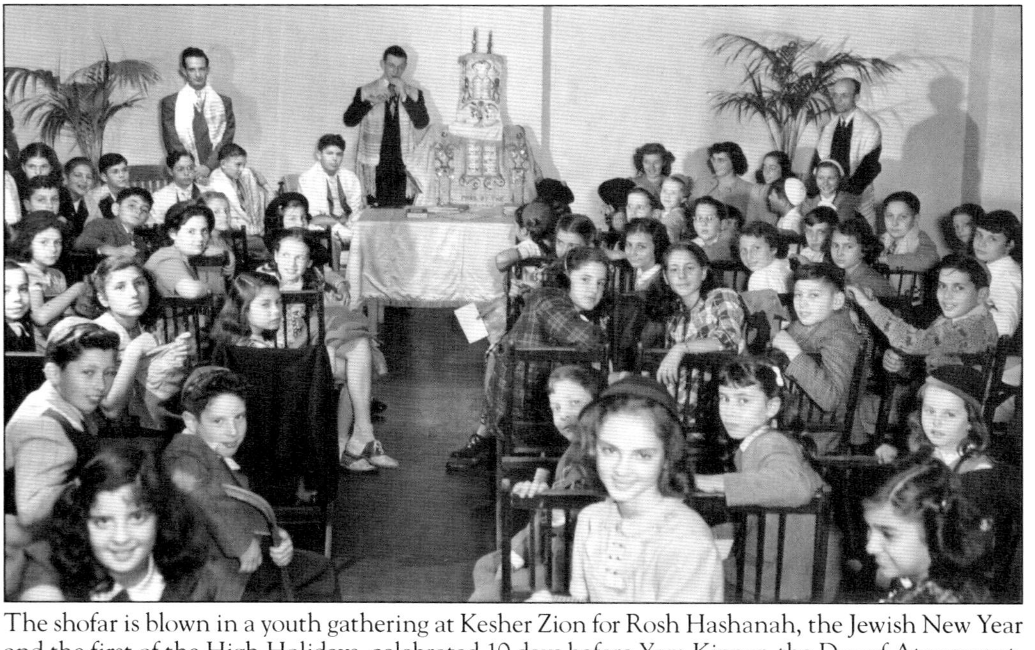

The shofar is blown in a youth gathering at Kesher Zion for Rosh Hashanah, the Jewish New Year and the first of the High Holidays, celebrated 10 days before Yom Kippur, the Day of Atonement. The Torah scrolls are seen in the background; to the right is Joseph M. Ravitz, a beloved teacher. The teacher on the left is Philip Yellin. (Courtesy of KZ.)

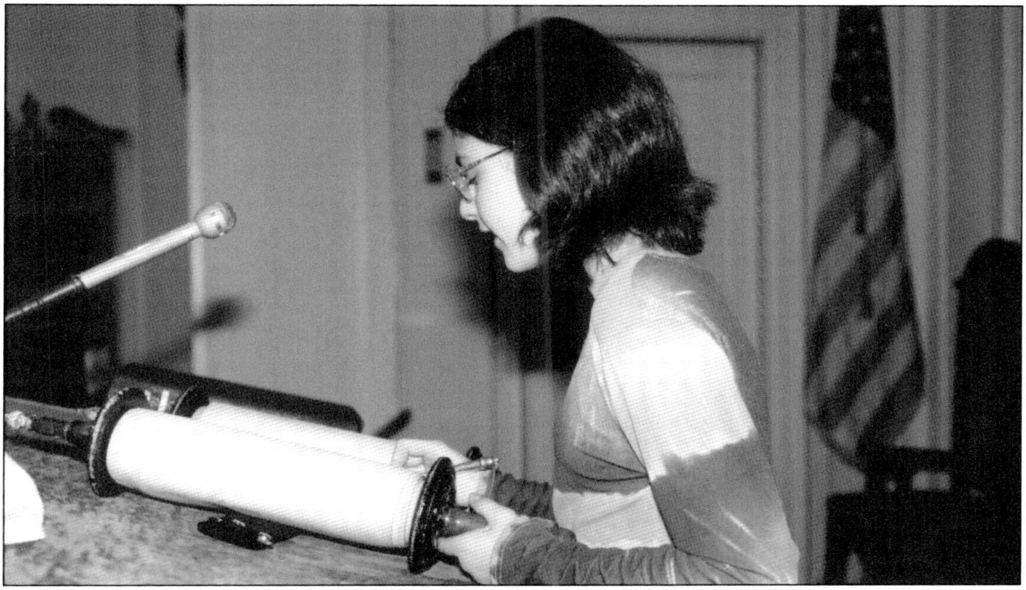

Sarah Pardo practices reading her Torah portion in 1997 at Reform Congregation Oheb Sholom in the Perkiomen Avenue location. Perhaps the most significant occurrence on this day is that the young person becomes fully responsible for keeping the commandments of the Torah as of that day. Below, three years later, Sarah's brother, Daniel Pardo, practices reading his Torah portion before his Bar Mitzvah ceremony at the newly completed building of Reform Congregation Oheb Sholom in Wyomissing. The pews were installed just one week before the ceremony. Daniel began preparing to become a Bar Mitzvah by going to Hebrew school several years before he actually turned Bar Mitzvah age. In the year leading up to the event, intense training focuses on the specific Torah portion and accompanying prayers (Both, courtesy of Michael Pardo.)

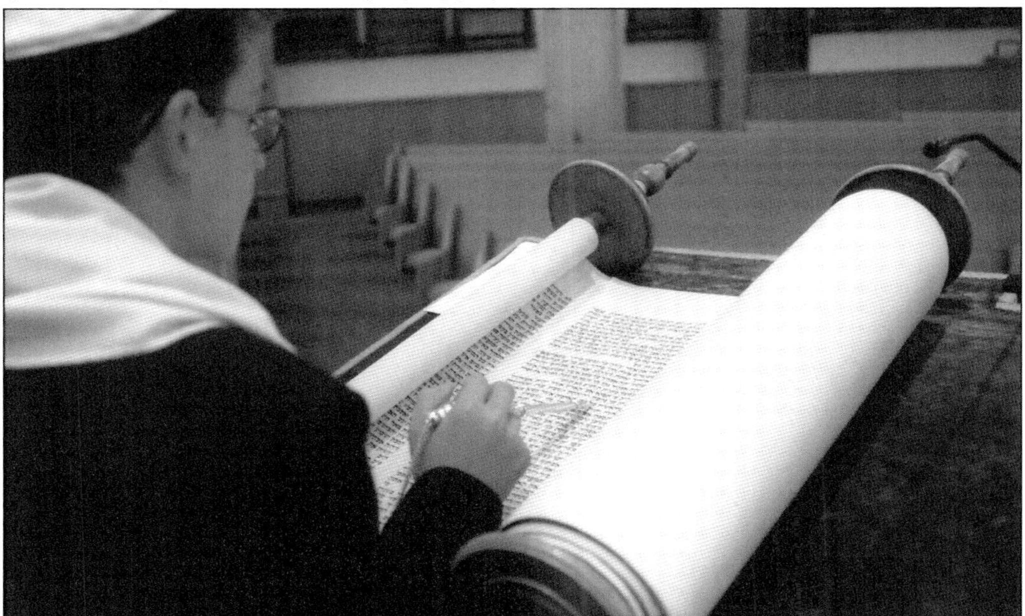

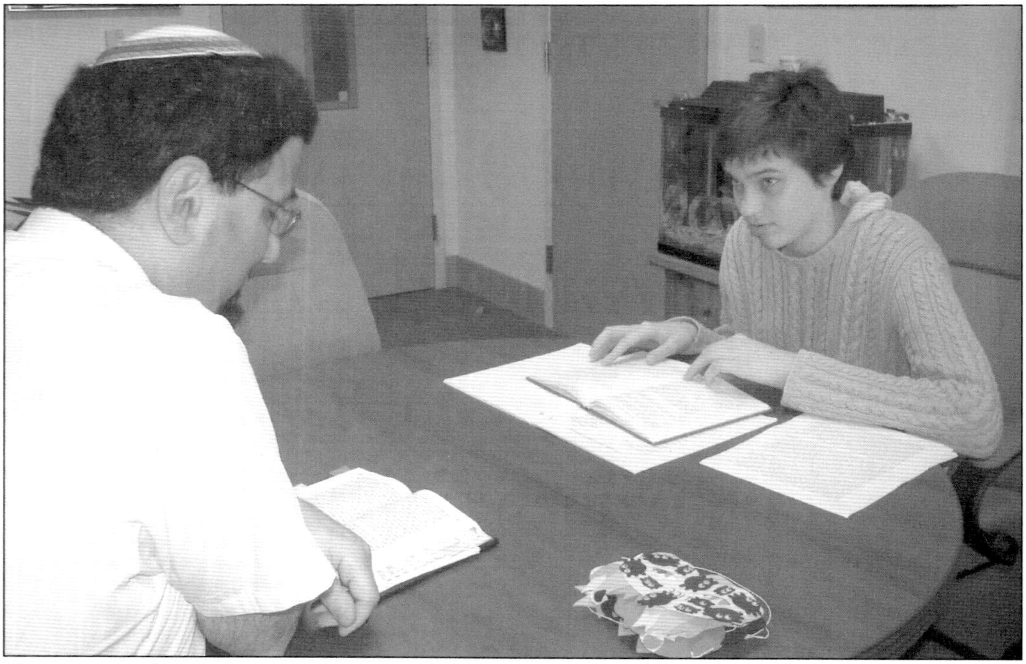

This picture shows Hannah Mart Walker, aged 13, preparing for her Bat Mitzvah. She started lessons with Rabbi Brian Michelson in August 2010 and met with him once per week until her Bat Mitzvah on May 21, 2011. During the Bat Mitzvah festivities, Hannah received the tallit, which her mother Michelle Mart presented to her. (Photograph by Dr. Laurie Grobman, courtesy of Michelle Mart.)

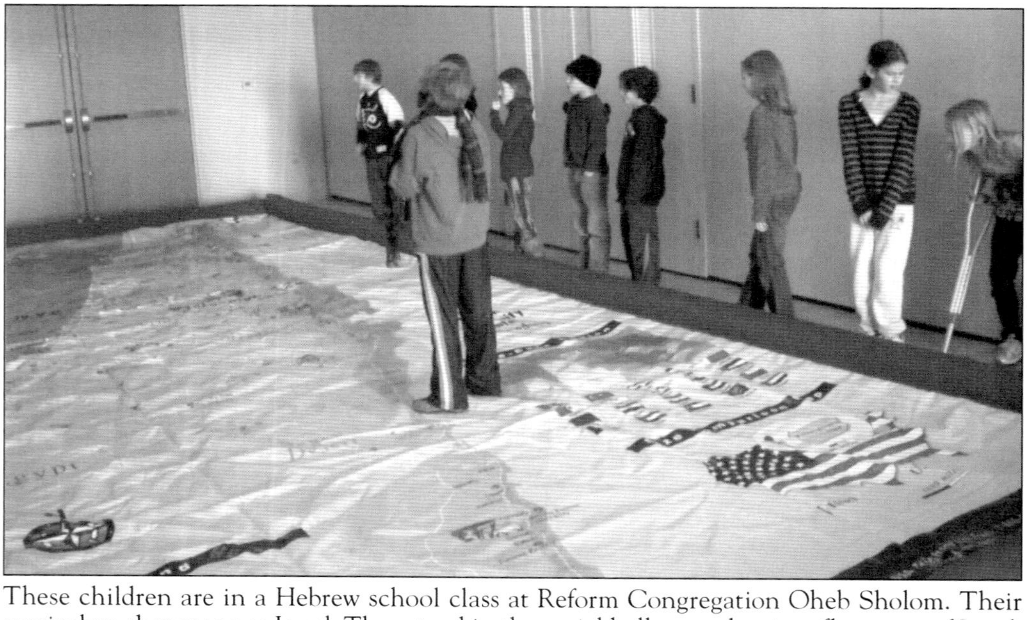

These children are in a Hebrew school class at Reform Congregation Oheb Sholom. Their curriculum that year was Israel. They stand in the social hall around a giant floor map of Israel, from which they learned geography of the country. The map helps the children understand the diverse geography of this small country. (Courtesy of Mark Nemirow.)

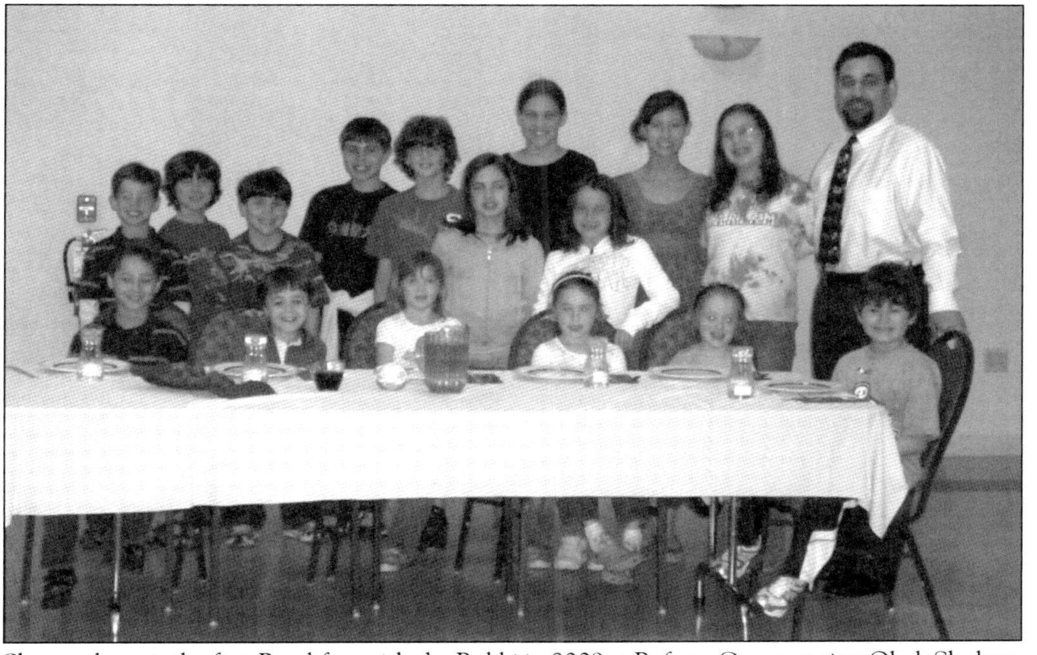

Shown above is the first Breakfast with the Rabbi in 2009 at Reform Congregation Oheb Sholom. This was a special Sunday morning that was started for the children in the congregation who came to the greatest number of Shabbat services over the course of the year. It was a Sunday morning with pancakes and the company of the rabbi. (Courtesy of Mark Nemirow.)

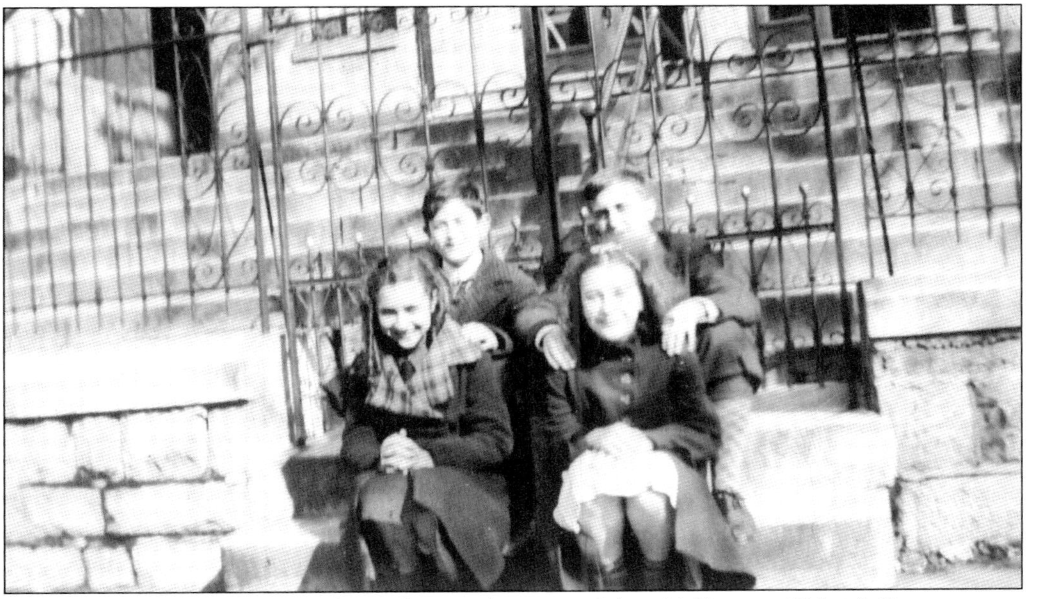

Local friends gather to talk and socialize on the steps of the old Shomrei Habrith Synagogue at 533 North Eighth Street. The two teens seated on the right, David Moyer and Marjorie Sulman at the age of 13, would later marry one another. On the left is Charlotte Levin, who graduated with honors from Southern Junior High School in 1938. They are accompanied by Jerold Sulman. (Courtesy of Marjorie Moyer.)

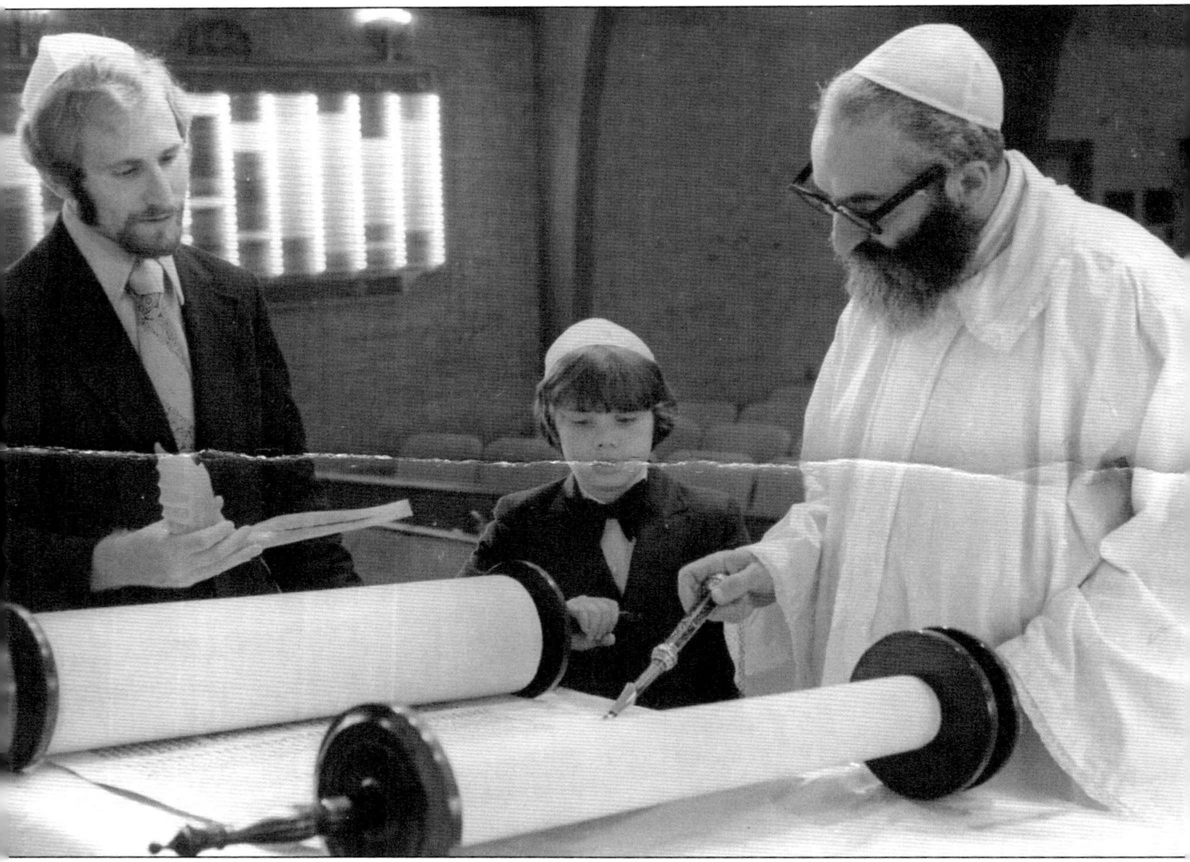

In this 1973 photograph at Shomrei Habrith Synagogue of Reading at Hampden Boulevard, Rabbi Mitchell Kornspan holds a shofar. A young Jewish boy stands with the older rabbi to the right in a pose depicting the Rosh Hashanah ceremony. The rabbi is translating the Torah from Hebrew to English as part of the boy's Hebrew education and Bar Mitzvah. This picture was taken in the sanctuary at the bimah, in front of the Holy of Holies. In 1893, Shomrei Habrith synagogue was built at 533 North Eighth Street, and in 1902, property at 415 Moss Street was purchased as a social hall. In 1960, Shomrei Habrith moved out of center city Reading to Hampden Boulevard, and in 1962, the building was dedicated. (Courtesy of SH.)

Four

Jewish Cultural Center, Federation, and Associated Groups and Activities

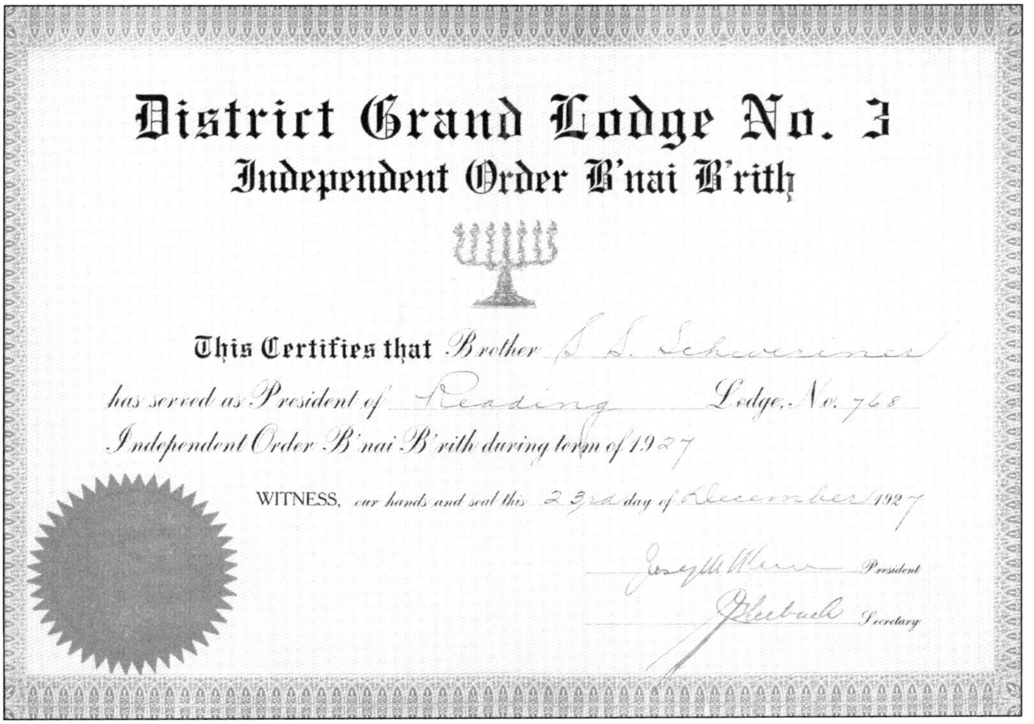

District Grand Lodge No. 3
Independent Order B'nai B'rith

This Certifies that Brother S. S. Schweriner
has served as President of Reading Lodge, No. 768
Independent Order B'nai B'rith during term of 1927

WITNESS, our hands and seal this 23rd day of December 1927

President

Secretary

The Independent Order of B'nai B'rith is the oldest continually operating Jewish service organization in the world, founded in New York City on October 13, 1843. Known today as B'nai B'rith International, it is engaged in a wide variety of community service and welfare activities. The certificate pictured here was presented to Sigmund Schweriner, who served as president of Reading Lodge No. 768, Independent Order of B'nai B'rith, in 1927. (Courtesy of RCOS.)

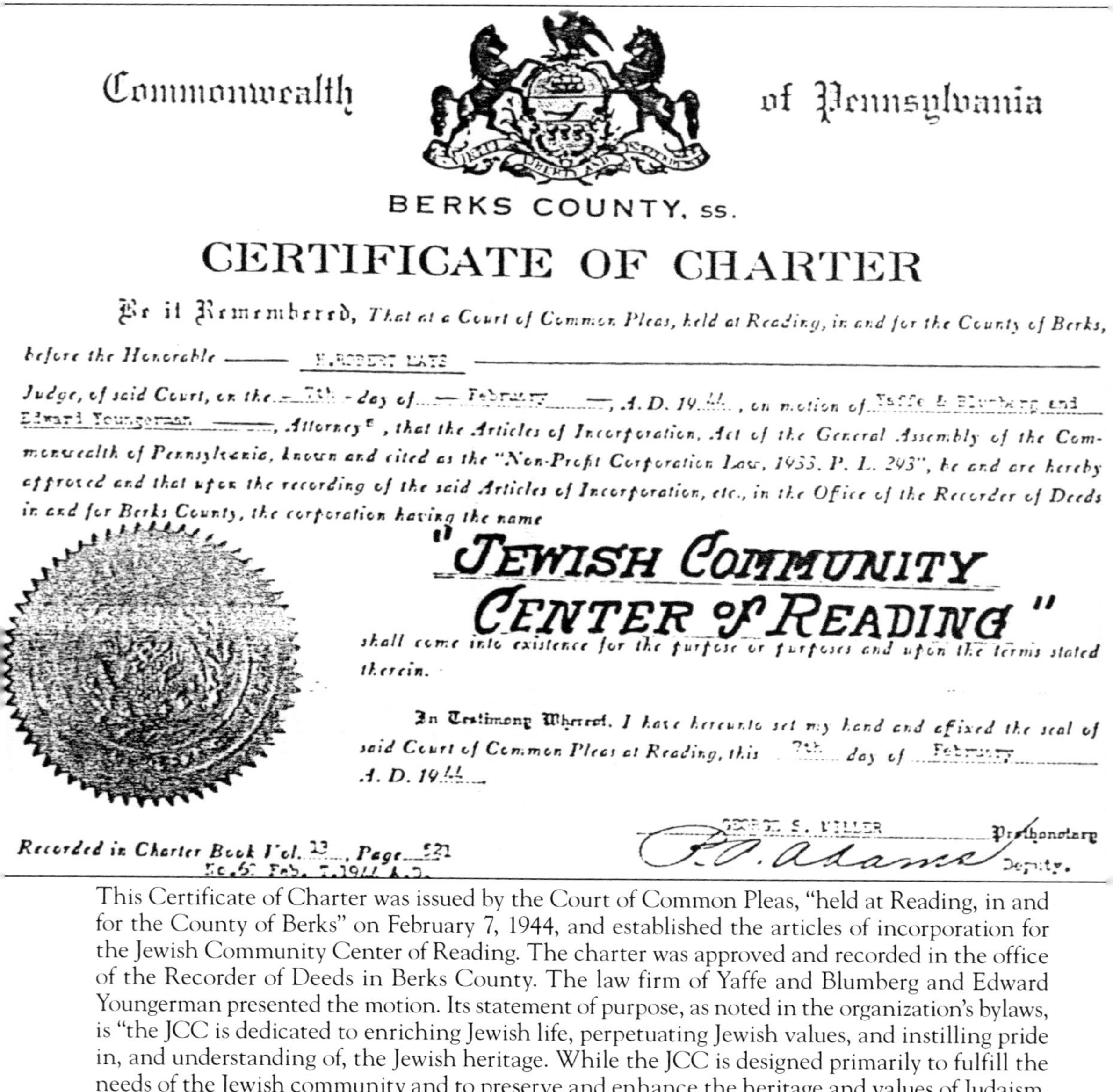

Commonwealth of Pennsylvania

BERKS COUNTY, ss.

CERTIFICATE OF CHARTER

Be it Remembered, That at a Court of Common Pleas, held at Reading, in and for the County of Berks, before the Honorable [illegible] Judge, of said Court, on the 7th day of February, A. D. 1944, on motion of Yaffe & Blumberg and Edward Youngerman, Attorneys, that the Articles of Incorporation, Act of the General Assembly of the Commonwealth of Pennsylvania, known and cited as the "Non-Profit Corporation Law, 1933, P. L. 293", be and are hereby approved and that upon the recording of the said Articles of Incorporation, etc., in the Office of the Recorder of Deeds in and for Berks County, the corporation having the name

"JEWISH COMMUNITY CENTER of READING"

shall come into existence for the purpose or purposes and upon the terms stated therein.

In Testimony Whereof, I have hereunto set my hand and affixed the seal of said Court of Common Pleas at Reading, this 7th day of February A. D. 1944

[illegible] Prothonotary

Deputy.

Recorded in Charter Book Vol. [illegible], Page [illegible]

This Certificate of Charter was issued by the Court of Common Pleas, "held at Reading, in and for the County of Berks" on February 7, 1944, and established the articles of incorporation for the Jewish Community Center of Reading. The charter was approved and recorded in the office of the Recorder of Deeds in Berks County. The law firm of Yaffe and Blumberg and Edward Youngerman presented the motion. Its statement of purpose, as noted in the organization's bylaws, is "the JCC is dedicated to enriching Jewish life, perpetuating Jewish values, and instilling pride in, and understanding of, the Jewish heritage. While the JCC is designed primarily to fulfill the needs of the Jewish community and to preserve and enhance the heritage and values of Judaism, its culture, traditions, ethics, and philosophy, participation in activities of the JCC is open to all." The Jewish Community Center of Reading was merged into the Jewish Federation of Reading on December 31, 1996. (Courtesy of JFR.)

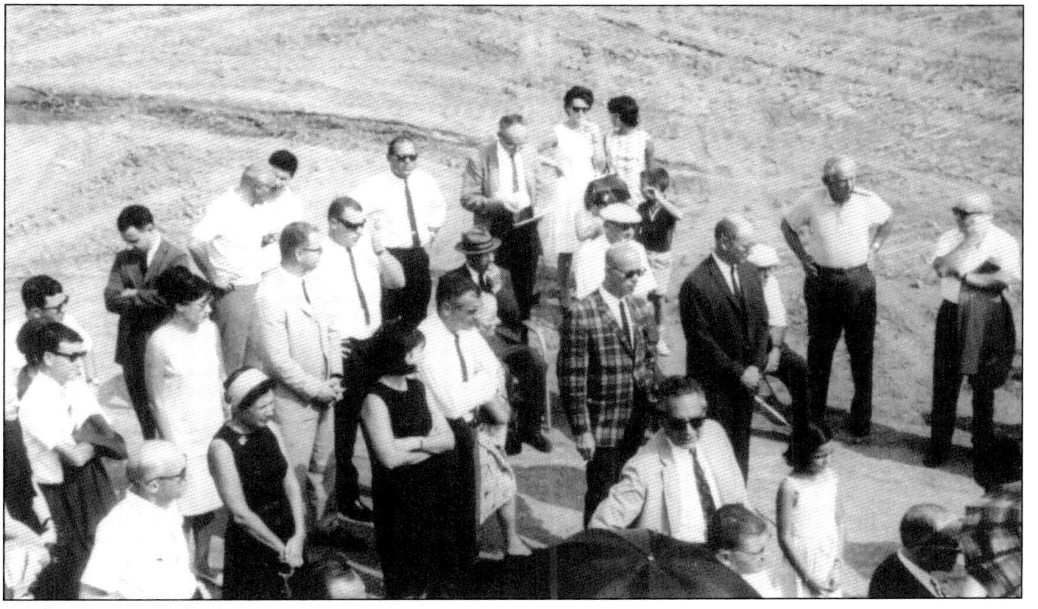

In the photograph above, individuals gather at the groundbreaking ceremony of the new Jewish Community Center of Reading in September 1965. The first Jewish Community Center of Reading was established in 1944. Leonard Sebrams was the first director, followed by Harry Sack in 1947. By 1954, it served over 1,500 youths and adults. Plans for the new location began to materialize in 1959, when the center purchased a 17-acre tract of land on Hampden Boulevard for a modern facility and day camp to better serve its members and the larger Berks County community. The second photograph is a letter from the governor's office of Harrisburg that was sent to the members of the Reading Jewish Community Center to congratulate them on the completion of the new Jewish Community Center on City Line Street in Reading. This recognition letter was a great honor for the Jewish Community Center. (Both, courtesy of JFR.)

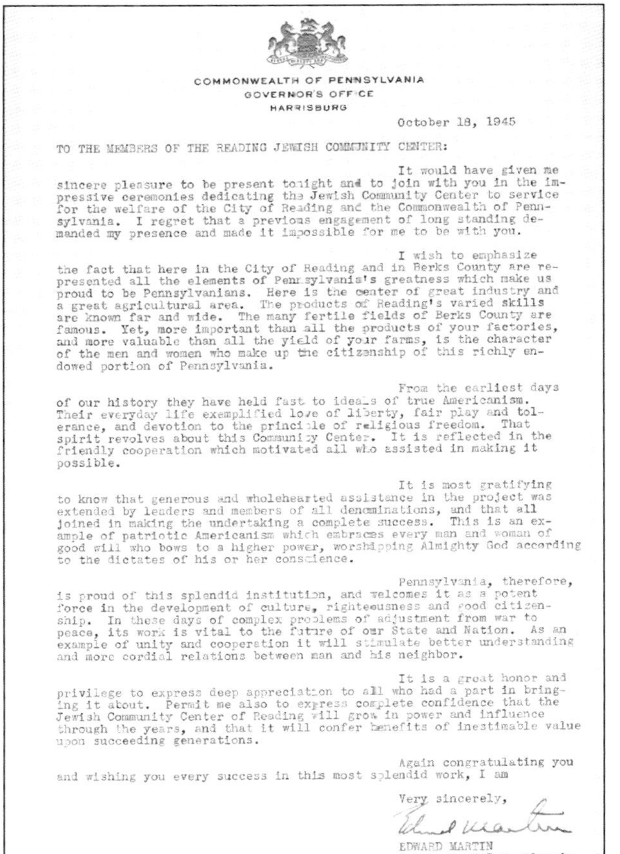

COMMONWEALTH OF PENNSYLVANIA
GOVERNOR'S OFFICE
HARRISBURG

October 18, 1945

TO THE MEMBERS OF THE READING JEWISH COMMUNITY CENTER:

It would have given me sincere pleasure to be present tonight and to join with you in the impressive ceremonies dedicating the Jewish Community Center to service for the welfare of the City of Reading and the Commonwealth of Pennsylvania. I regret that a previous engagement of long standing demanded my presence and made it impossible for me to be with you.

I wish to emphasize the fact that here in the City of Reading and in Berks County are represented all the elements of Pennsylvania's greatness which make us proud to be Pennsylvanians. Here is the center of great industry and a great agricultural area. The products of Reading's varied skills are known far and wide. The many fertile fields of Berks County are famous. Yet, more important than all the products of your factories, and more valuable than all the yield of your farms, is the character of the men and women who make up the citizenship of this richly endowed portion of Pennsylvania.

From the earliest days of our history they have held fast to ideals of true Americanism. Their everyday life exemplified love of liberty, fair play and tolerance, and devotion to the principle of religious freedom. That spirit revolves about this Community Center. It is reflected in the friendly cooperation which motivated all who assisted in making it possible.

It is most gratifying to know that generous and wholehearted assistance in the project was extended by leaders and members of all denominations, and that all joined in making the undertaking a complete success. This is an example of patriotic Americanism which embraces every man and woman of good will who bows to a higher power, worshipping Almighty God according to the dictates of his or her conscience.

Pennsylvania, therefore, is proud of this splendid institution, and welcomes it as a potent force in the development of culture, righteousness and good citizenship. In these days of complex problems of adjustment from war to peace, its work is vital to the future of our State and Nation. As an example of unity and cooperation it will stimulate better understanding and more cordial relations between man and his neighbor.

It is a great honor and privilege to express deep appreciation to all who had a part in bringing it about. Permit me also to express complete confidence that the Jewish Community Center of Reading will grow in power and influence through the years, and that it will confer benefits of inestimable value upon succeeding generations.

Again congratulating you and wishing you every success in this most splendid work, I am

Very sincerely,

EDWARD MARTIN
Governor of Pennsylvania

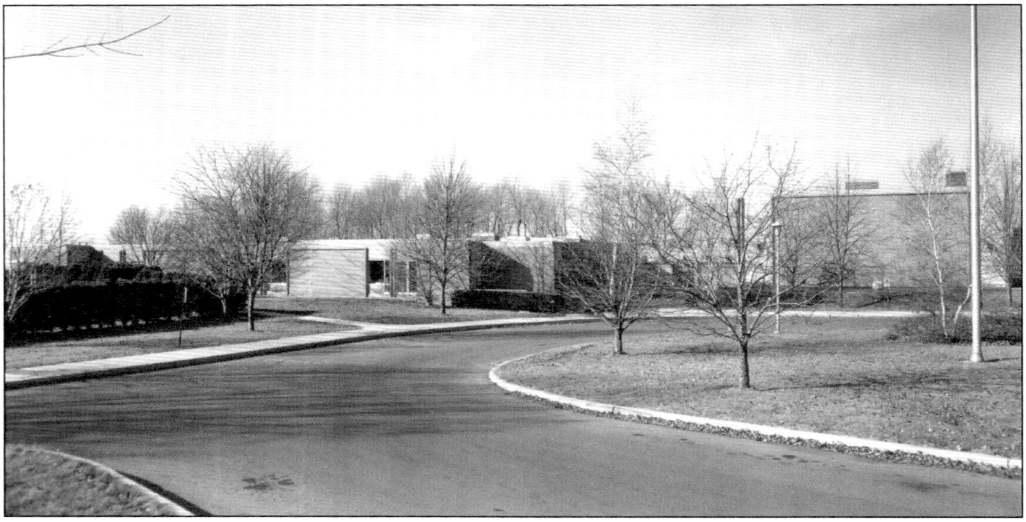

Pictured here is the building at 1700 City Line Street in Reading, home to the Jewish Community Center from 1969 to 2008. Although closely tied to Jewish culture and identity, the JCC was also a recreational and sporting facility for many non-Jews. It housed a large gymnasium, racquetball courts, an exercise room, and a large indoor swimming pool. (Courtesy of JFR.)

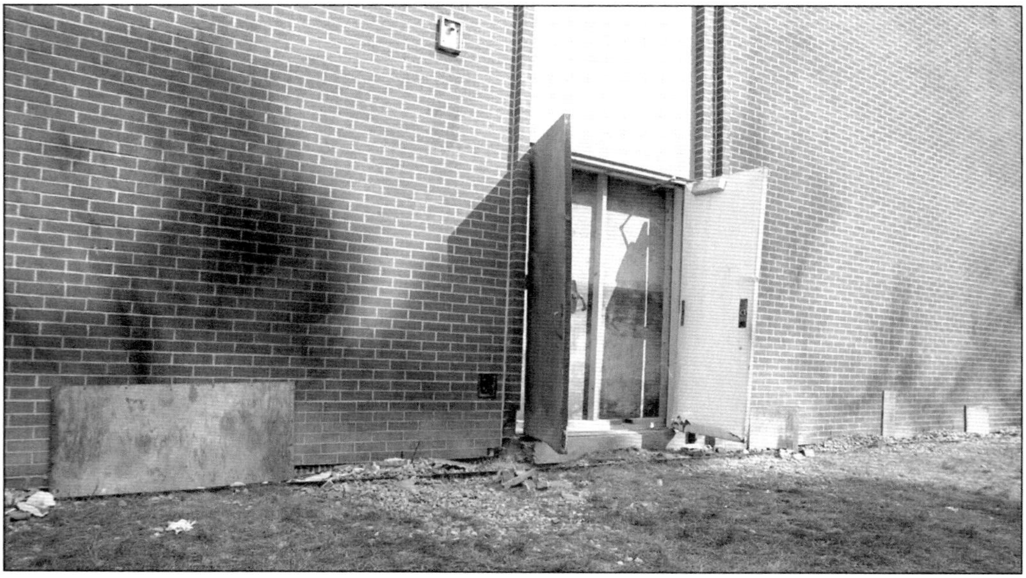

On August 28, 1973, five simultaneous bomb charges ripped through the Jewish Community Center's rear wall, damaging doors, windows, and a handball court. Within a week, ATF agents, as well as a colonel from the US Army, converged in Reading to aid the local police in the investigation. Outraged over the bombing, the community was quick to condemn such acts. Nancy J. Knoblauch, president of the League of Women Voters of Berks County, expressed concern on behalf of the league at such brutal acts of vandalism. Such acts were not representative of the majority of the community in Reading. Sister M. Charlene Altemost, a teacher of comparative religion in the theology department at Alvernia College, expressed her sympathy towards the Jewish community and questioned why such blatant acts of evil are still prevalent in our society. The ensuing investigation failed to uncover who was behind the bombing. (Courtesy of JFR.)

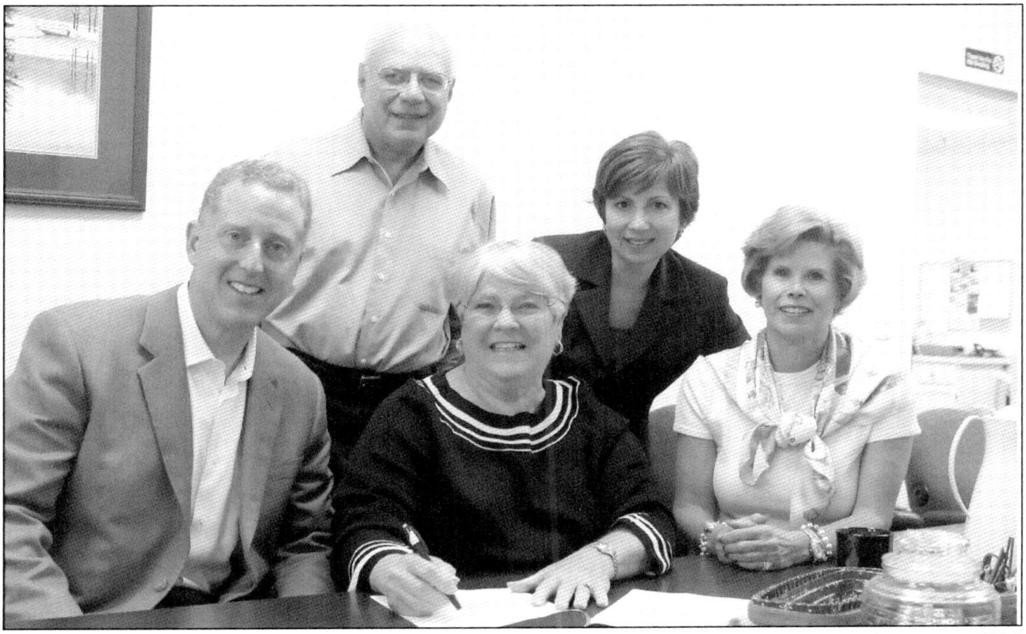

This photograph was taken on September 17, 2008, when the Jewish Community Center at 1700 City Line Street was sold to the Reading School District. Pictured from left to right are Michael Fromm, past president of the federation; Dr. Gordon Perlmutter, past president of the federation; Yvonne Oppenheimer, past president of the federation; Tammy K. Mitgang, current executive director of the federation; and Kate Mohn, secretary to the board. (Courtesy of JFR.)

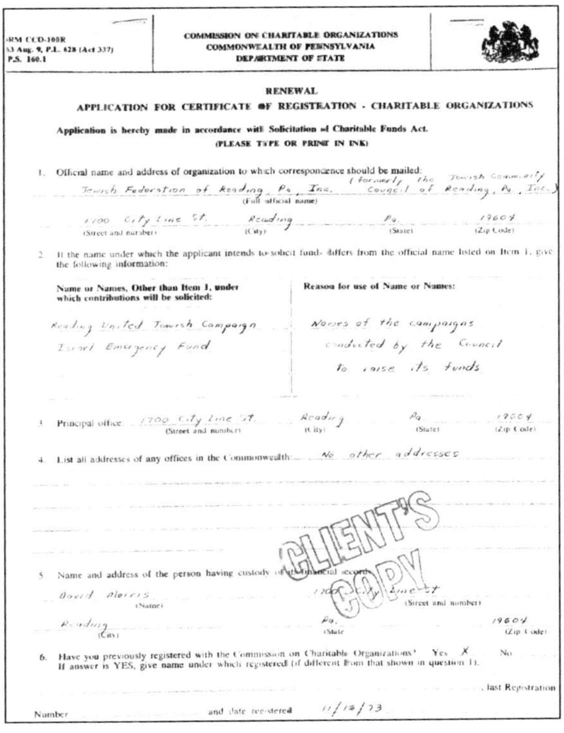

RM CCD-100R
53 Aug. 9, P.L. 628 (Act 337)
P.S. 160.1

COMMISSION ON CHARITABLE ORGANIZATIONS
COMMONWEALTH OF PENNSYLVANIA
DEPARTMENT OF STATE

RENEWAL
APPLICATION FOR CERTIFICATE OF REGISTRATION - CHARITABLE ORGANIZATIONS

Application is hereby made in accordance with Solicitation of Charitable Funds Act.
(PLEASE TYPE OR PRINT IN INK)

1. Official name and address of organization to which correspondence should be mailed:
Jewish Federation of Reading, Pa., Inc. (formerly the Jewish Community Council of Reading, Pa., Inc.)
(Full official name)
1700 City Line St. (Street and number) Reading (City) Pa. (State) 19604 (Zip Code)

2. If the name under which the applicant intends to solicit funds differs from the official name listed on Item 1, give the following information:

Name or Names, Other than Item 1, under which contributions will be solicited:	Reason for use of Name or Names:
Reading United Jewish Campaign Israel Emergency Fund	Names of the campaigns conducted by the Council to raise its funds

3. Principal office: 1700 City Line St. (Street and number) Reading (City) Pa (State) 19604 (Zip Code)

4. List all addresses of any offices in the Commonwealth: No other addresses

CLIENT'S COPY

5. Name and address of the person having custody of its financial records
David Morris (Name) 1700 City Line St (Street and number)
Reading (City) Pa. (State) 19604 (Zip Code)

6. Have you previously registered with the Commission on Charitable Organizations? Yes X No
If answer is YES, give name under which registered (if different from that shown in question 1).
, last Registration
Number and date registered 11/16/73

The renewal application for certificate of registration officially changed the name of the Jewish Community Council of Reading, Pennsylvania, Inc., to the Jewish Federation of Reading, Pennsylvania, Inc., on November 16, 1973, and lists the Reading United Jewish Campaign and Israel Emergency Fund as the names under which contributions could be solicited. Originally, the collective fundraising organization had been created in Reading in 1935 by representatives of Jewish community organizations. (Courtesy of JFR.)

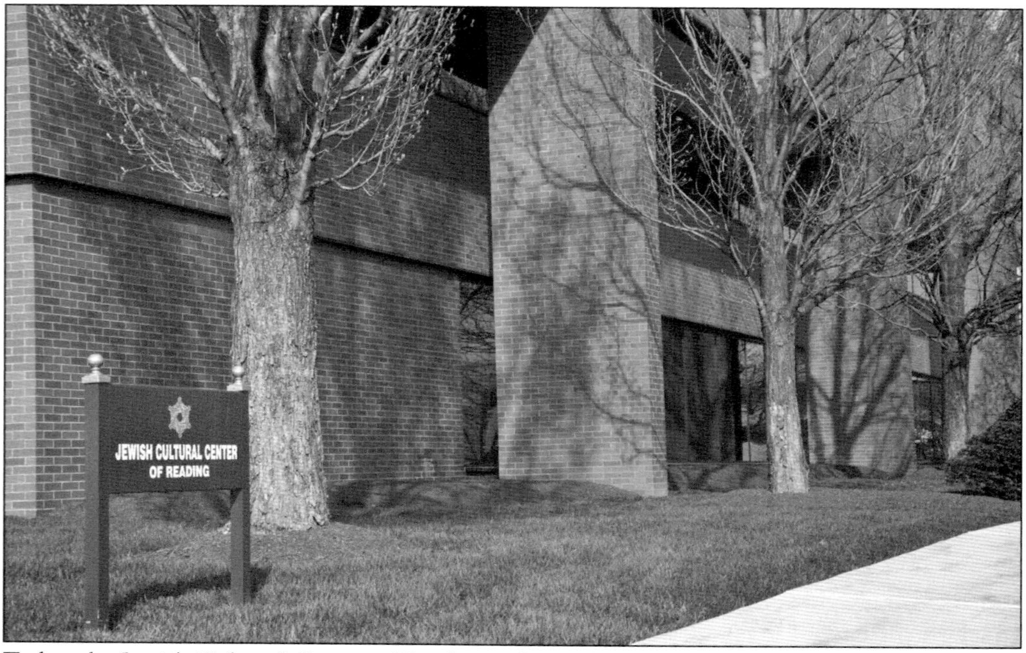

Today, the Jewish Cultural Center of Reading is located on Berkshire Boulevard in Wyomissing and remains a hub of the Jewish community, offering classes, lectures, bus trips, holiday programs, a book fair, bridge club, mah-jongg, and a senior club. The Jewish Federation of Reading and the Jewish Cultural Center are committed to celebrating Jewish life, maintaining Jewish connections, and educating about Jewish culture. (Photograph by Jeffrey Watts, courtesy of Jeffrey Watts.)

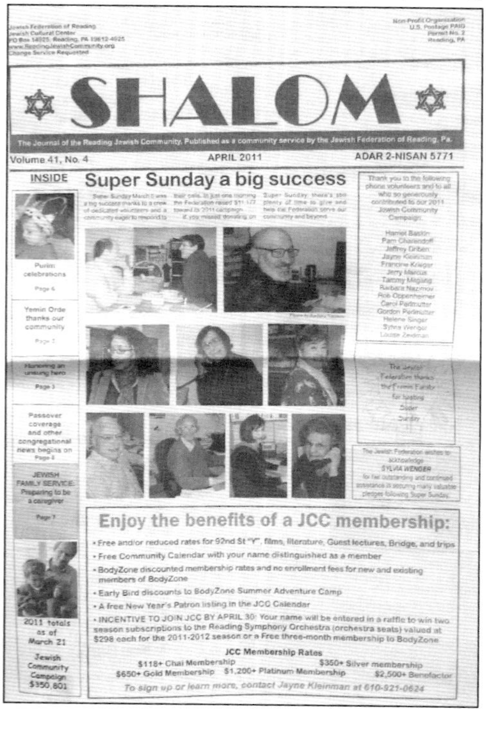

Non-Profit Organization
U.S. Postage PAID
Permit No. 2
Reading, PA

SHALOM

The Journal of the Reading Jewish Community. Published as a community service by the Jewish Federation of Reading, Pa.

Volume 41, No. 4 APRIL 2011 ADAR 2-NISAN 5771

INSIDE

Purim celebrations

Yemin Orde thanks our community

JEWISH FAMILY SERVICE: Preparing to be a caregiver

2011 totals as of March 21 Jewish Community Campaign $350,801

Super Sunday a big success

SYLVIA WENGER

Enjoy the benefits of a JCC membership:

- Free and/or reduced rates for 92nd St "Y", films, literature, Guest lectures, Bridge, and trips
- Free Community Calendar with your name distinguished as a member
- BodyZone discounted membership rates and no enrollment fees for new and existing members of BodyZone
- Early Bird discounts to BodyZone Summer Adventure Camp
- A free New Year's Patron listing in the JCC Calendar
- INCENTIVE TO JOIN JCC BY APRIL 30: Your name will be entered in a raffle to win two season subscriptions to the Reading Symphony Orchestra (orchestra seats) valued at $298 each for the 2011-2012 season or a Free three-month membership to BodyZone

JCC Membership Rates

$118+ Chai Membership $350+ Silver membership
$650+ Gold Membership $1,200+ Platinum Membership $2,500+ Benefactor

To sign up or learn more, contact Jayne Kleinman at 610-921-0624

Shalom, the journal of the Reading Jewish community, is published as a community service by the Jewish Federation of Reading, Pennsylvania. The first *Shalom* was published as volume 1, no. 1 in December 1971. *Shalom* goes to everyone in the Jewish community. *Shalom* reports on everything happening in the Jewish community locally as well as nationally and internationally. (Photograph by Laurie Grobman, courtesy of Laurie Grobman.)

Reading Jewish Voice was first published in September 1922 (volume 1). The bound copies pictured here are dated from 1922 through 1923, and the Jewish Cultural Center has copies of the Voice from the 1930s. Voice was published in English and Yiddish by Jewish Voice Publishing, with J. Koralsky serving as editor and publisher. Volume 1 includes a call for a Jewish Community Center: "This is the cry of the day!" (Courtesy of JFR.)

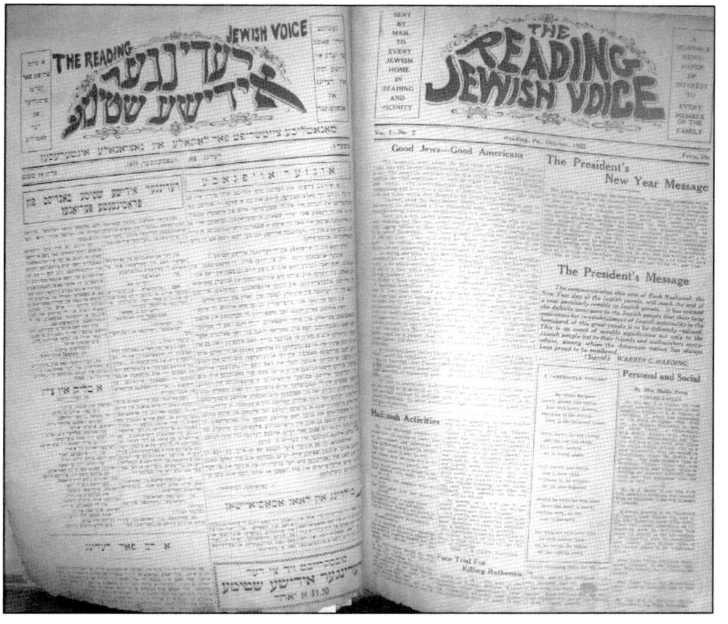

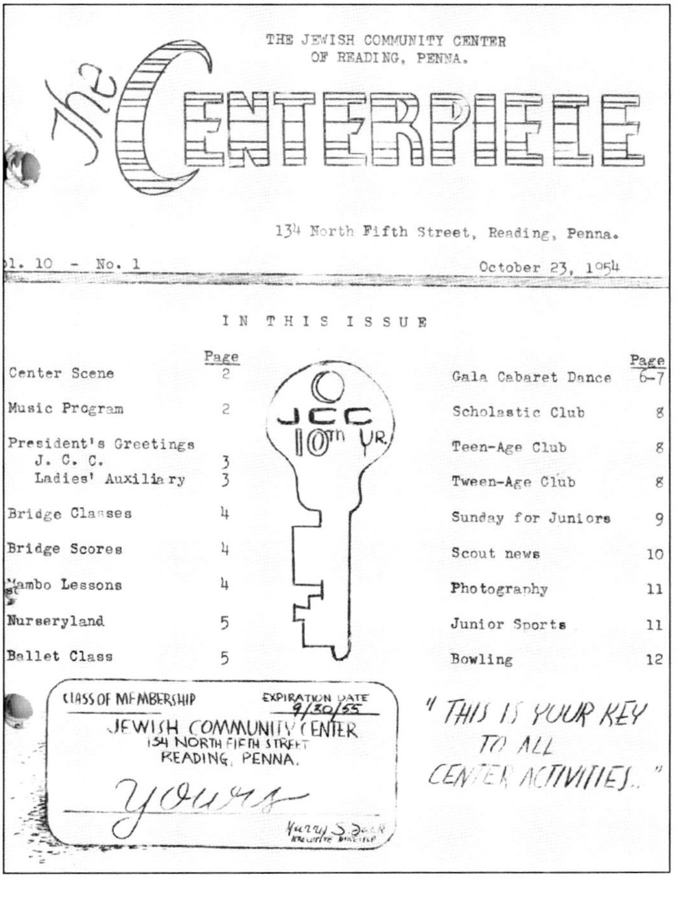

THE JEWISH COMMUNITY CENTER
OF READING, PENNA.

The CENTERPIECE

134 North Fifth Street, Reading, Penna.

Vol. 10 - No. 1 October 23, 1954

IN THIS ISSUE

	Page		Page
Center Scene	2	Gala Cabaret Dance	6-7
Music Program	2	Scholastic Club	8
President's Greetings J. C. C.	3	Teen-Age Club	8
Ladies' Auxiliary	3	Tween-Age Club	8
Bridge Classes	4	Sunday for Juniors	9
Bridge Scores	4	Scout news	10
Mambo Lessons	4	Photography	11
Nurseryland	5	Junior Sports	11
Ballet Class	5	Bowling	12

The Centerpiece pictured here is volume 10 from 1954. Volume 1 most likely began in 1945. The Centerpiece informed all members of the activities of the Jewish Community Center and was sent to everyone who went to the center. The Centerpiece exists today as part of the Shalom. (Courtesy of JFR.)

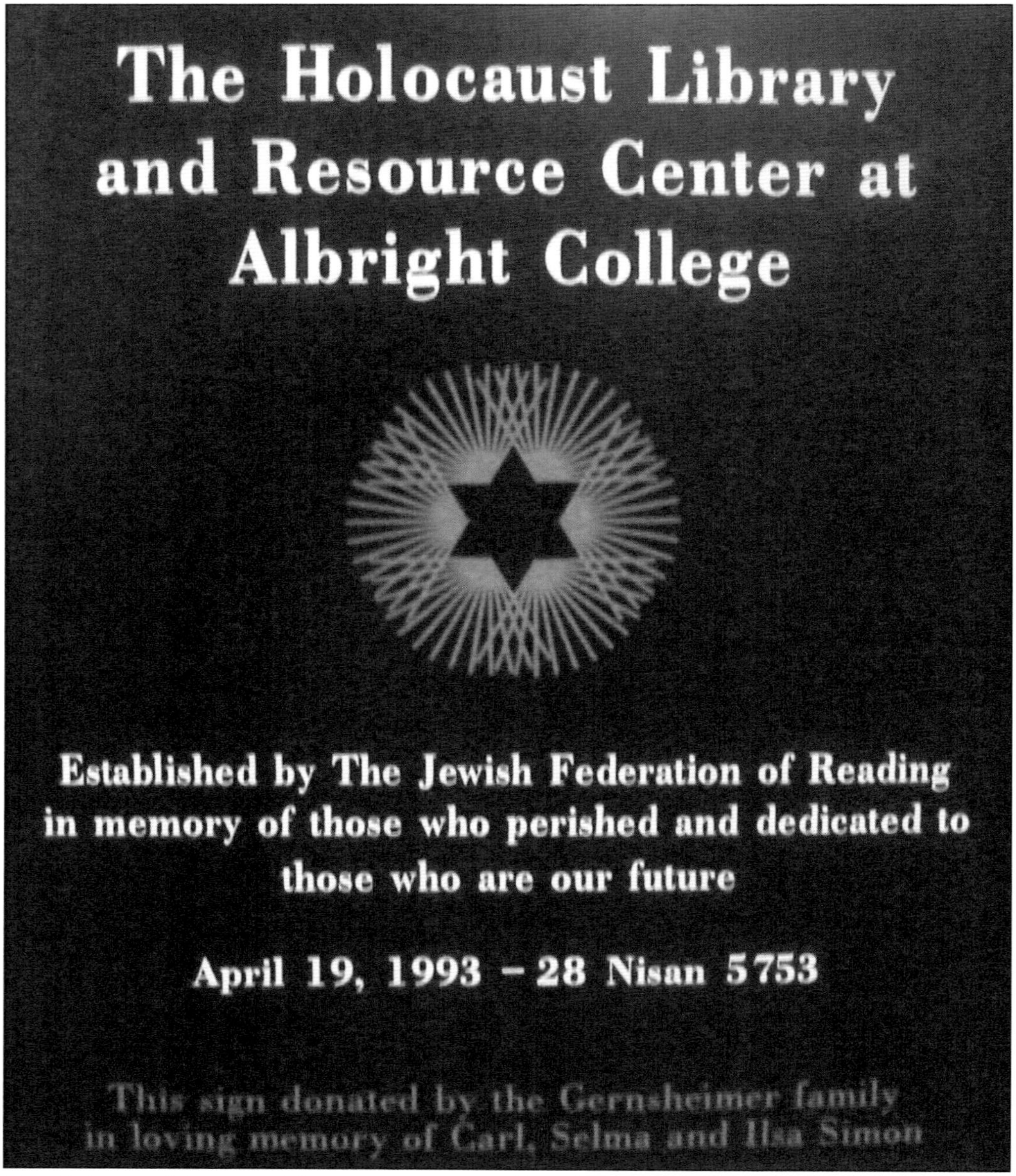

The Holocaust Library and Resource Center at Albright College was founded in 1993 as a joint venture between the college and the Jewish Federation of Reading. The center serves to educate the Berks County community about the Holocaust and other world genocides. Support is offered to faculty and students at Albright and other institutions of higher learning in the Berks County area. Particular emphasis is also placed in outreach to local teachers. Events are offered to help teachers expand their knowledge, and materials are also provided. Additional events are also planned for the community, including the annual Richard J. Yashek lecture. The center assists community groups in planning annual Yom Hashoah and Kristallnacht commemorations. Daniel Tannenbaum served as the first center coordinator after his retirement from the Jewish Federation. In 2011, Jennifer L. Goss was appointed to replace Tannenbaum. (Photograph by Laurie Grobman, courtesy of Laurie Grobman.)

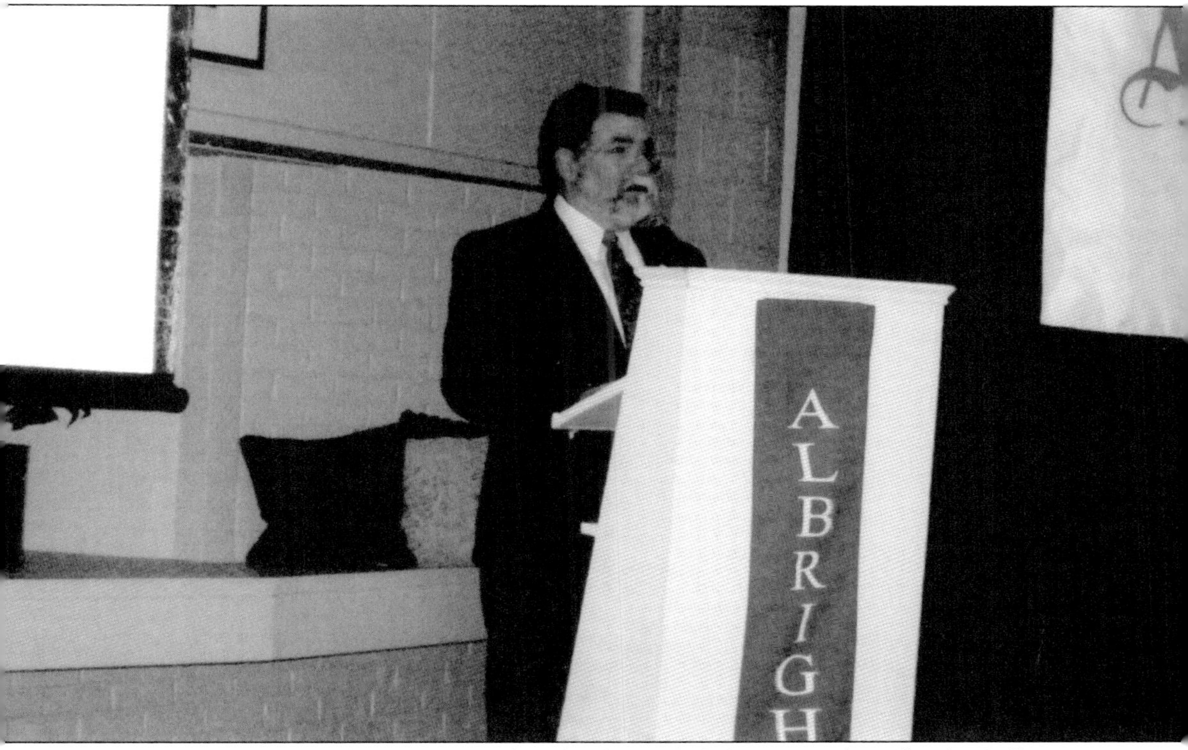

John Incledon speaks at the 2009 annual Richard J. Yashek lecture at the Albright College in Reading. The lecture was named in honor of Yashek, a Holocaust survivor. Yashek returned to his hometown of Luebeck, Germany, in 1993 and again with his daughter, Kim, in 2000. When the Yasheks went back in 2004, the town of Luebeck commemorated Yashek's brother and parents with plaques on the anniversary of Kristallnacht. Yashek and his wife, Rosalye, funded the Electronic Music Program, offered to participants in Olivet Boys and Girls Club. There is also a Richard J. Yashek Memorial Fund for Congregation Leadership by the Berks County Community Foundation that provides grants to Reform Congregation Oheb Sholom and various other charities to support programs that promote and enhance leadership in the congregation. Incledon is a professor of Spanish and serves as director of the Holocaust studies program at Albright College. (Courtesy of JFR.)

LEO CAMP 1912 - 1980

Leo Camp was the youngest of three children born to Carl and Irma ımperlik, proprietors of a small grocery store in the working class district Vienna, Austria.

He was privileged to enjoy a formal education until the age of fourteen, ;er which he went to work in a nearby textile factory. By the age of twenty-e, Mr. Camp already had established himself in the business world rough the founding - together with his brother, Erwin, of a successful ınufacturing company for jersey fabrics.

At the time of the Nazi Anschluss in Austria in 1938, Mr. Camp was Switzerland on business. On his return to Austria to spirit his mother and ster out of the country, he was arrested and confined for a time at Dachau d Buchenwald. His ultimate release in 1939 was secured though the eless efforts of his sister, Pepa.

"Every day of life that I live is a gift to be deeply appreciated," Mr. ımp remarked occasionally on reflection of his survival of that experience. ıat same experience also clarified his strong sense of purpose and, as well, stilled in him a very real commitment to champion the cause against ustice.

Immigrating to the United States in 1939, Mr. Camp lived in New York til 1942 when he joined the U.S. Army. He served as an intelligence ncommissioned officer and participated in the Normandy invasion and bsequent European campaigns.

Following military discharge, he moved to Reading, Pennsylvania, to n the firm of Camp & McInnes that had been founded by his brother win. Shortly thereafter, in 1948, he married the former Henrietta Greenfield. ıey had two sons, David and Jonathan.

Active in the affairs of his community, Leo Camp served as chairman the Reading United Jewish Campaign and was a founder and president of : Jewish Community Council, a predecessor of the Jewish Federation of ading. He contributed significantly to educational and cultural endeav-s, and to a fostering of a better understanding of daism.

An original director of the Reading Area Community College, he rved on the boards of directors of the Reading Hospital and Medical nter, Chamber of Commerce of Reading and Berks County, Reading usical Foundation, Foreign Affairs Council, Threshold of Berks County, :., and the Reading Y.M.C.A.

Preview of Exhibitions and Reception to follow in Freedman Gallery, Center for the Arts

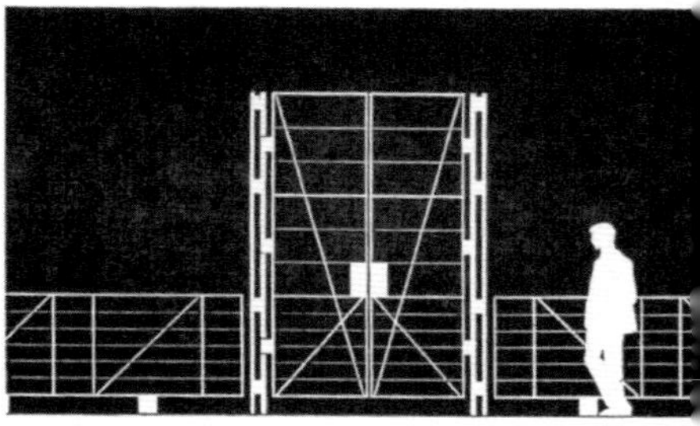

40. Gate at Hall of Witness

Fifteenth Anniversary

THE LEO CAMP MEMORIAL LECTURE

JAMES INGO FREED
- Distinguished Lecturer -

November 3, 1994 - 8 pm
Memorial Chapel

The Leo Camp Lecture Series was founded in 1979 at Albright College in Reading by the Jewish Federation of Reading in honor of Leo Camp, a Holocaust survivor. The annual lectures are significant to the Jewish culture and educate the Reading and Berks community. Leo Camp was born in 1912 in Vienna, Austria. At the time of Nazi invasion of Austria, Camp was in Switzerland on business; however, when he returned home to help his mother and sister out of the country, he was arrested and confined at Dachau and Buchenwald. After immigrating to the United States in 1939, Camp joined the US Army and served as an noncommissioned officer in intelligence and participated in the Normandy invasion. Camp moved to Reading, Pennsylvania, to join the firm Camp & McInnes, which was founded by his brother, Erwin. In 1948, he married Henrietta Greenfield, and they had two sons, David and Jonathon. (Courtesy of JFR.)

Five

Entrepreneurial Spirit

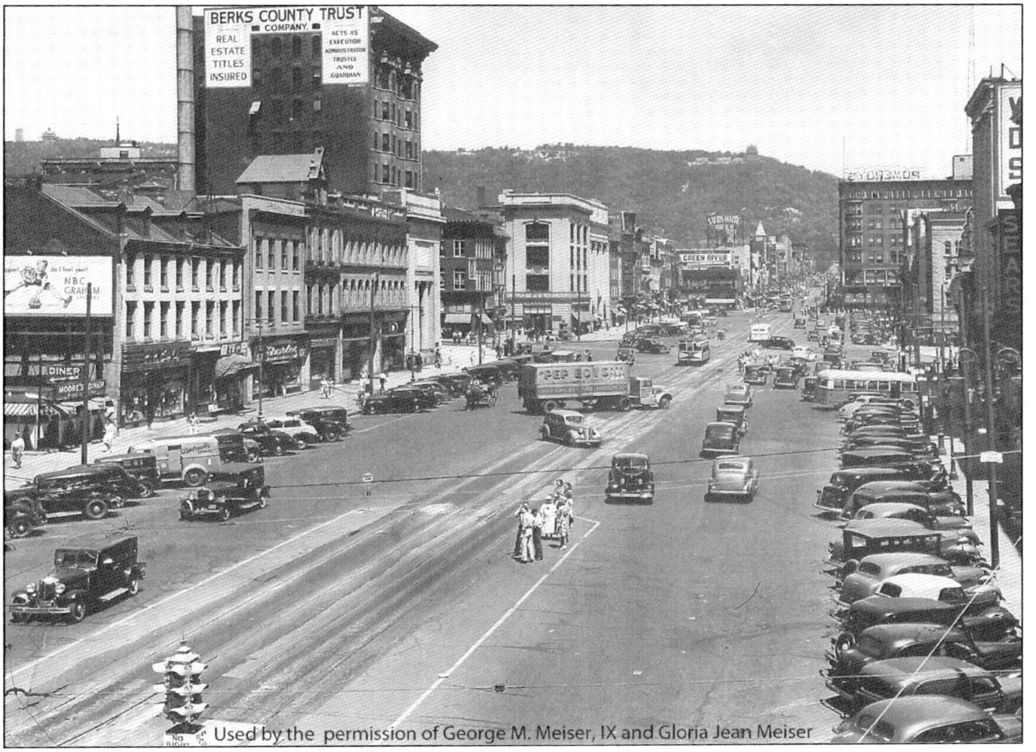

Pictured in 1940 looking east toward the Pagoda, a replica Japanese Shogun Dynasty castle constructed in 1908, is Penn Square, the former shopping hub in Reading. Many businesses on Penn Street were Jewish-owned. When the shopping malls were built, most of the Penn Street stores were unable to survive. (Courtesy of George M. Meiser IX and Gloria Jean Meiser.)

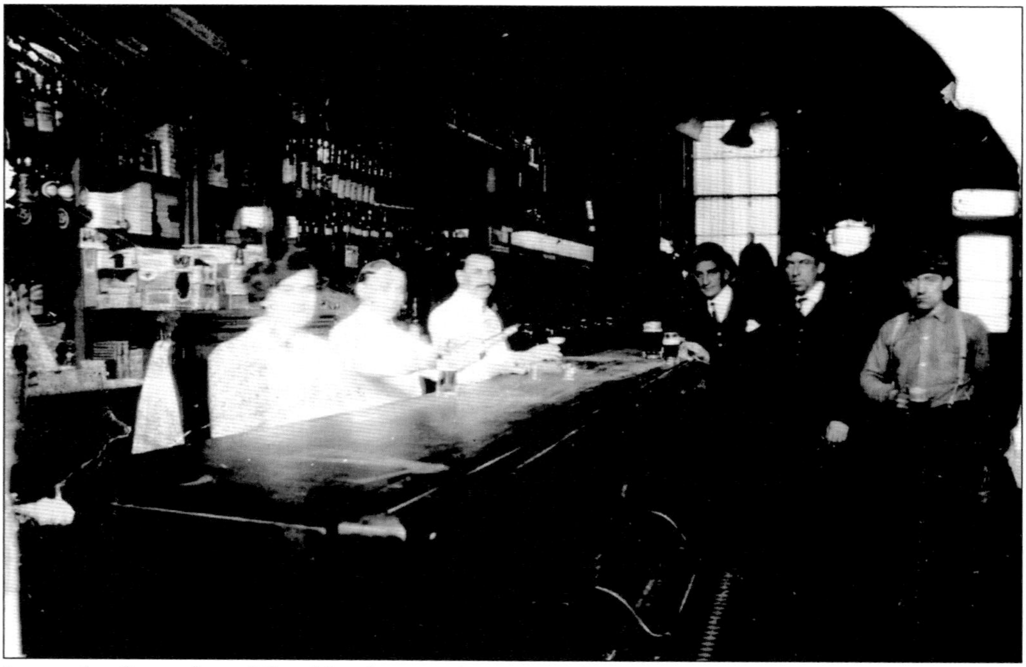

Located at Seventh and Franklin Streets, the Terminal Hotel was aptly named for the train stop right next door. Operated and owned by Morris Knoblauch, this bar sold Sunshine beer, which was produced in Reading. It also had several rooms upstairs for travelers. (Courtesy of Eileen Knoblauch-Wagner.)

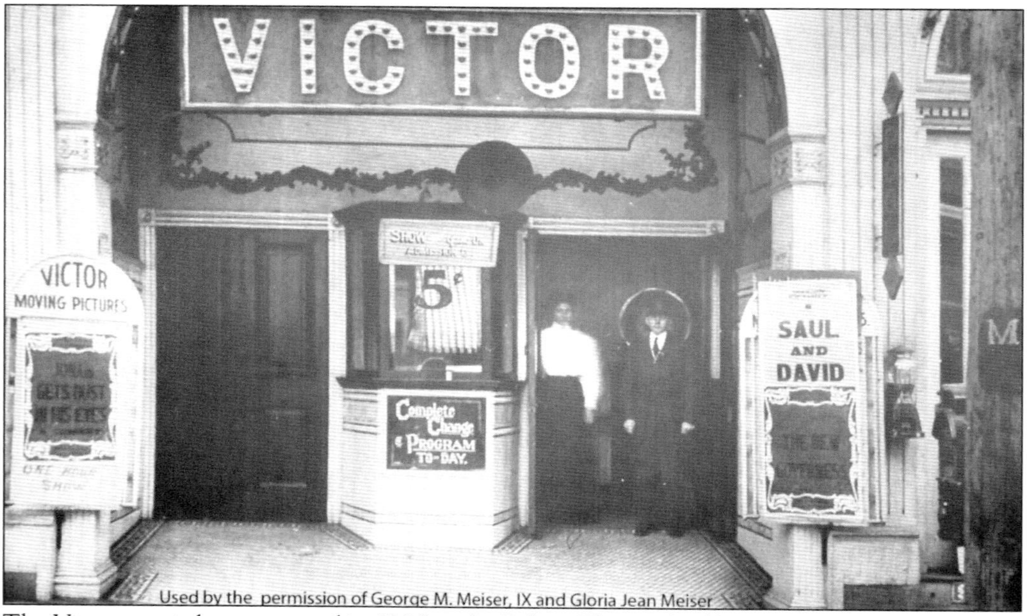

The Victor movie house opened in 1906 in the Palace Theatre building and existed for two years at this site. The 142-seat auditorium measured 15 by 98 feet. The first film operators were Bert Schantz and Winfeld Steele. As shown on the ticket booth, admissions at the time were only 5¢. (Courtesy of George M. Meiser IX and Gloria Jean Meiser.)

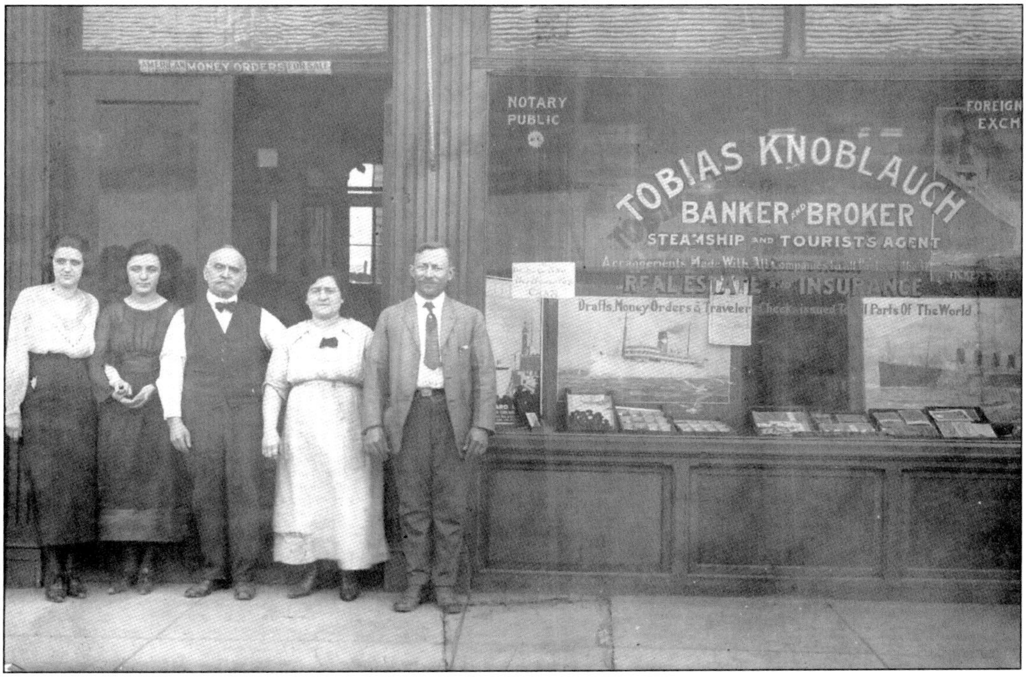

The Knoblauch Bank was founded in 1900 by Tobias Knoblauch, an Austrian immigrant who became a naturalized American citizen that same year. Building the bank from his own personal funds, Tobias lent money to needy Jewish families without charging interest and with no repayment deadline. Tobias Knoblauch and his son, Leo C. Knoblauch, who would eventually take over the business, expanded the bank by meeting the needs of the community. The Knoblauch Bank funded construction projects around the area to build houses for Jewish families. The families rented the houses, and their monthly rent went toward paying for the house so that the renter would eventually own it. Tobias Knoblauch felt it was important for immigrant families to have ownership of a house for financial stability and growth. (Both, courtesy of Eileen Knoblauch-Wagner.)

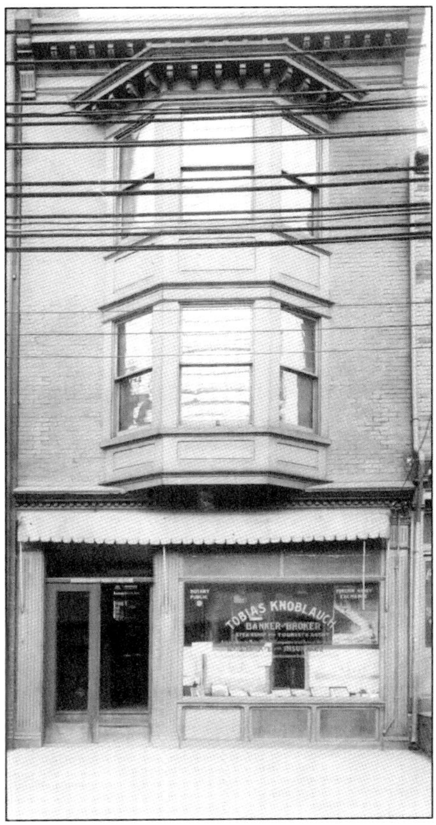

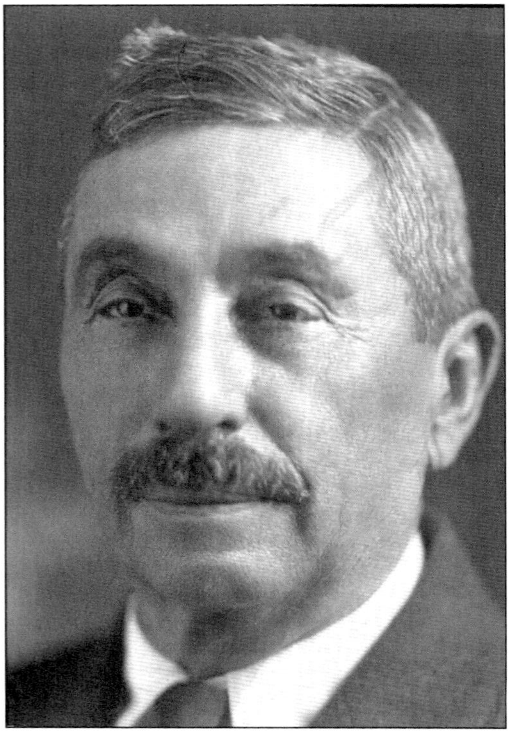

Emigrating from Russia in 1888, Jacob Fogelman, pictured at left, made his living by being a junk man. In 1917, Fogelman was found not guilty by Judge Warner in criminal court on a charge of false pretense involving the sale of a tank. Fogelman was president of Shomrei Habrith Synagogue in 1918. Jewish-owned businesses were already thriving in Reading in the late 1800s. (Courtesy of Mildred Ruttenberg.)

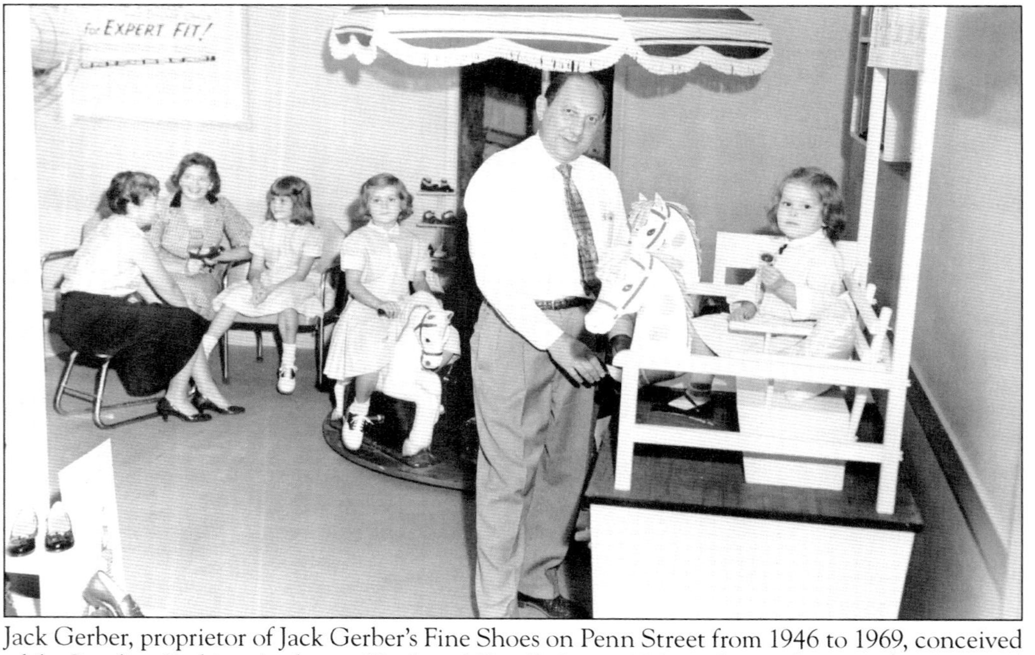

Jack Gerber, proprietor of Jack Gerber's Fine Shoes on Penn Street from 1946 to 1969, conceived of the Reading Parking Authority "Park and Shop" plan in 1964 and was subsequently appointed to the authority by Reading mayor Victor R.H. Yarnell. Gerber was married to Mollie (Lipsitz) Gerber and had one son, Bernard Gerber, who returned to Reading to practice law after earning his JD at the University of Pennsylvania. (Courtesy of Bernie Gerber.)

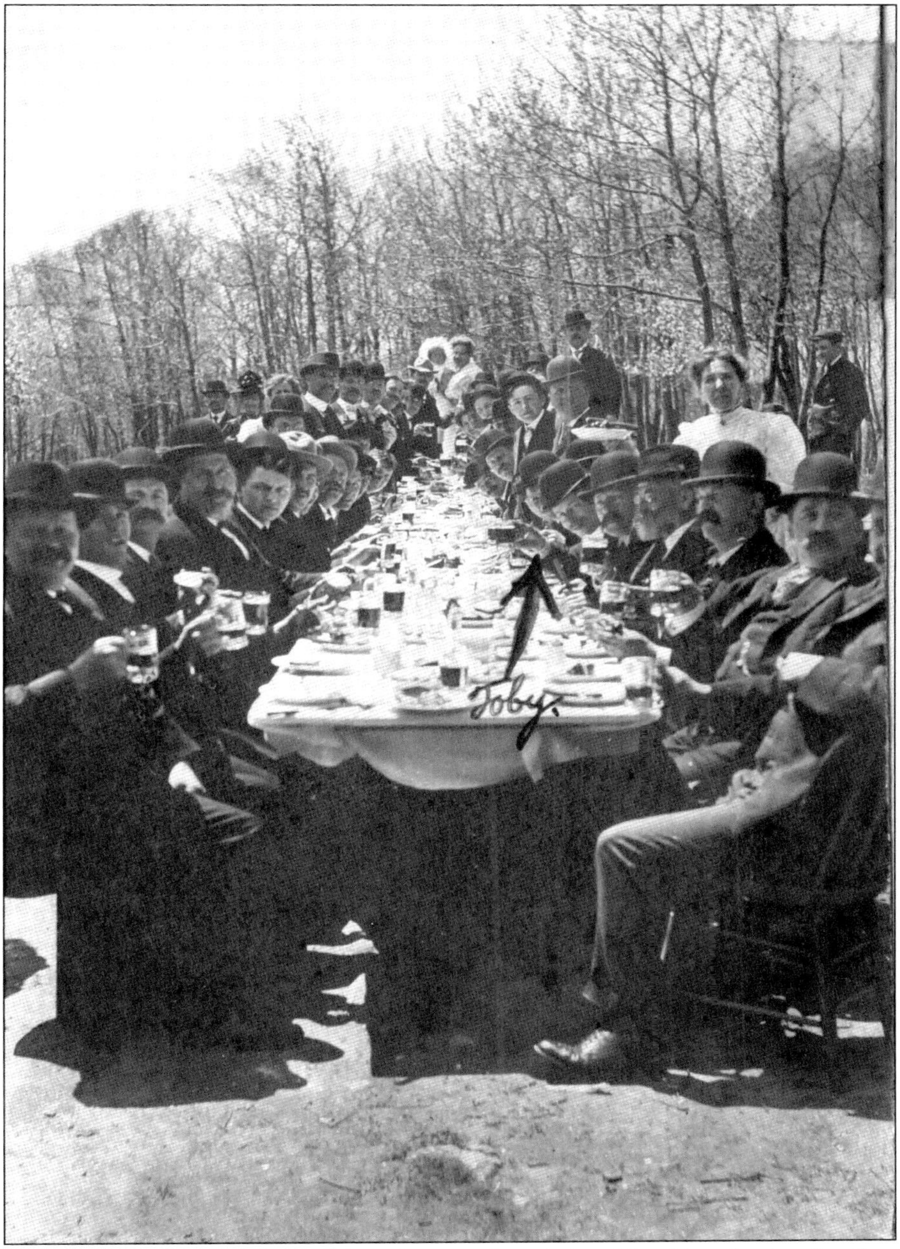

This is a portrait of the Hassel Free Loan Society, founded by Max Hassel, who distributed his wealth generously. At his funeral in 1933, Rabbi Max J. Routtenberg told the congregation, "His was always the desire to help his fellow man. He did not want his wealth to be buried with him. He wanted his generosity to continue after his death," and lamented the loss of Hassel, saying, "the Jewish community had lost a great and devoted friend, and the city of Reading had lost a great benefactor." The Hassel Free Loan Society provided loans to Reading's most needy. However, Max Hassel's reputation in the Reading Jewish community is ambivalent. Despite his recognized philanthropy, he was also known to be a bootlegger and was nicknamed Reading's "Beer Baron." (Courtesy of Eileen Knoblauch-Wagner.)

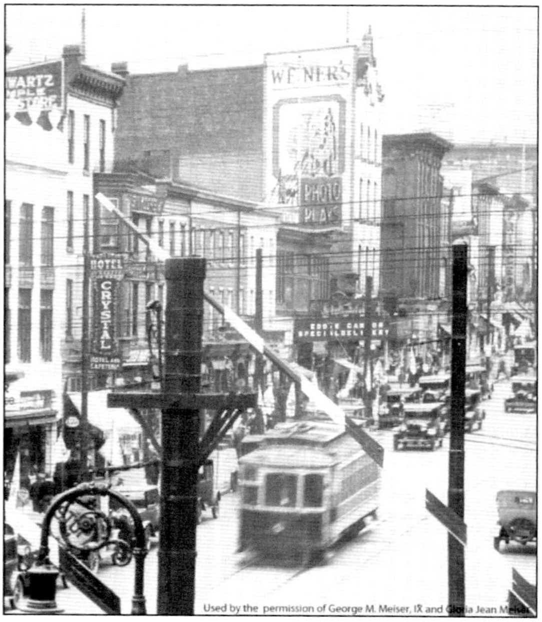

This very early photograph showcases several prominent advertisements of Jewish-owned businesses painted on the walls of Reading buildings. They include Schwartz's shoe store, Weiner's clothing store, the Princess Blouse shop, and Bloom's furniture store. Also visible is the Crystal Hotel and Cafeteria, a favorite meeting place for Jewish families. (Courtesy of George M. Meiser IX and Gloria Jean Meiser.)

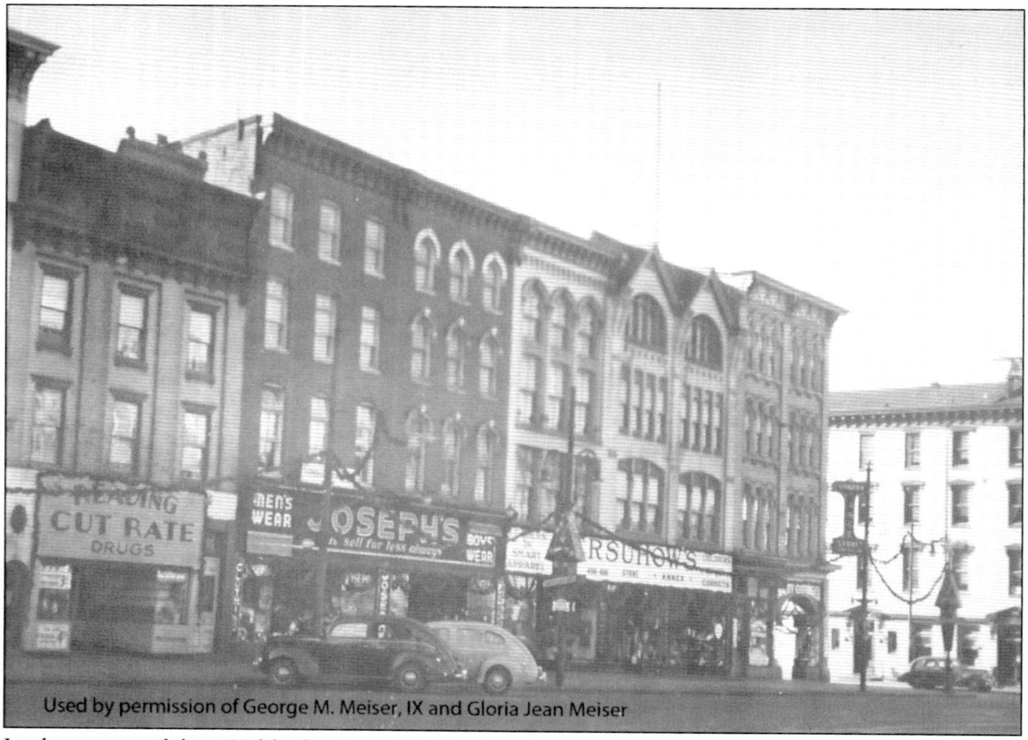

In the center of the 400 block is Joseph's Men's and Boys' Wear, a Jewish-owned clothing store on Penn Street operated by Charles, Frieda, Julius, and Ralph Joseph. Other Jewish-owned businesses in the picture are Reading Cut Rate drugstore, owned by Louis Filderman, and Quality Clothing Company, owned by Robert Mendelsohn and F.J. Zaffiro. (Courtesy of George M. Meiser IX and Gloria Jean Meiser.)

Here is a 1930s photograph of the 800 block of Penn Street's Jewish-owned businesses including Kagen's, a sporting goods store operated by Alex and Sara Kagen, and the Princess Blouse shop, operated by Abraham Goldstein. Other Jewish businesses in the photograph are Henry Eisenberg's Adeline Shop and Ozan's furs, owned by Ralph Ozan. (Courtesy of George M. Meiser IX and Gloria Jean Meiser.)

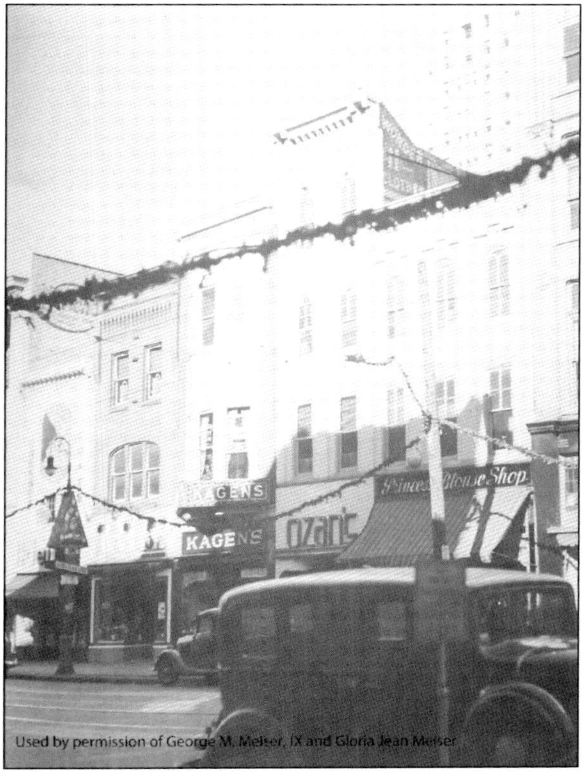

This is a 1930s photograph of "The Live Store" Charles Auto Supply, a Jewish-owned business at 431 Penn Street. It was operated by Jacob and Pauline Charles and Herman T. Wiener. Reading's changing downtown architecture is evident in the photograph. The early-19th-century building on the left, originally known as the United States Hotel, is a Penn Street landmark. (Courtesy of George M. Meiser IX and Gloria Jean Meiser.)

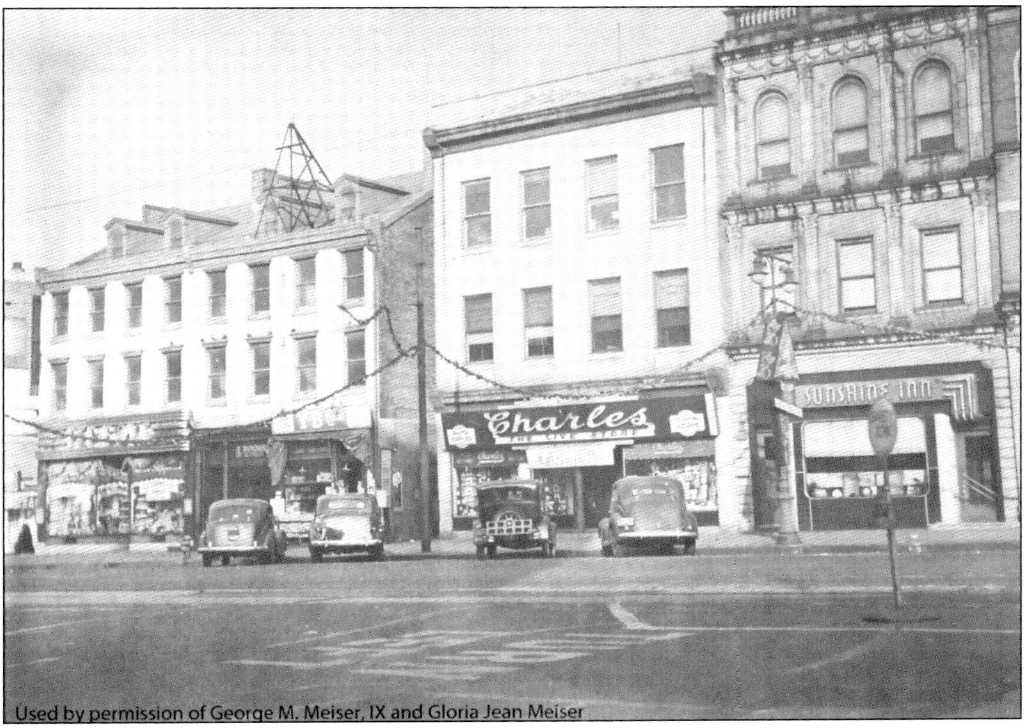

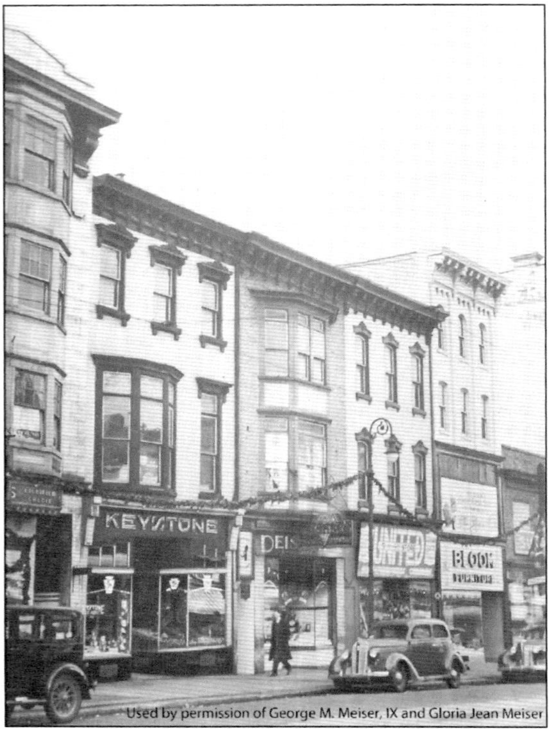

Pictured here are several more Jewish-owned businesses in the 400 block of Penn Street, including Bloom Furniture, owned and operated by Hyman Bloom. To the left is Nathan Weiner's United 5¢ to $5 Store. Other visible businesses are Schlechter Jewelry, owned by Ida Schlechter and Alfred Aron; Keystone Meat Market, owned by Barney Klevansky; and the A&P Supermarket. (Courtesy of George M. Meiser IX and Gloria Jean Meiser.)

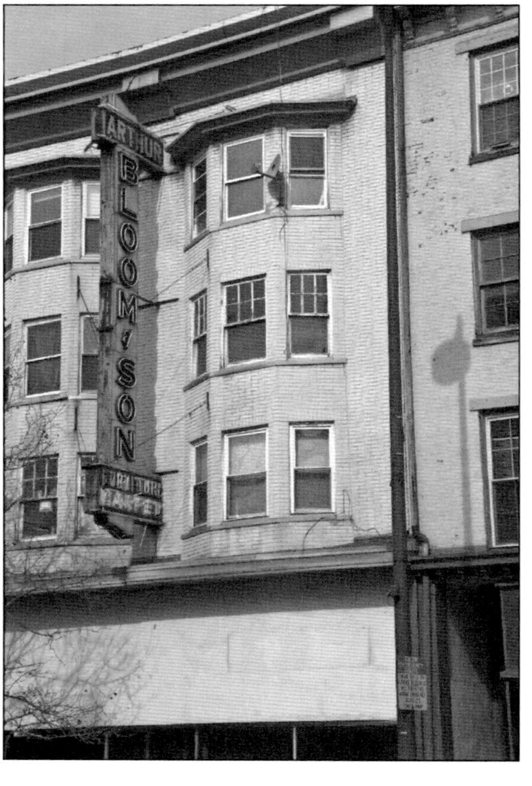

Hyman Bloom founded the Bloom Furniture store in 1914 at 339 South Sixth Street. He was the only worker in the beginning, but as time passed, he added employees and moved to the larger quarters shown here on Penn Street. Bloom Furniture closed in 1992. (Photograph taken by Jeffrey Watts, courtesy of Jeffrey Watts.)

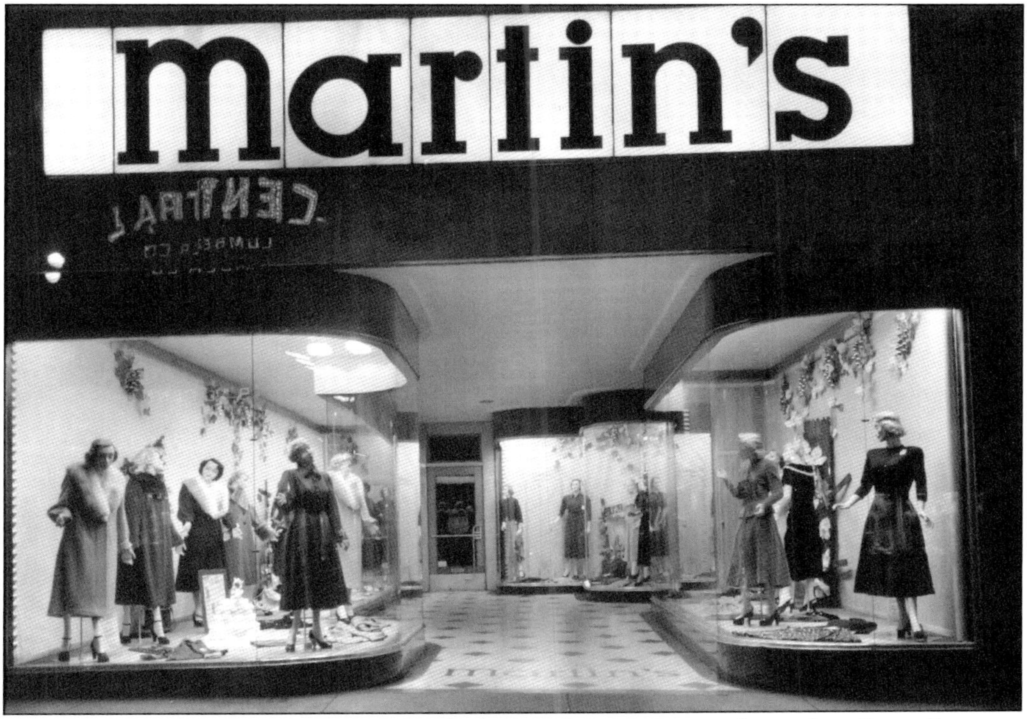

Pictured above is the Martin's, a mid-to-high priced women's store located on Penn Street in Reading. Abraham Goldstein opened the store in 1926 and named it after his infant son, Martin Goldstein. Martin's also featured men's athletic wear. Martin Goldstein would later take over the store and move it to a smaller space at 536 Penn Street, next to the old City Bank. Martin's display windows were always beautifully decorated and showcased new styles. In the photograph below in front of the new Martin's store are, from left to right, Abraham Goldstein, unidentified, Ed Daniels, Martin Goldstein, Reading mayor Eugene Shirk, and Jack Leifer. (Both, courtesy of Marty Goldstein.)

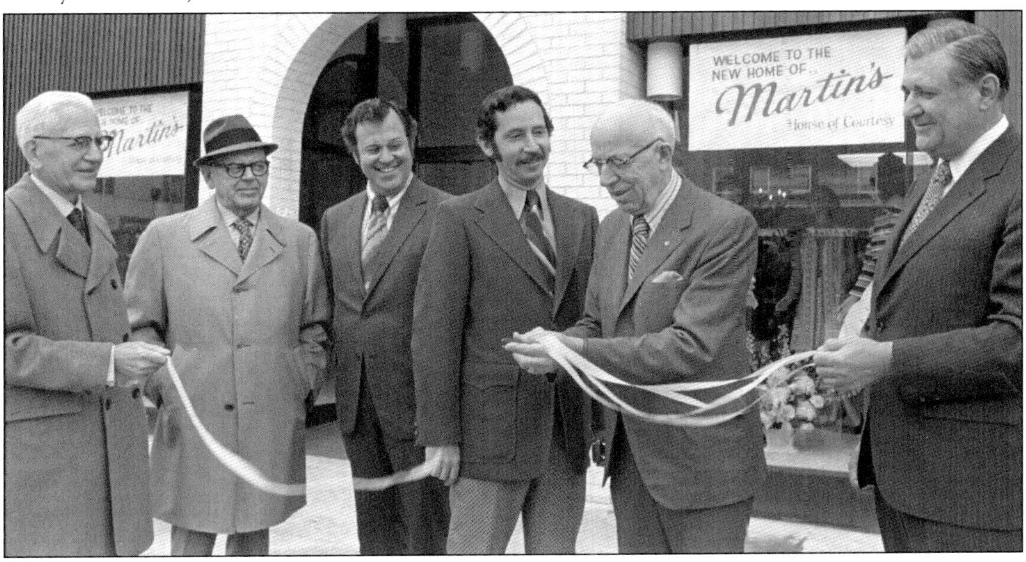

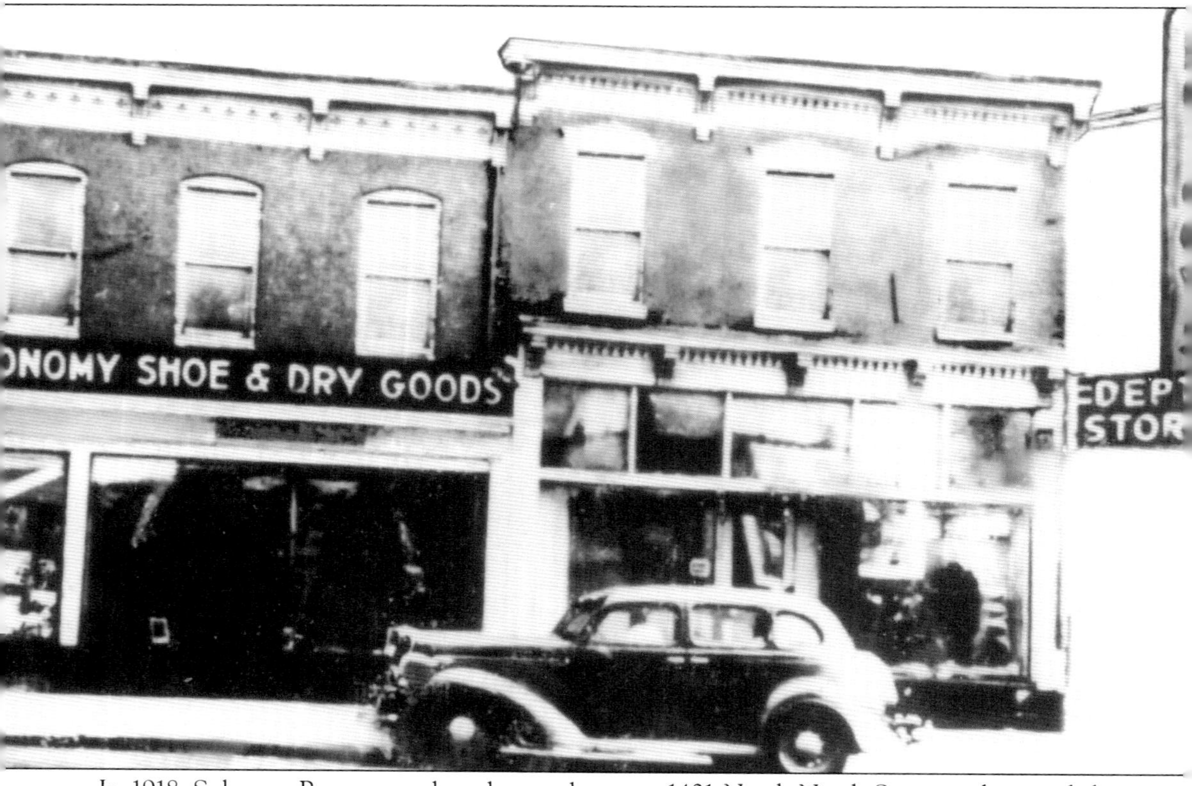

In 1918, Solomon Boscov purchased a row home at 1401 North Ninth Street and opened the Economy Shoe and Dry Goods store. The family lived upstairs, above the store. During the Depression, he kept the store going by extending credit to his neighborhood customers until they could pay for their purchase. By 1939, Boscov bought the neighboring store. As time went by, he was able to purchase first one and then another adjoining house, and the store continued to grow. Always careful to control expenses, Solomon purchased a new neon sign that was mounted in the corner. However, since he had already paid for the old Economy Shoe and Dry Goods sign, he kept that sign up as well. (Courtesy of Ken Lakin.)

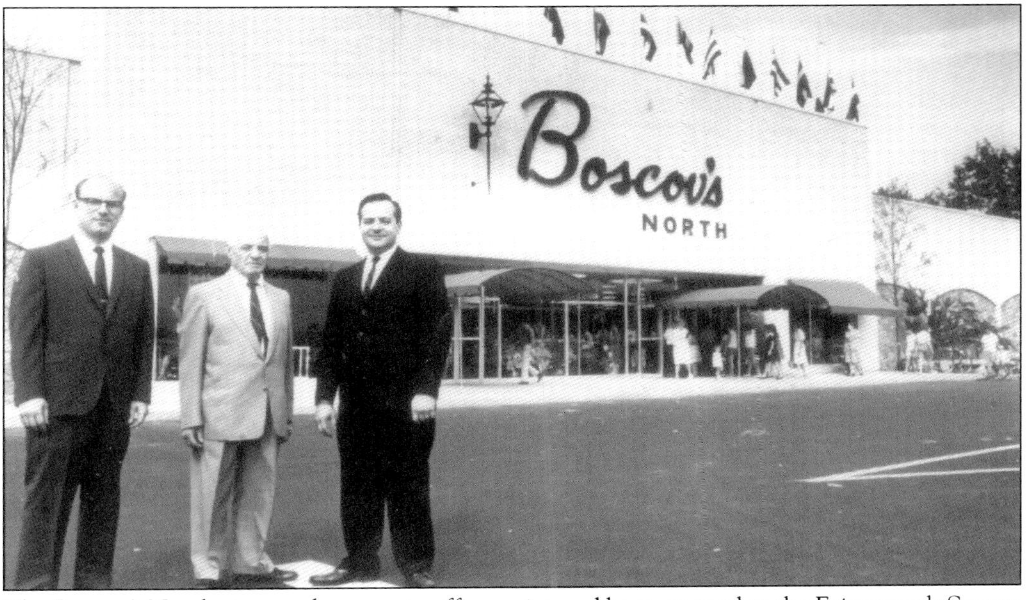

The Boscov's North store and corporate offices, pictured here, opened at the Fairgrounds Square Mall in 1964. Later, when Boscov's East opened on Perkiomen Avenue, the corporate offices moved there, where they are still located today. This well-known chain of department stores extends throughout Pennsylvania, New York, New Jersey, Delaware, and Maryland, with 39 stores currently open. Pictured from left to right are Ed Lakin, Solomon Boscov, and Albert Boscov. (Courtesy of Ken Lakin.)

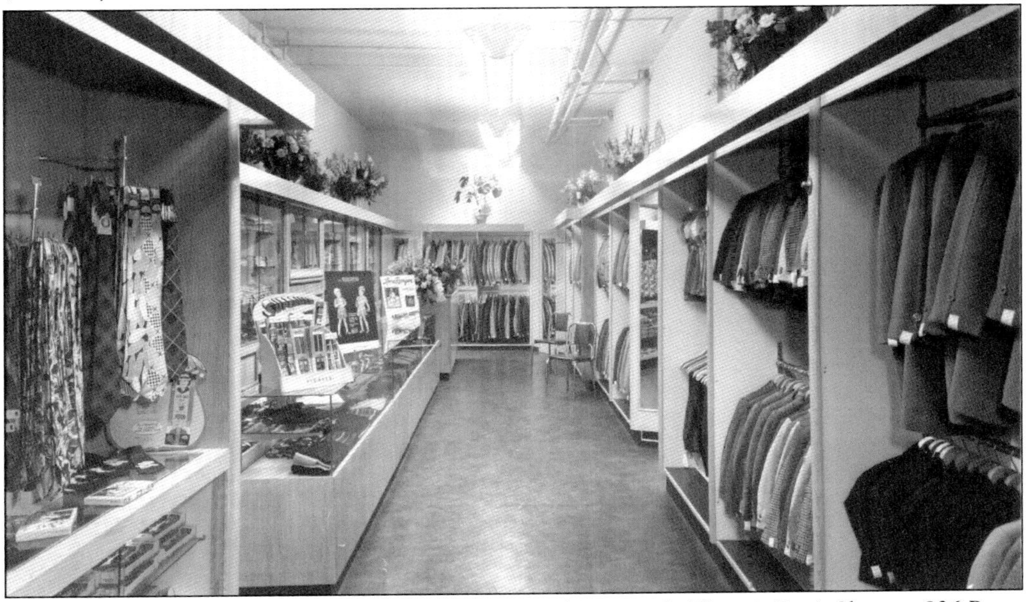

This is the inside of Pauline Goodman Goldberg and Bernie Goldberg's Boy's Shop at 836 Penn Street, which sold boys clothing. This store opened in 1946, a year after Bernie Goldberg returned from his post in the Army in World War II. They moved the store to a larger location in 1958 at 756 Penn Street and were able to add larger sizes of boys clothing. This location was a former Planters Peanut Store. (Courtesy of Pauline Goodman Goldberg.)

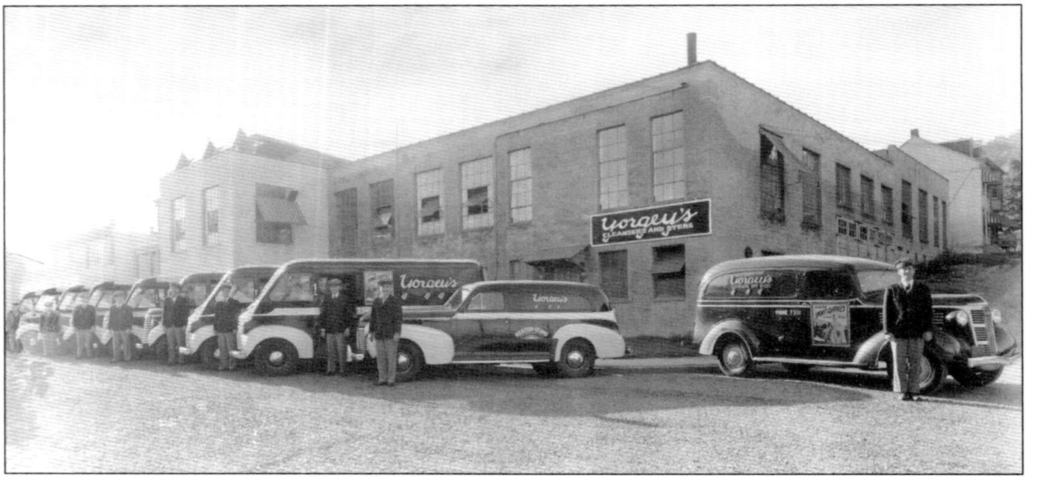

This is the Yorgey's Fine Cleaning processing plant, located at Seventeenth and Fairview Streets in Reading. Taken on June 1, 1942, the picture depicts the expansion of the plant. Also visible outside the building is Yorgey's trucking fleet. The trucks delivered clothes to the manufacturing plant for dry cleaning and then back to either customers' homes or to the many stores throughout Reading where customers had dropped off their clothes. Below is the production area and pressing department in the 1940s. Efficiency and high standards enabled the business to thrive in the Reading area and to provide high-quality dry cleaning at a low cost to its customers. Presently, the operation is run by Richard and Mickey Roeberg. (Both photographs by Jeffrey Watts, courtesy of Jeffrey Watts.)

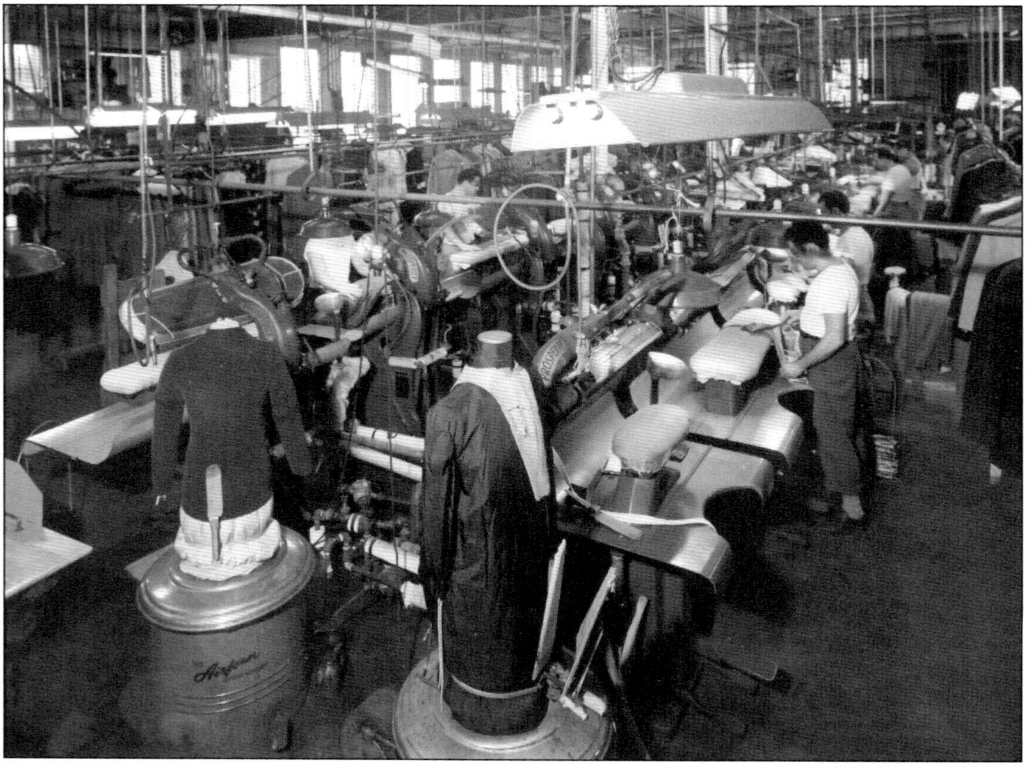

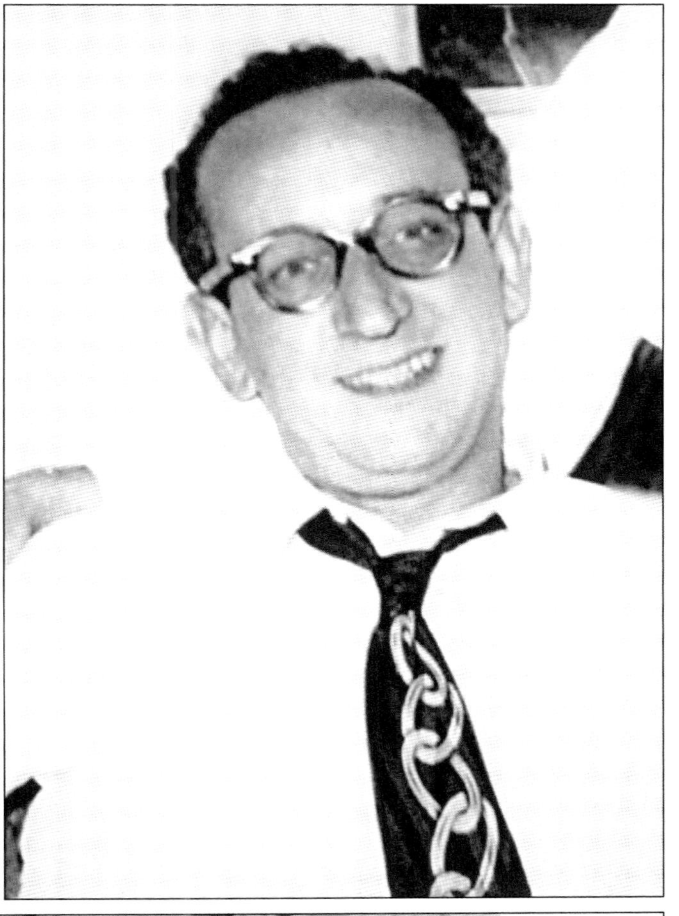

Fromm Electric Supply was founded in Reading in 1958 by Louis D. Fromm, pictured at right, with the purchase of Silver Electric Supply. The company had four employees and operated in a row home at 428 North Ninth Street. Louis Fromm's son, Bernie Fromm, was the company's first salesman. Pictured below is the four-story building at Fourth and Elm Streets that Fromm Electric moved to in 1961. Because the company did not yet need all of the space, it rented one floor to Boscov's—which only had two stores then—and another to a local motorcycle dealer. (Both, courtesy of Michael Fromm.)

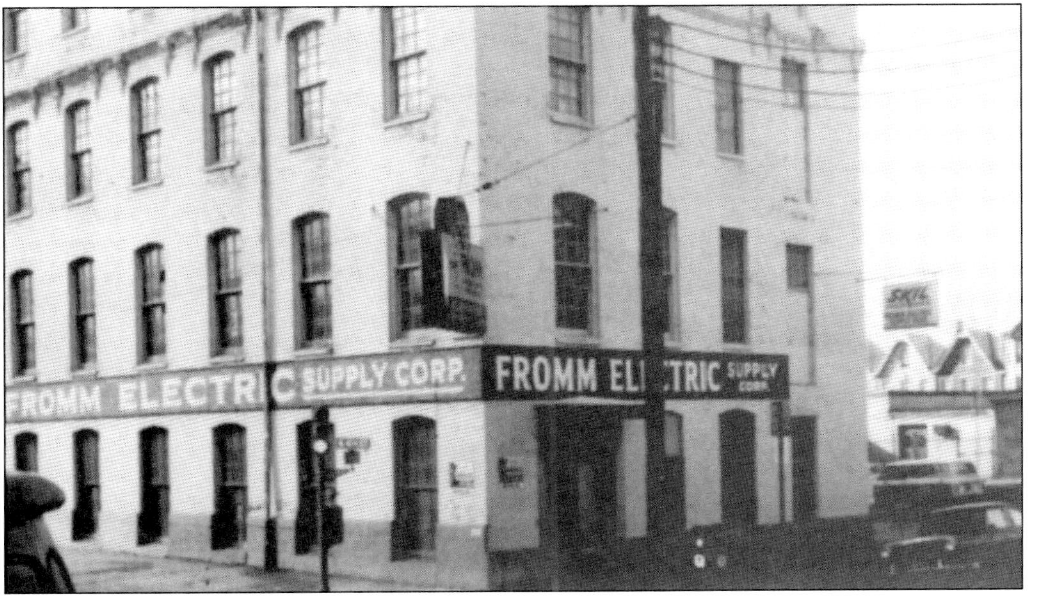

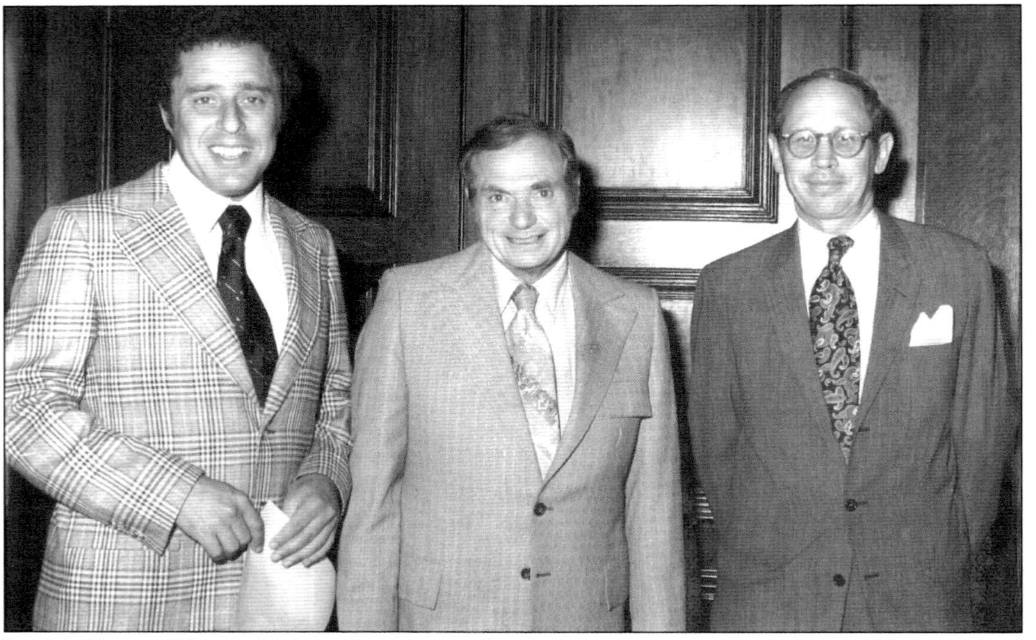

In 1974, Fromm Electric built a 40,000-square-foot headquarters on Centre Avenue after receiving a state loan. Bernie Fromm is pictured with Gov. Milton J. Shapp, Pennsylvania's first Jewish governor, and executive deputy secretary George E. Bartoll III. In 1962, Louis Fromm died, and his 27-year-old son, Bernie, stepped in to run the business. (Courtesy of Michael Fromm.)

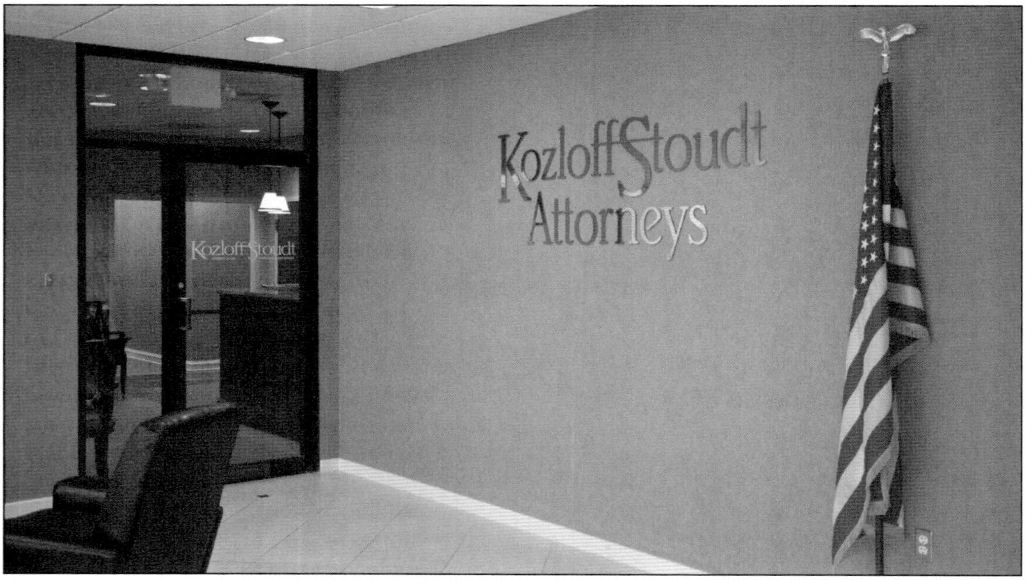

Kozloff Stoudt Attorneys was formed in 2000 as the result of the merger of two Berks County firms—Kozloff, Diener, Payne & Fegley and Rhoda, Stoudt & Bradley. Rhoda, Stoudt & Bradley was founded in 1936. James W. Stoudt was inducted as a fellow in the American College of Trial Lawyers in 1963, a very high honor in the legal profession. David Kozloff was selected for inclusion in *2011 Super Lawyers*, published by Thomson Reuters Business. (Photograph by Jeffrey Watts, courtesy of Jeffrey Watts.)

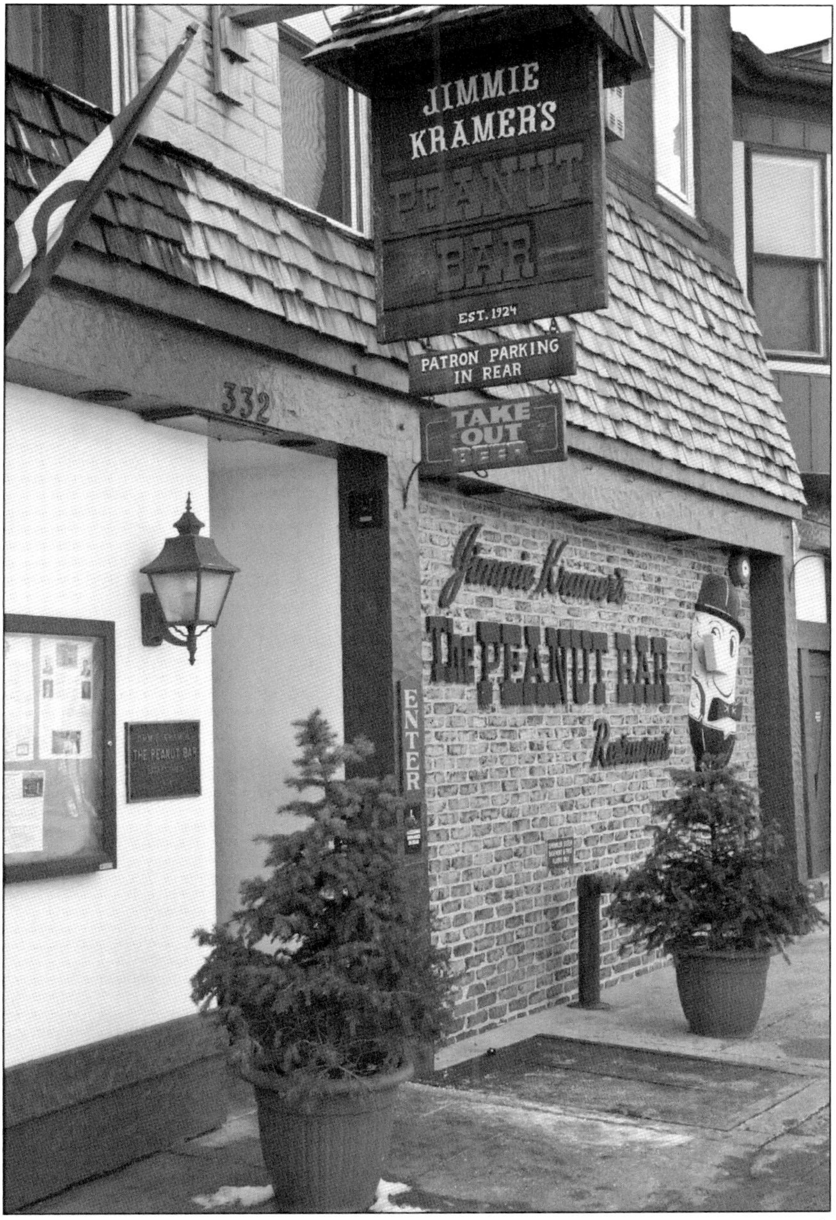

Jimmie Kramer's Peanut Bar has been at this location at 332 Penn Street since 1933, when it was called Jimmie Kramer's Olde Central Café. The giant peanut outside represents a tradition of cracking peanuts and tossing them on the floor; introduced by Kramer in 1935, it has become a trademark of the restaurant and continues today. Kramer's parents were Russian immigrants who came to America in the early 1900s. In 1935, Jimmie Kramer's wife, Annie "Mom" Kramer, joined the company and expanded the menu. Harold B. Leifer, the Kramers' son-in-law, came into the business in the 1950s. He retired in 2006 and passed away in November 2010. His and Beatie Kramer Leifer's son, Michael Leifer, now owns the restaurant. The restaurant first opened in 1924 in the resort community of South Mountain in Wernersville, Pennsylvania, as the Green Terrace Hotel. (Photograph by Jeffrey Watts, courtesy of Jeffrey Watts.)

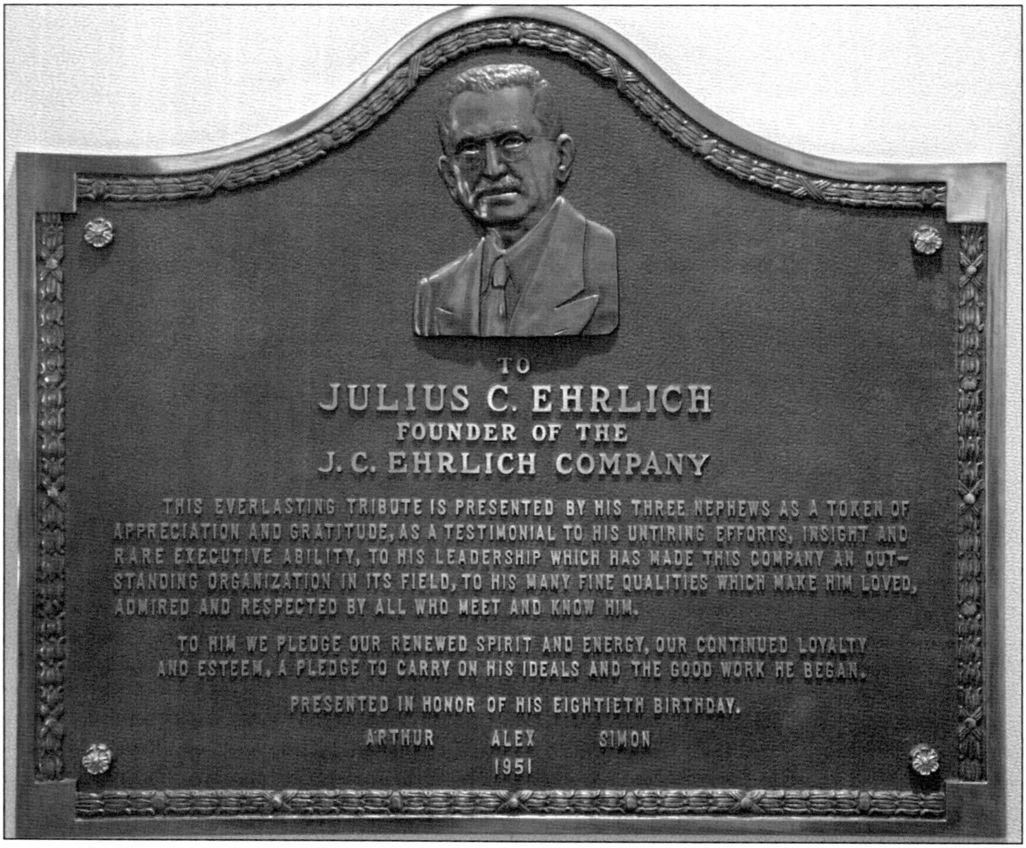

Pictured above is a plaque honoring Julius C. Ehrlich, who founded J.C. Ehrlich Co., Inc., in Reading in 1928. He sold insecticides and fogging equipment. Ehrlich's innovation was to help a customer apply insecticide in the department store. The plaque below recognizes the third generation of owners. In 2006, J.C. Ehrlich joined Rentokil to become the North American base for the company's pest control operations. Here in North America, Rentokil operates Ehrlich in the Mid-Atlantic, Presto-X in the Midwest, and Watch All in New England. Victor Hammel, the great-grandson of Julius Ehrlich, currently serves as Chairman of Rentokil North America Pest Control. (Both photographs by Jeffrey Watts; courtesy of Jeffrey Watts.)

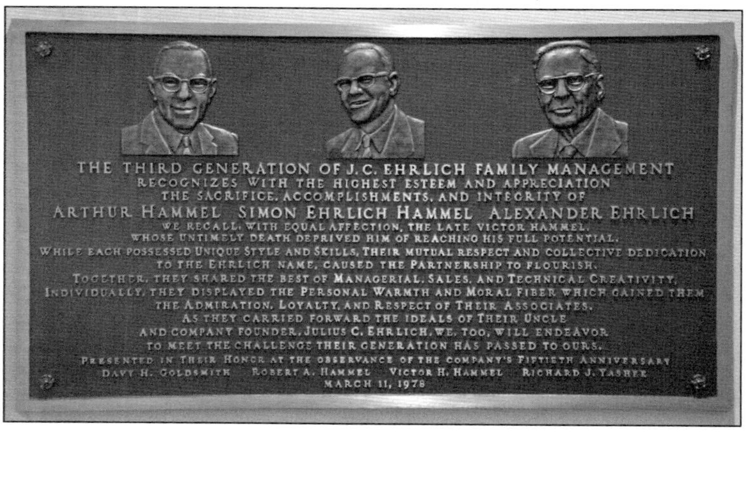

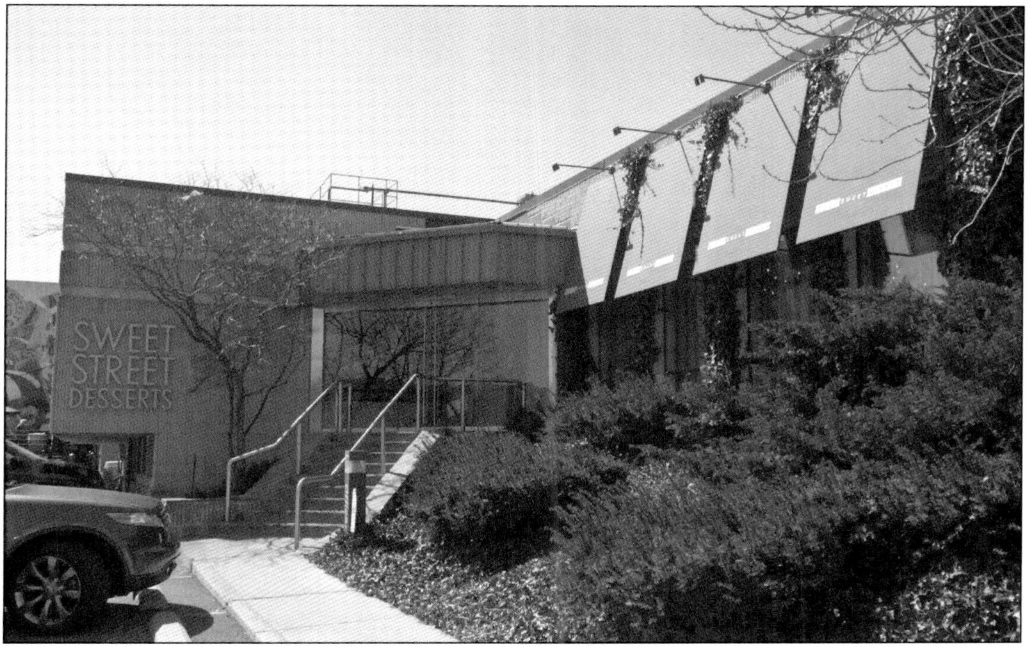

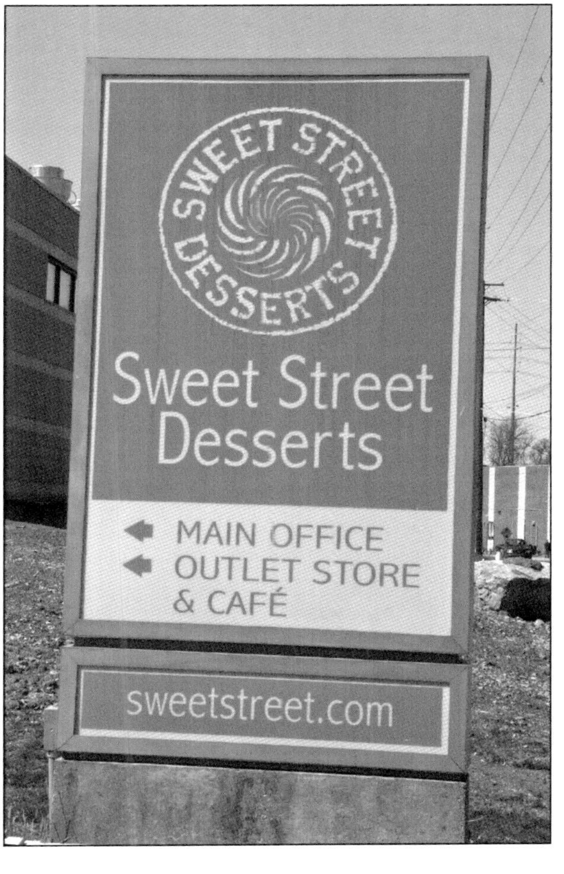

Sweet Street Desserts is located in Reading on Heister's Lane. Founder Sandy Solmon, who graduated from the University of California, Berkley, started Sweet Street as a manufacturer of cookies in 1979. Her first year was not an easy one. Commodity prices for sugar and chocolate skyrocketed, doubling in price. Her first distributor, Aramark, which is now U.S. Foodservice, and Woodhaven Food helped her to distribute goods throughout most of Pennsylvania and parts of New Jersey. Her second distributor, now Cisco, helped to expand that market to all of Pennsylvania, New Jersey, and Michigan. Though most of her business is wholesale, Solmon has a bakery that patrons are able to walk right into and buy her goodies directly. Currently, Sweet Street provides goods for all 50 states and 49 countries, including Saudi Arabia, Vietnam, Mexico, and most of Europe. Solmon is also admired as a philanthropist who gives her time and money to many community organizations. (Both photographs by Jeffrey Watts, courtesy of Jeffrey Watts.)

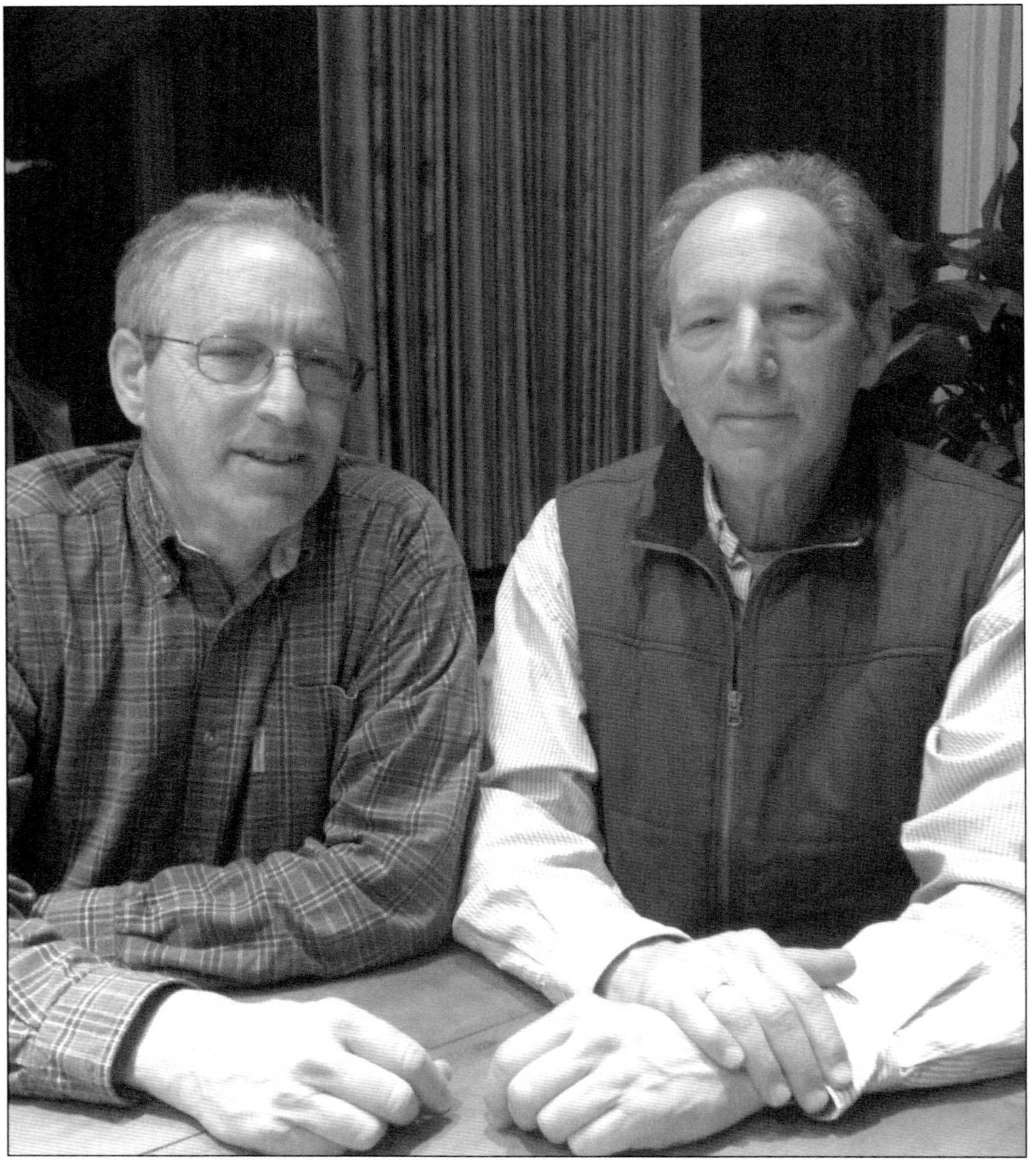

Twin brothers Jack (right) and Jeff Gernsheimer (left) returned to Bernville in 1971 after college and several years of employment and military duty to open Partners Design, Inc. The Gernsheimers' mother, Hildegard (Hilde) Simon Gernsheimer, is a Holocaust survivor. Partners Design has designed logos for many local businesses, including Boscov's, National Penn Bank, Berks Packing Company, Reading Phillies, Canal Street Pub and Restaurant, C.H. Briggs Hardware, and the former Bernville Bank. Jack Gernsheimer also designed a logo for Bernville's 150th anniversary celebration in 2001. He designed five logos using the Star of David for organizations such as the Jewish Cultural Center, Reform Congregation Oheb Sholom, Sinai Academy, and Albright College Holocaust Research Center. They also designed a logo in response to the Yom Kippur War of 1973. Partners Design is located in an old farmhouse at 187 Koenig Road on a farm once owned and operated by their father, Solly Gernsheimer. (Photograph by Jeffrey Gernsheimer, courtesy of Jeffrey Gernsheimer.)

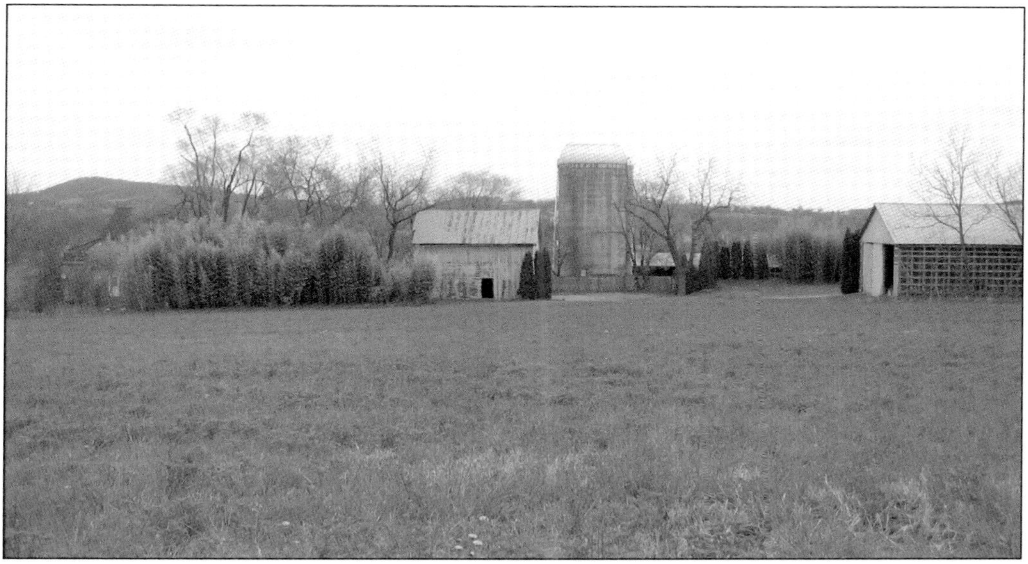

Solly Gernsheimer's former farm on Koenig Road in Bernville, which was later burned down by arsonists in 1975, is pictured here. Gernsheimer's second farm, which he bought in 1955 from Solly Katz's widow, Elsie Katz, is just off New Shaefferstown Road. Jeff Gernsheimer and his wife, Jan, and Jack Gernsheimer and his wife, Nancy Wolff, built houses and reside on this farm. Solly Katz was Robert Katz's older brother. In 1977, Solly and Hilde Gernsheimer won their case in US District Court over 26.64 acres of their farmland taken by the federal government for the Blue Marsh Lake Project. Robert Katz's son, Lee Katz, owned the farm pictured below. Lee Katz had a second farm nearby. Both farms are believed to be on Centerport Road in Bernville. (Both photographs by Jeffrey Gernsheimer; courtesy of Jeffrey Gernsheimer.)

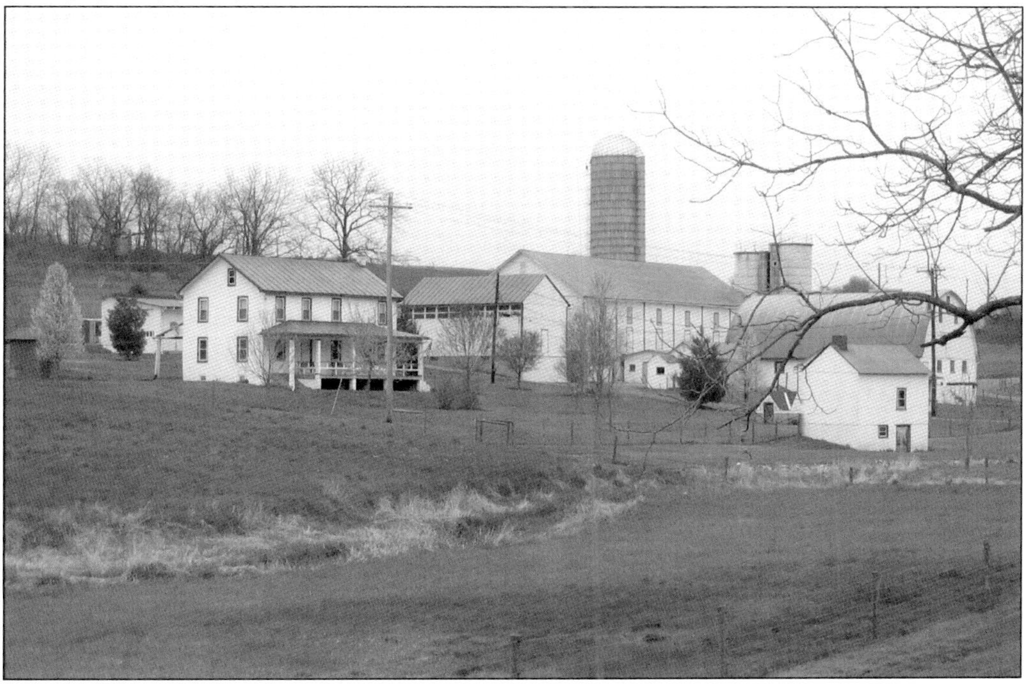

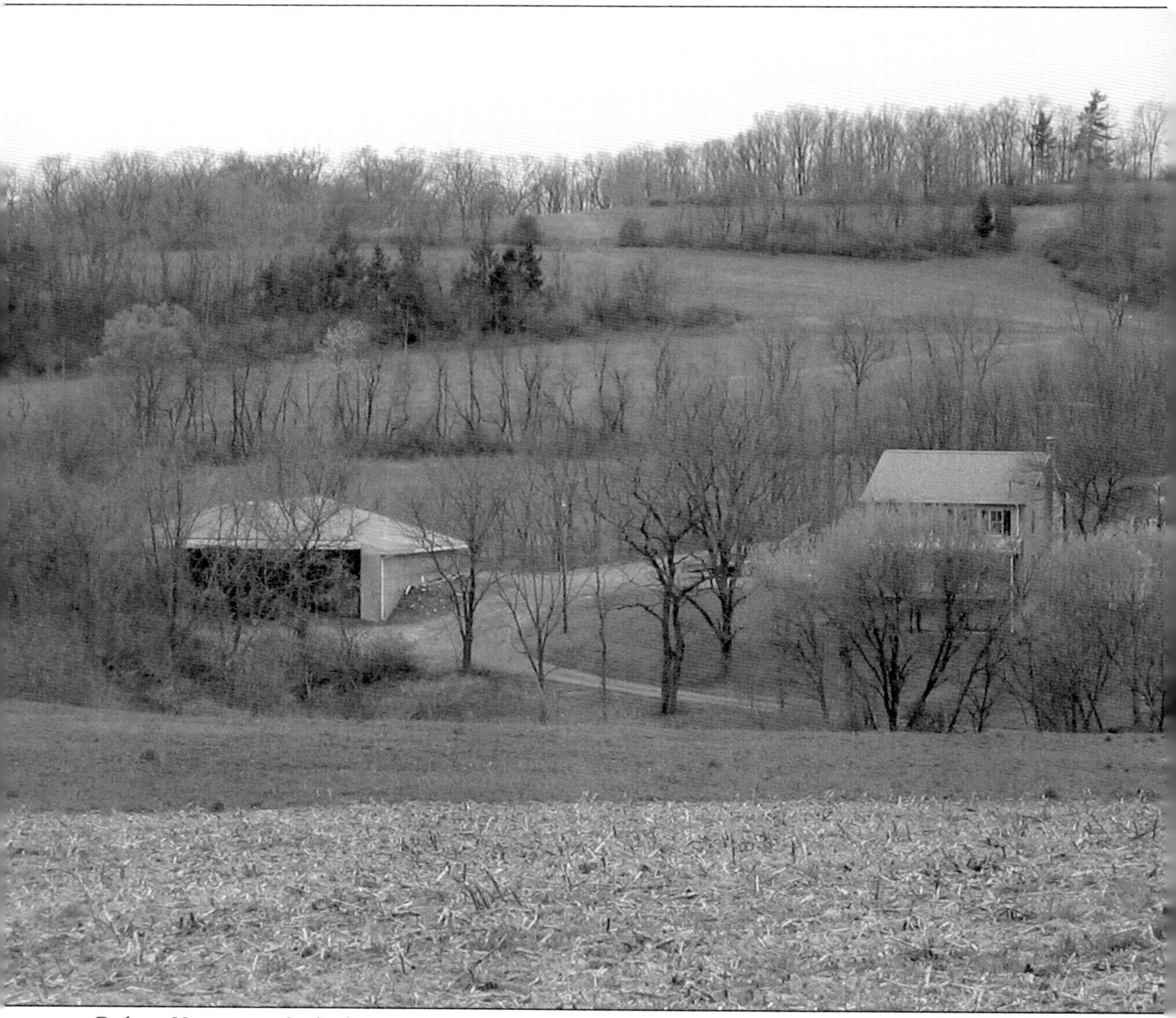

Robert Katz, a cattle dealer, owned several farms in Bernville, including the one pictured here. The barn on this farm burned down in the early 1960s. It sat where the shed now is. Katz had several more farms, including one near the Green Valley Country Club on Cacoosing Road in Sinking Spring and one off Route 183 near Strausstown. Katz was born on January 7, 1900, in Giesson, Germany. He had two older brothers and two older sisters. In Germany, Katz served as a soldier in World War I. Katz immigrated to the United States in 1923. He sponsored over 50 German families' immigration to the United States, ultimately rescuing them from the Nazis. He was a practicing Jew and attended Temple Oheb Sholom. Robert Katz died on September 9, 1976. He left the bulk of his estate to his wife, Paula, and his son, Lee. A portion of his small fortune was donated to various charities in the Reading area. (Photograph by Jeffrey Gernsheimer, courtesy of Jeffrey Gernsheimer.)

Six

Recreation

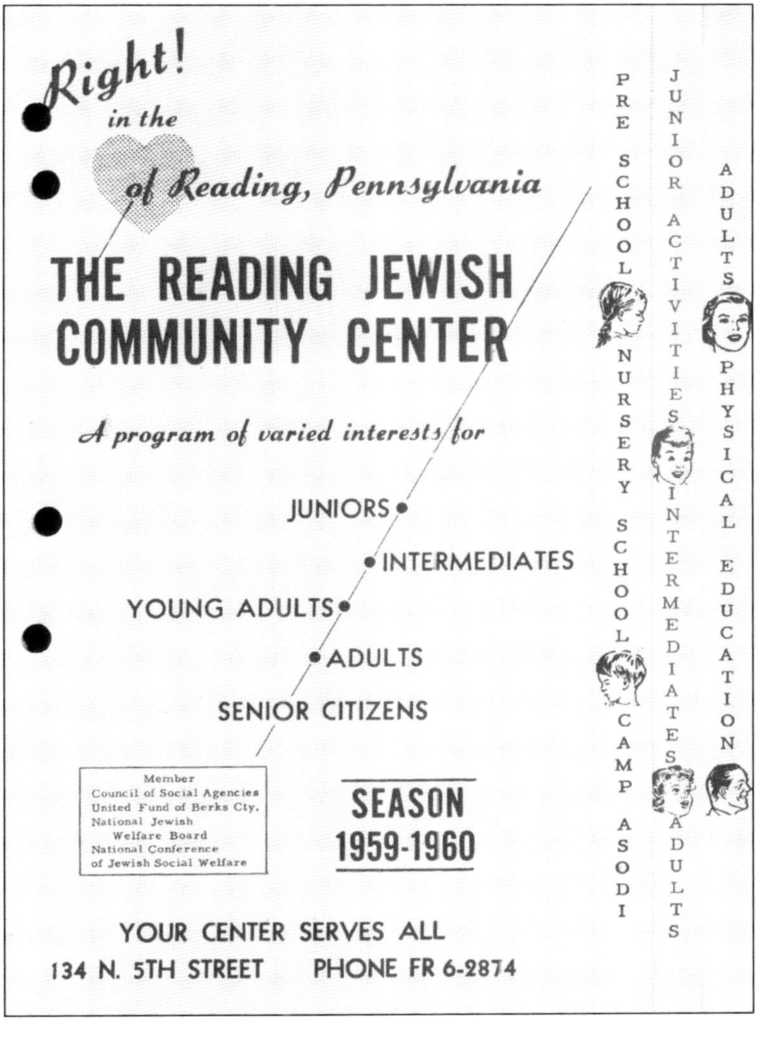

This image of the Reading Jewish Community Center 1959–1960 Season brochure lists the center's varied activities for the community. The brochure highlights the center's philosophy that "Your Center Serves All." Community members of all faiths, ethnicities, and races participated in preschool, Camp Asodi, and year-round athletic activities. (Courtesy of JFR.)

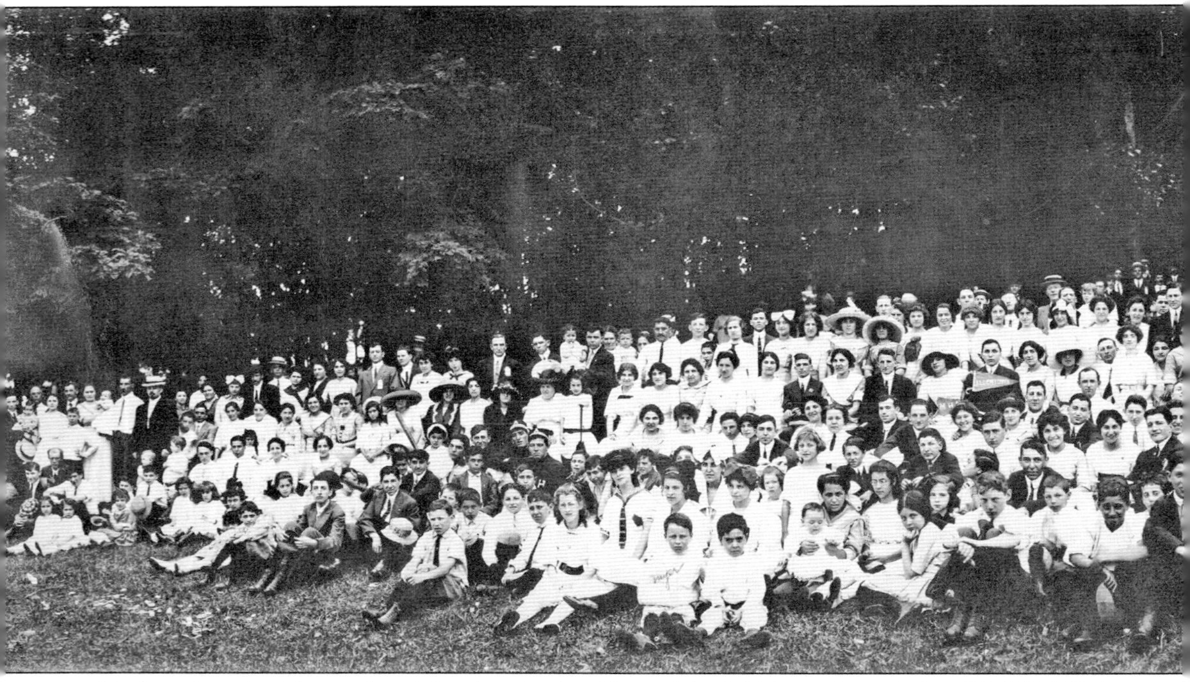

Gathered are Jewish people celebrating the first Young Men's Hebrew Association (YMHA) Gala Day, held in August 1912 at Black Bear Inn. Members from Berks County and beyond joined together to celebrate the accomplishment of the organization. E. Louis Kotzen was the recording secretary of the YMHA. The Jewish community in Reading was concerned that the YMHA and Young Women's Hebrew Association (YWHA) did not have an adequate facility. The October

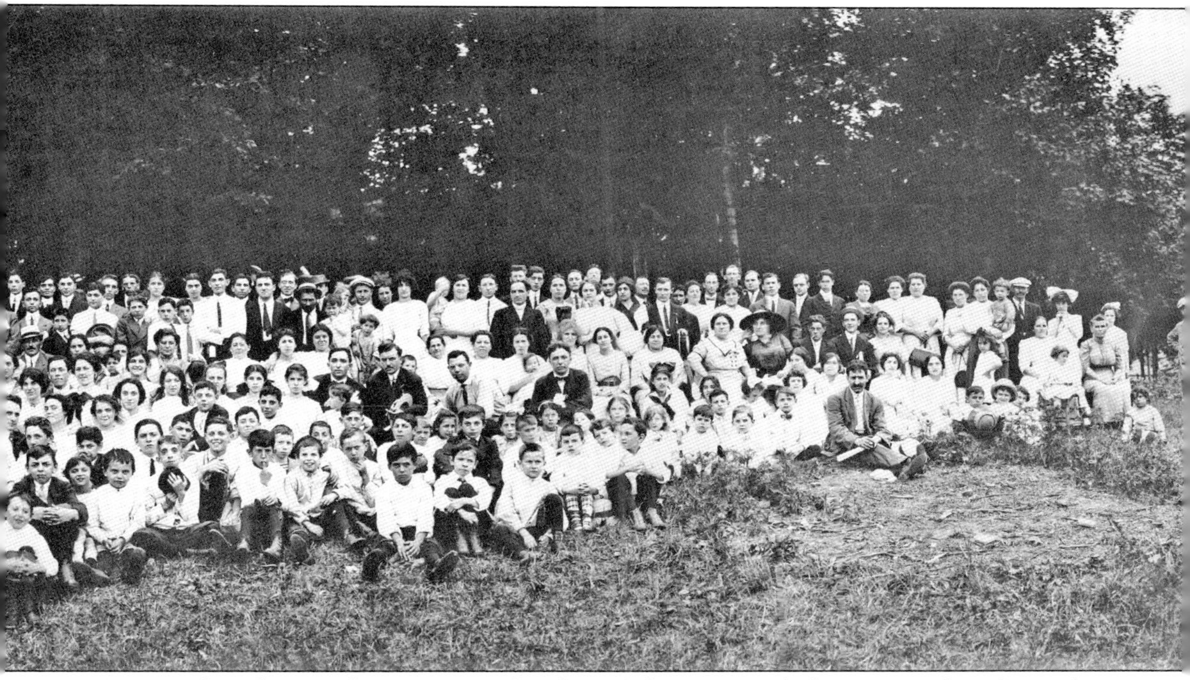

1922 issue of *Reading Jewish Voice* states, "Reading's failure to provide for its young Jewish people is in sorry contrast with what other Jewish communities are doing. The time has come when we must prepare our young men and young women to assume their share of civic responsibility, even to step into the shoes of leadership." (Courtesy of JFR.)

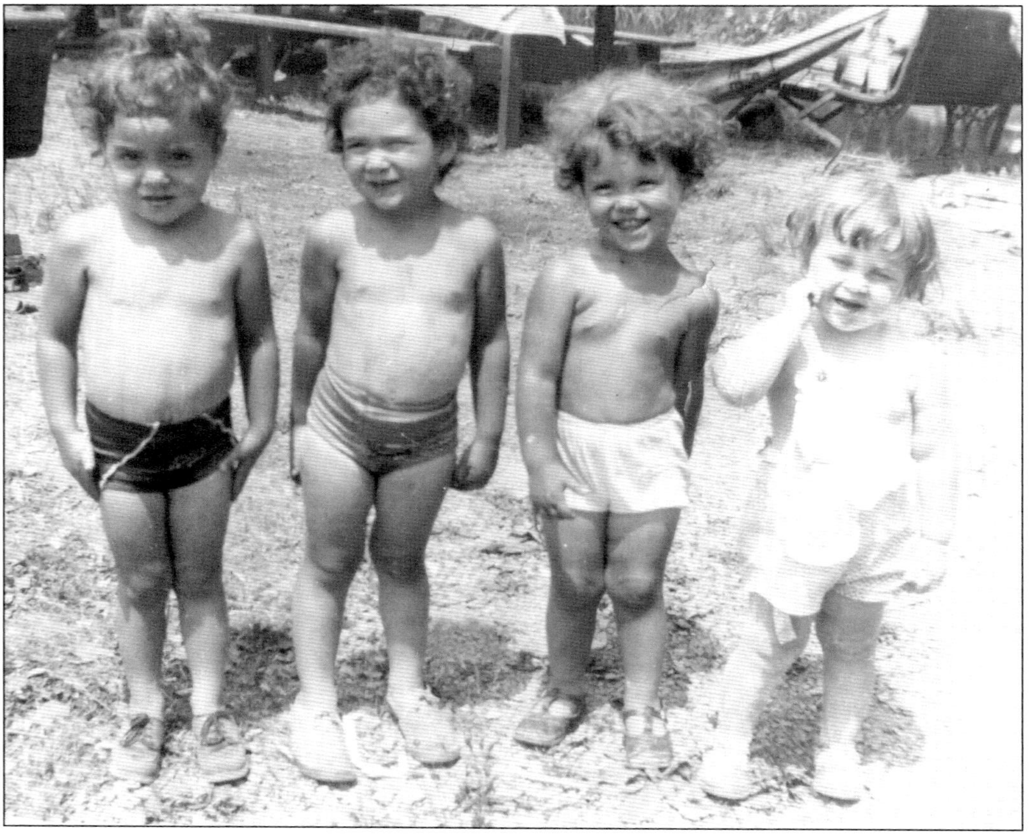

Four girls stand together for a picture outside the community pool on a hot summer day in 1938. Several social and residential exclusions were placed on those of the Jewish faith in the area at this time, but this pool was an exception. Sunday was the day to come and socialize at the pool with one another, enjoying lunch, swimming, and friendship. Even on a rainy day, the children gathered, placing picnic tables on their sides to protect them from the weather. (Courtesy of Marjorie Moyer.)

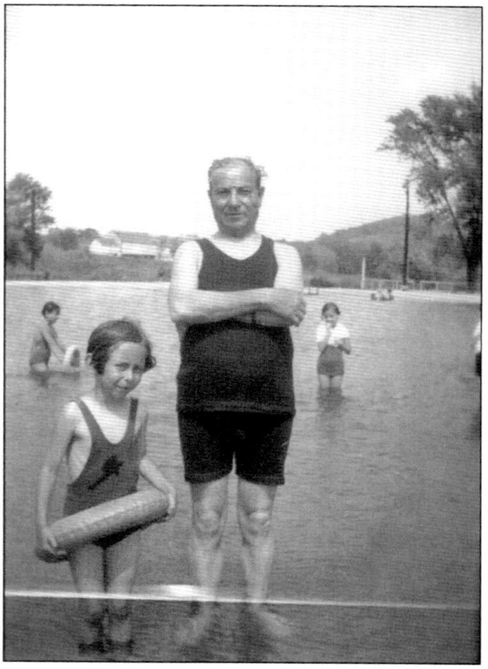

Rosalye Levine, now Rosalye Yashek, and her grandfather, Harry Katz, spend a summer day at Kutztown pool in 1933. As a child, her family did not have a car, and on hot summer days, they walked two miles to the Kutztown pool. She recalls hundreds of people traveling to the pool on summer weekends. Rosalye Levine married Richard Yashek, a Holocaust survivor who moved to Reading in 1949. (Courtesy of Kim Yashek.)

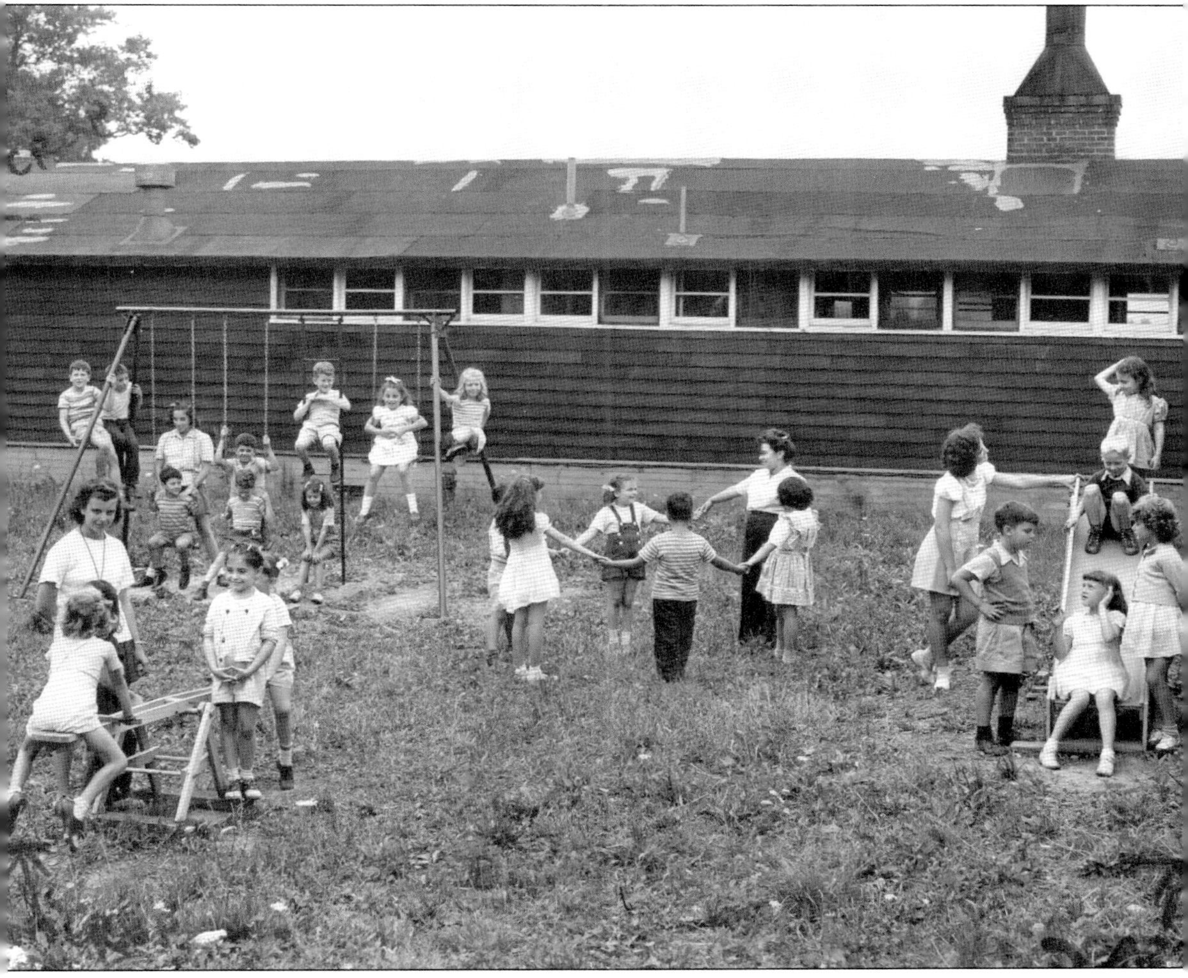

Camp Asodi, pictured in 1946, was organized and run by the Reading Jewish Community Center and was an integral part of the JCC's year-round youth program. The camp directors, Vivian Levine and Harry "Pop" Polter, met at Camp Asodi and later married. Camp Asodi was geared to the needs of children age four to 12 years. Since the first JCC had little land, the first years of camp were held at several locations, including the South Temple Pool and a former Civilian Conservation Corps (CCC) location. Organized every year during summer, the camp was a favorite with kids in the Reading community, providing activities and games for children to enjoy during the summer break, such as box hockey, table tennis, and skits. The camp was called Asodi for several years after moving to the City Line Street facility. (Courtesy of JFR.)

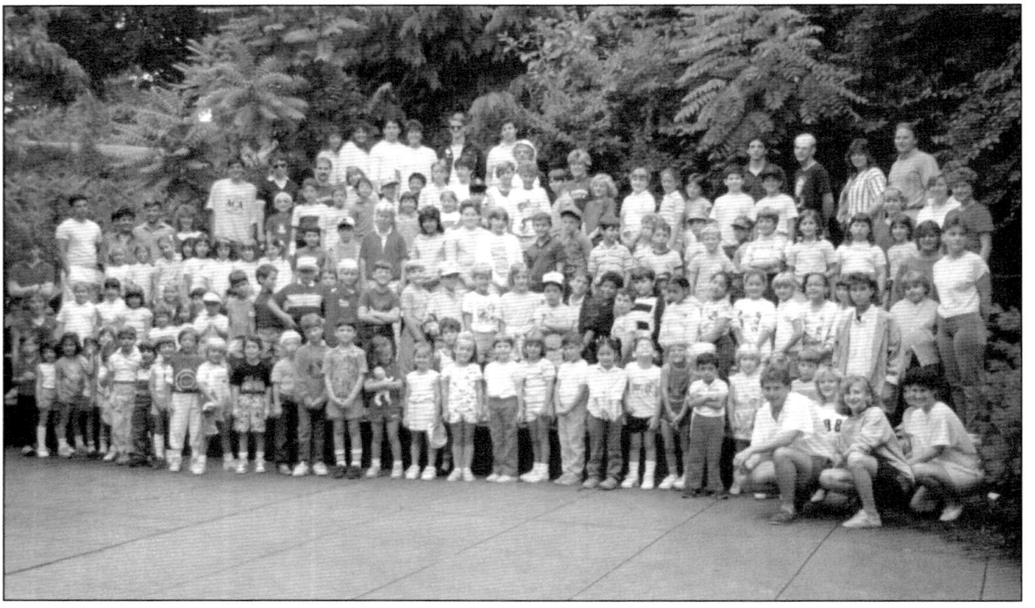

Pictured here are campers and counselors at the campgrounds of the Jewish Community Center day camp at the City Line Street location. This camp was held behind the City Line Street Jewish Community Center building. With woods, playing fields, playground equipment, and an indoor pool, the new location provided superb facilities for a day camp. The Jewish Community Center summer day camp is now closed. (Courtesy of JFR.)

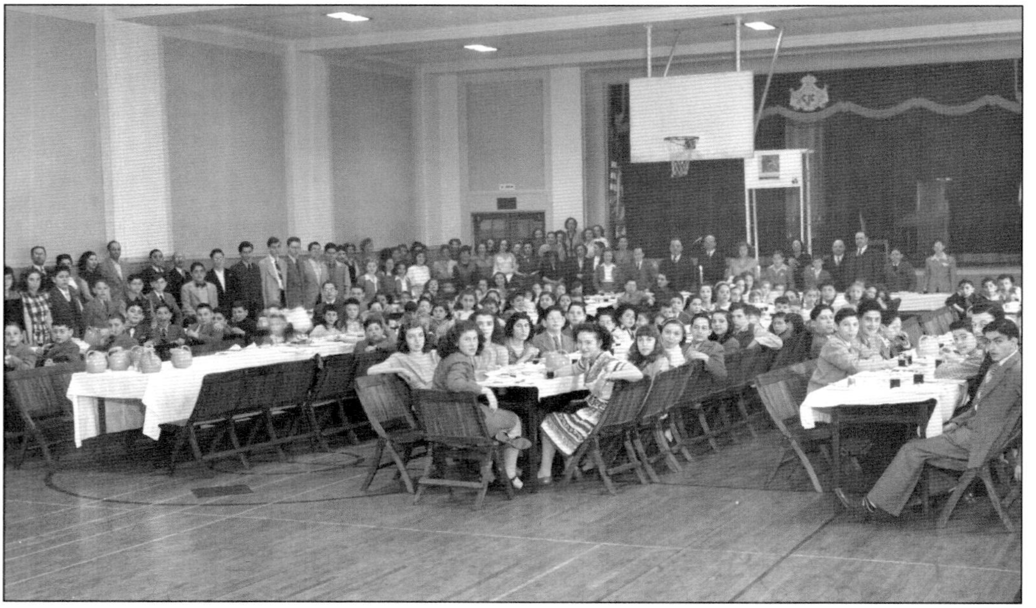

During a Model Seder in 1946, children and faculty enjoy the festivities in the auditorium at the Jewish Community Center. Children from all classes enjoy food and soda. Teachers and faculty stand lining the walls in the background as children remain sitting. High Holiday services were also held at the JCC at this time due to the small size of Kesher Zion Synagogue facilities. (Courtesy of KZ.)

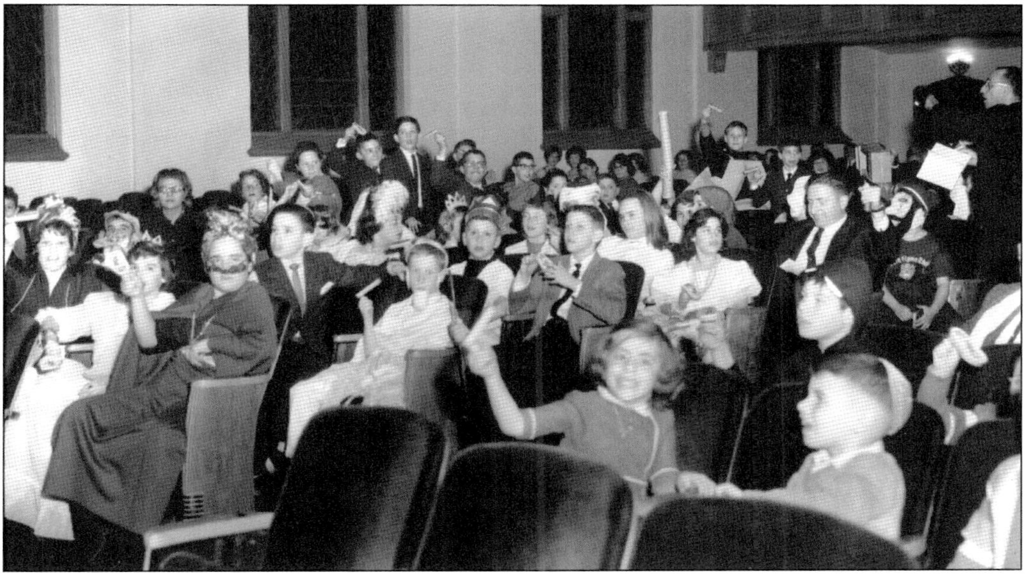

This 1963 photograph is of the Kesher Zion Hebrew School during the Megillah reading. The children are dressed to celebrate Purim and are holding their groggers, or noisemakers. Children use these noisemakers during the Megillat Esther to drown out the evil Haman whenever his name is mentioned in the story. (Courtesy of KZ.)

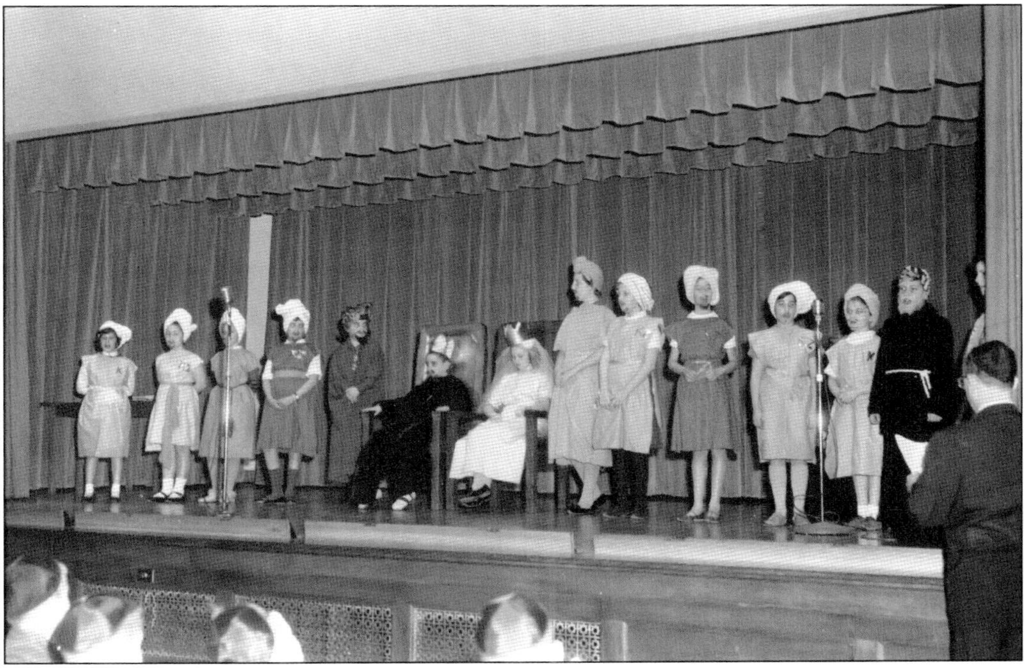

Also from 1963, the children of Kesher Zion's Hebrew School are shown acting out a scene from the Purim play. Children are dressed in costumes and makeup, portraying the beautiful new queen, Esther; the evil advisor, Haman; and King Ahasuerus of ancient Persia. The students could also celebrate the holiday by eating Hamantashen, or "Haman's ears," which are sweet pastries with a variety of fillings. The musical director of the show is Cantor Ben Klonsky. (Courtesy of KZ.)

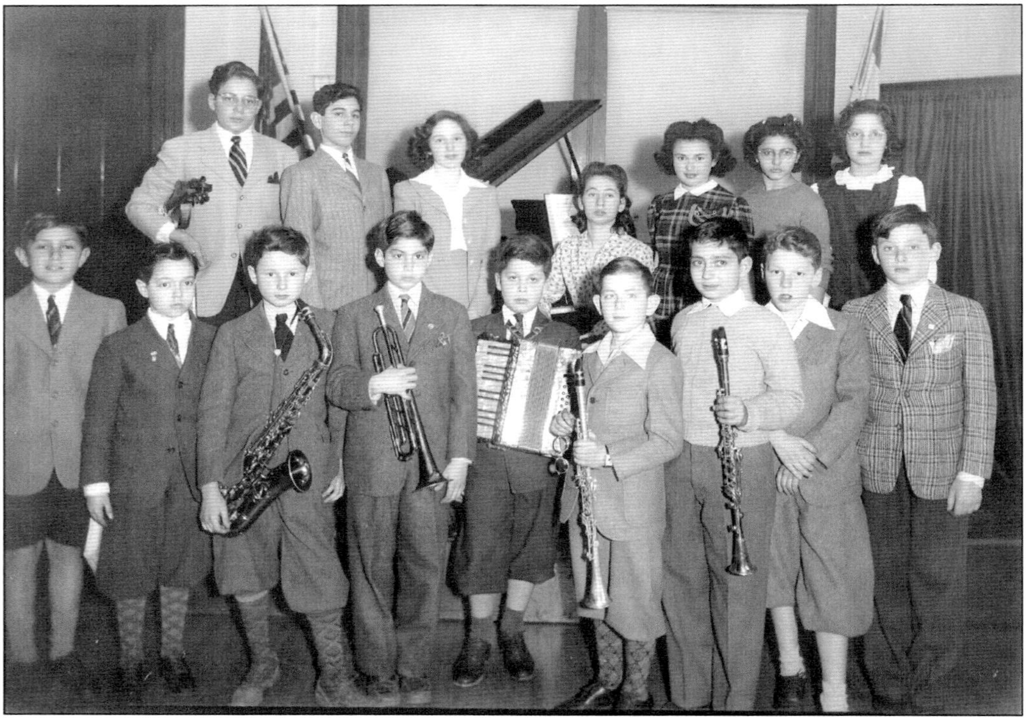

This is a picture of a music recital taken at Kesher Zion. For the photograph, some children were required to stand on chairs to not only be seen but to show off their instruments. Frederic Fidler is in first row with the trumpet. Irving Fidler, a cousin of Frederic Fidler, obtained the trumpet from Frederic's family after Frederic's death. (Courtesy of KZ.)

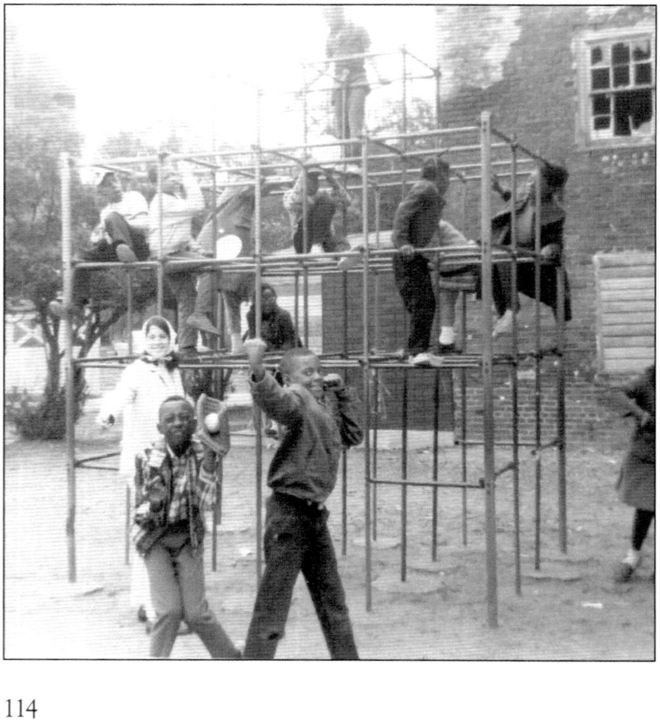

A group of children from Reform Congregation Oheb Sholom helps to clean the WeVol playground in Reading. After a weekend of cleaning, some of the children and the WeVol group posed for a few photographs, such as this one from May 12, 1966. Children from Oheb Sholom also collected food for the needy. Adults and children alike volunteered during Christian holidays to help with local soup kitchens. (Courtesy of RCOS.)

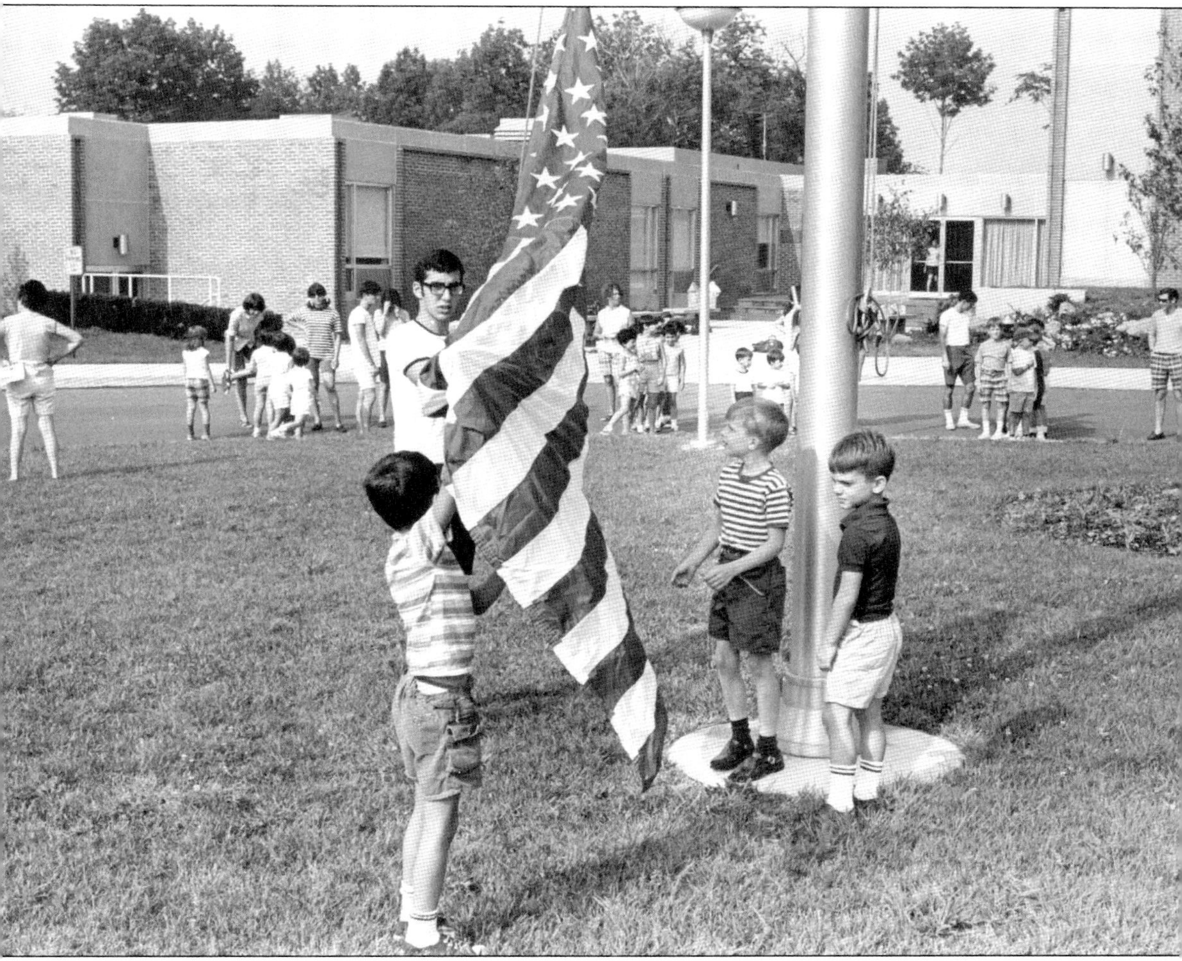

At the Jewish Community Center on City Line Street, children from the Reading community were involved in a number of fun activities. These included sports teams, camp, theatrical productions, and much more. The raising of the flag shows that Americanism and patriotism were very important to the Jewish community in Reading. (Courtesy of JFR.)

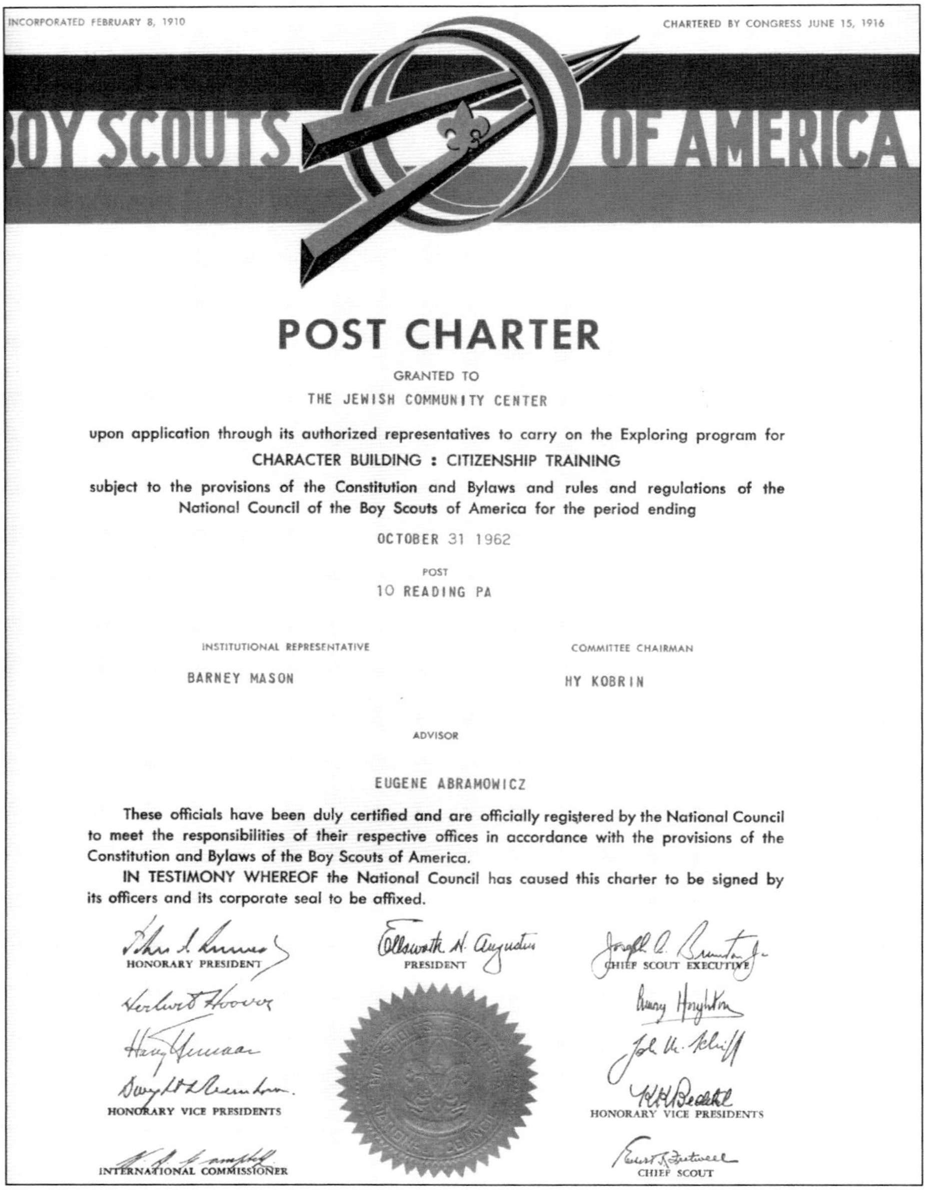

INCORPORATED FEBRUARY 8, 1910

CHARTERED BY CONGRESS JUNE 15, 1916

BOY SCOUTS OF AMERICA

POST CHARTER

GRANTED TO

THE JEWISH COMMUNITY CENTER

upon application through its authorized representatives to carry on the Exploring program for

CHARACTER BUILDING : CITIZENSHIP TRAINING

subject to the provisions of the Constitution and Bylaws and rules and regulations of the National Council of the Boy Scouts of America for the period ending

OCTOBER 31 1962

POST

10 READING PA

INSTITUTIONAL REPRESENTATIVE

BARNEY MASON

COMMITTEE CHAIRMAN

HY KOBRIN

ADVISOR

EUGENE ABRAMOWICZ

These officials have been duly certified and are officially registered by the National Council to meet the responsibilities of their respective offices in accordance with the provisions of the Constitution and Bylaws of the Boy Scouts of America.

IN TESTIMONY WHEREOF the National Council has caused this charter to be signed by its officers and its corporate seal to be affixed.

HONORARY PRESIDENT

PRESIDENT

CHIEF SCOUT EXECUTIVE

HONORARY VICE PRESIDENTS

HONORARY VICE PRESIDENTS

INTERNATIONAL COMMISSIONER

CHIEF SCOUT

The document pictured here is the official post charter for the Jewish Community Center's Boy Scout Post 10 Reading, Pennsylvania, dated 1962. The JCC Scouting program promoted the values of the Boy Scouts and also aimed to improve understanding and cooperation among racial, ethnic, and religious groups in Berks County, one of many steps that helped to integrate the Jewish community into the larger Berks community. A 1955 article in the *Reading Eagle* states that the Jewish Community Center already had a Scouting program serving 130 boys and girls under the supervision of the center's youth activities committee, chaired by Dr. Reidenberg. Thus, the history of the JCC Scouting program remains somewhat unclear. Since 1916, Scouting programs have been a part of Jewish organizations, and Jewish national leaders such as Dr. Cyrus Adler, Frank Weil, and Mortimer Schiff have helped guide the program in the United States. (Courtesy of JFR.)

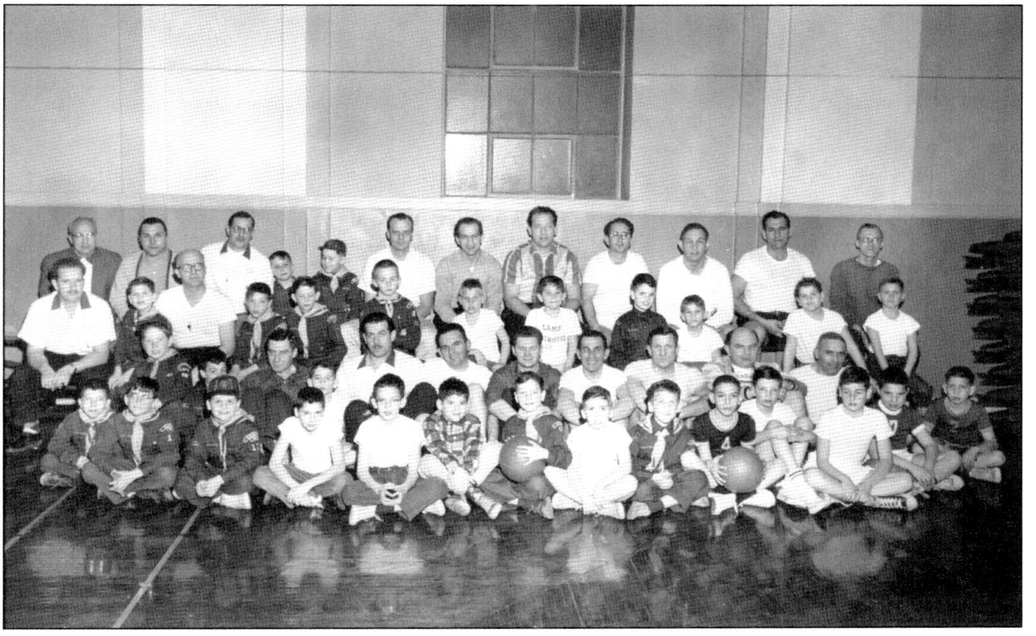

Pictured above is a father-son night of Cub Scout Pack 10 in the Jewish Community Center's gymnasium. After the charter was recognized in 1962, the Jewish Community Center began to hold many Boy Scouts of America events. Below, young Jewish girls participate in the Jewish Community Center's Girl Scouts program. By 1955, the Jewish Community Center had two Brownie troops and two Girl Scout troops. Like Scouting programs nationally, the Jewish Community Center program is geared to developing citizenship and character, focusing values such as honesty, fairness, courage, compassion, character, sisterhood, and confidence through activities that include camping and the earning of badges. (Both, courtesy of JFR.)

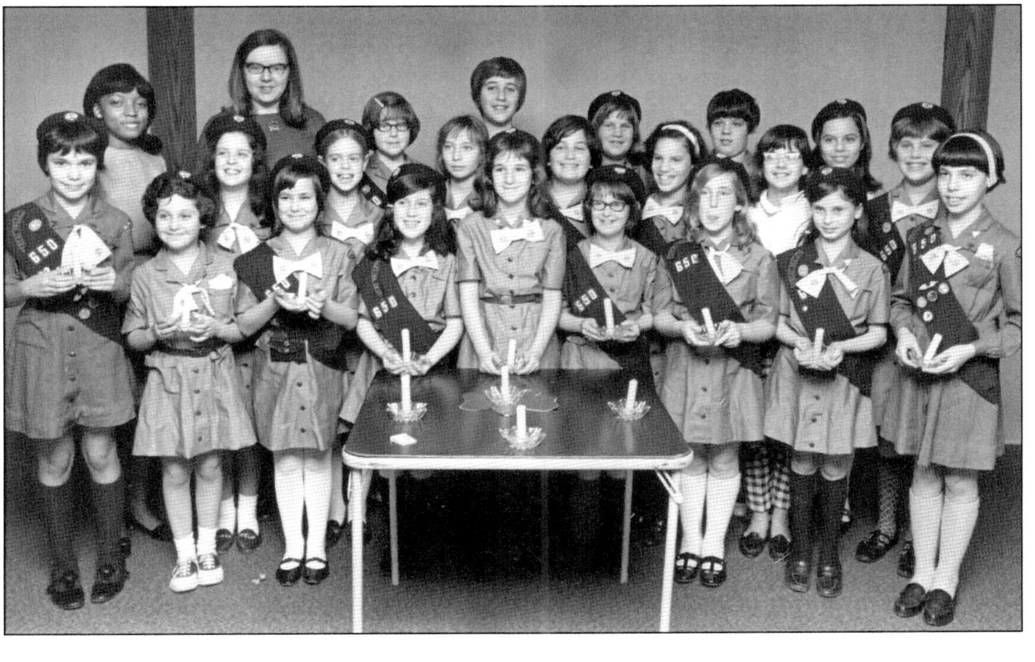

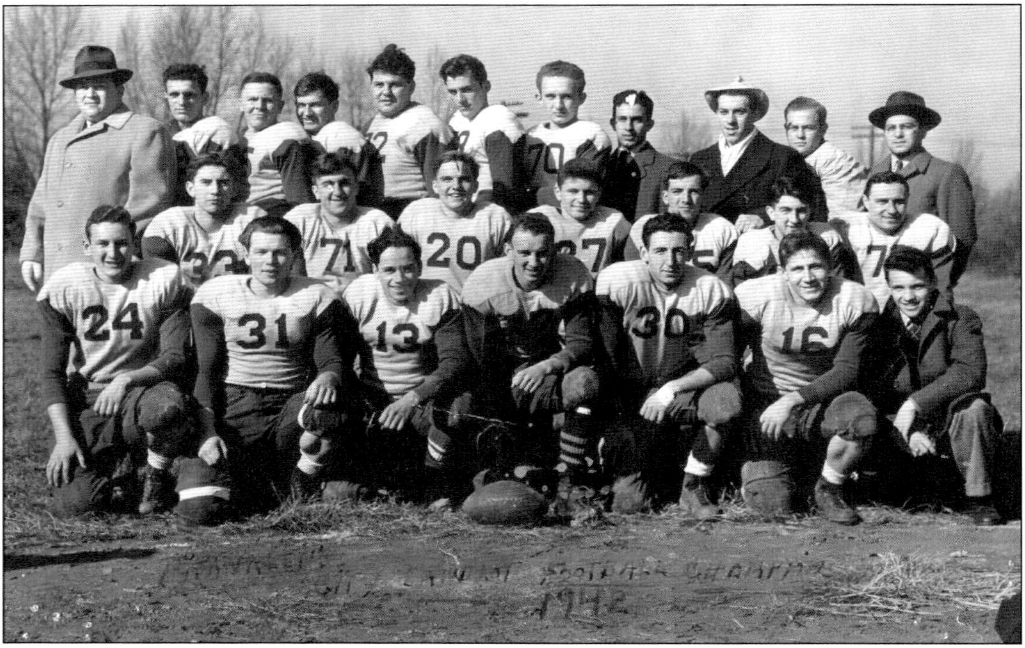

Berks County's championship high school students gather in 1942 for a group photograph of their locally compiled football team. The team featured all the best local players, such as David Moyer, no. 73. Having such athletic talent and the chance to integrate within the community, many Jews were welcomed into secular sports teams. (Courtesy of Marjorie Moyer.)

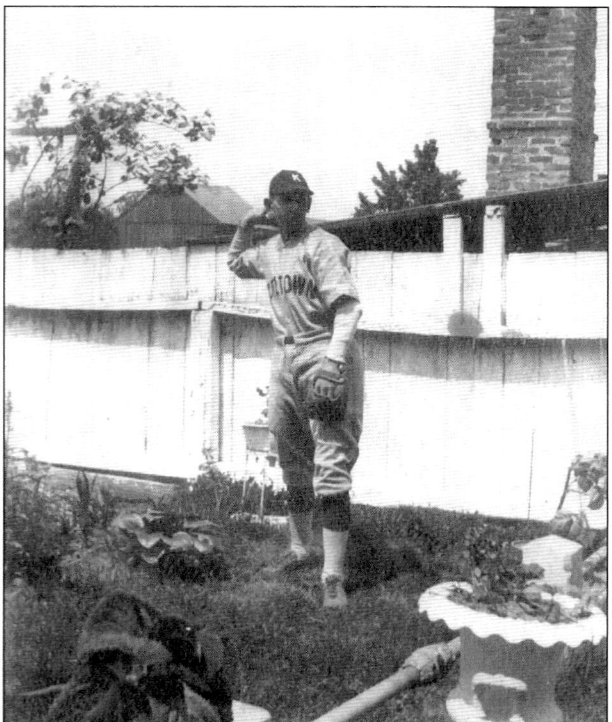

Samuel Levine played on a Kutztown men's league in 1928. Born in Kutztown, Pennsylvania, in 1900, Levine attended Kutztown High School and excelled in athletics. He was awarded a basketball scholarship to Kutztown State Teachers College, now Kutztown University. Levine worked with the Kutztown Publishing Company for 45 years. (Courtesy of Kim Yashek.)

Pictured here is the souvenir program for the Reading Community Center basketball team's 1930–1931 season. In the second game of the season, the team beat Bethlehem Community Center by a score of 43–30. The team was comprised of H. Paris, J. Saul, V. Finkle, Goodman, L. Finkle, B. Finkle, Blumberg, S. Paris, G. Saul, Bloom, and Crystal. H. Paris and L. Pinkle led the team with 12 points apiece. (Courtesy of JFR.)

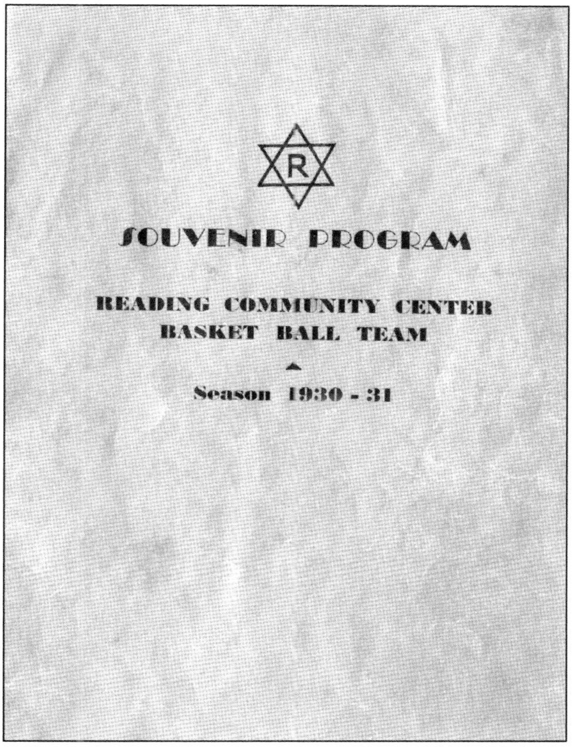

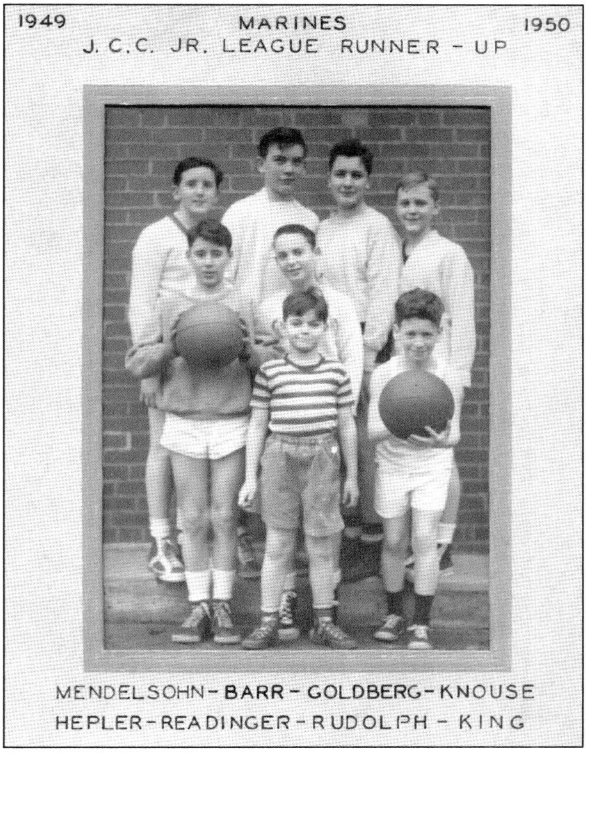

These eight boys make up Jewish Community Center's Junior League basketball team and are celebrating their achievement in a local basketball tournament. Boys and girls of all ages played sports and competed in local and national tournaments. The boys, from left to right, are (first row) Ross Rudolph and Michael King; (second row) Ivan Mendelsohn, Edward Barr, and Louis Goldberg. (Courtesy of JFR.)

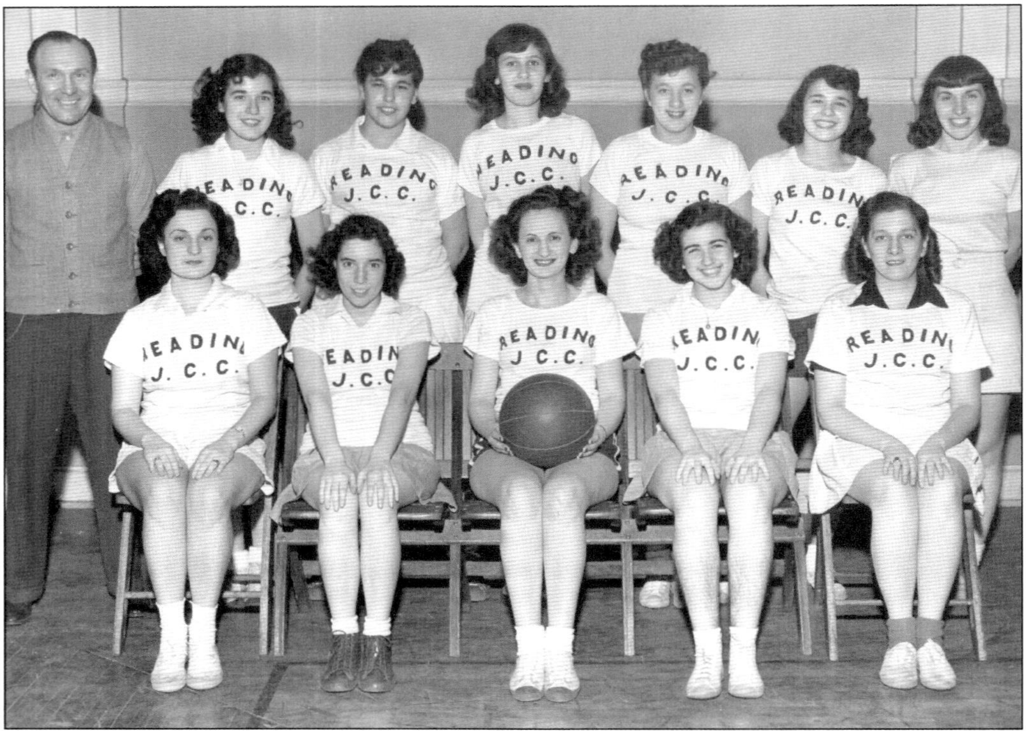

Pictured above is the Reading Jewish Community Center's women's basketball team during the 1948–1949 season. The Jewish Community Center of Reading was one of the first places in the area to have girls' sports teams and host events. The coaches are Harry "Pop" Polter and Betty Smith. The players, in no particular order, are Mildred Fishkin, Lenore Lonker, Frances Rudolph, Rose Wagman, Goldie Jacobson, Sue Paroly, Betty Krichmar, ? Krimen, Sandy Farber, and Rachel Ravitz. Pictured below is a Jewish Community Center men's basketball team picture from the 1950s. The teams included Jews and non-Jews. The coach is Harry "Pop" Polter. (Both, courtesy of JFR.)

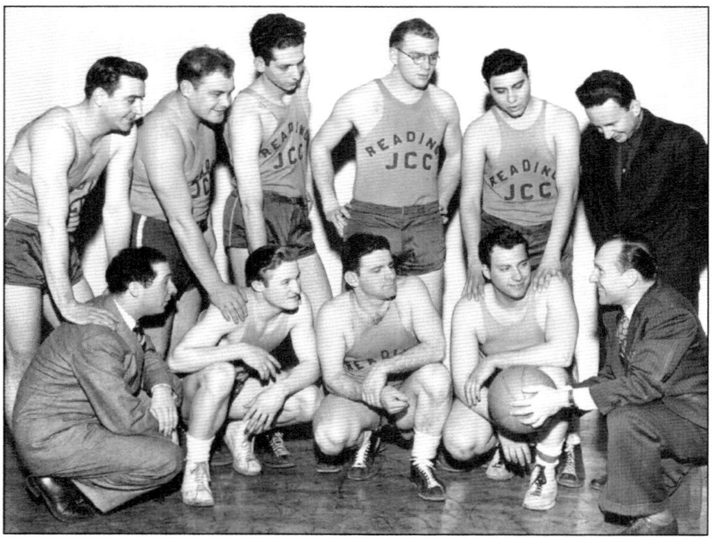

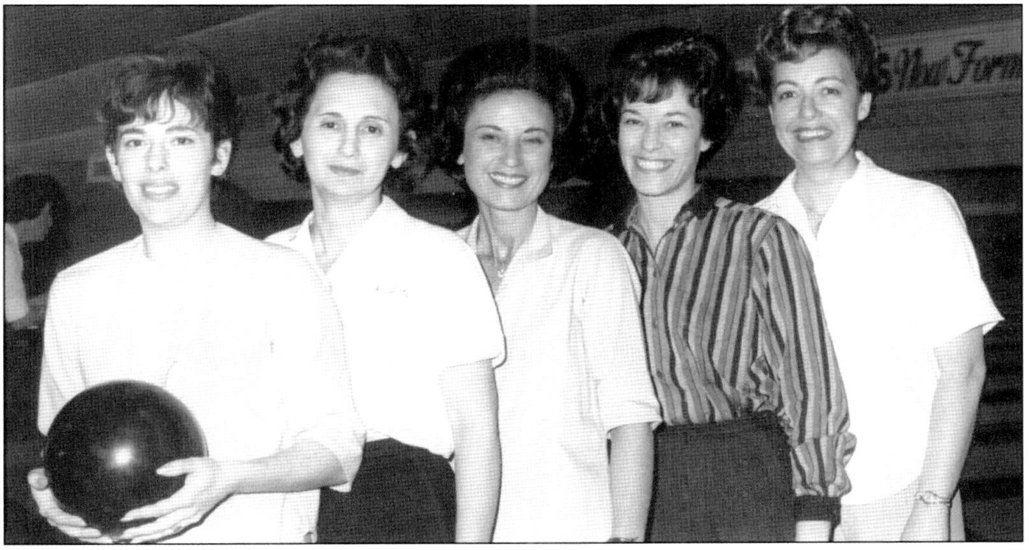

In 1955, approximately 18 husband-wife teams competed in the Jewish Community Center bowling leagues. The Jewish Community Center also had a bowling program for children. Many Jewish women's leagues played at Bowl-O-Rama on Perkiomen Avenue in Reading. This picture is from a women's bowling league in 1962. Pictured from left to right are Rosalie Stein, unidentified, Francine Suknow, unidentified, and Florence Sakin. (Courtesy of JFR.)

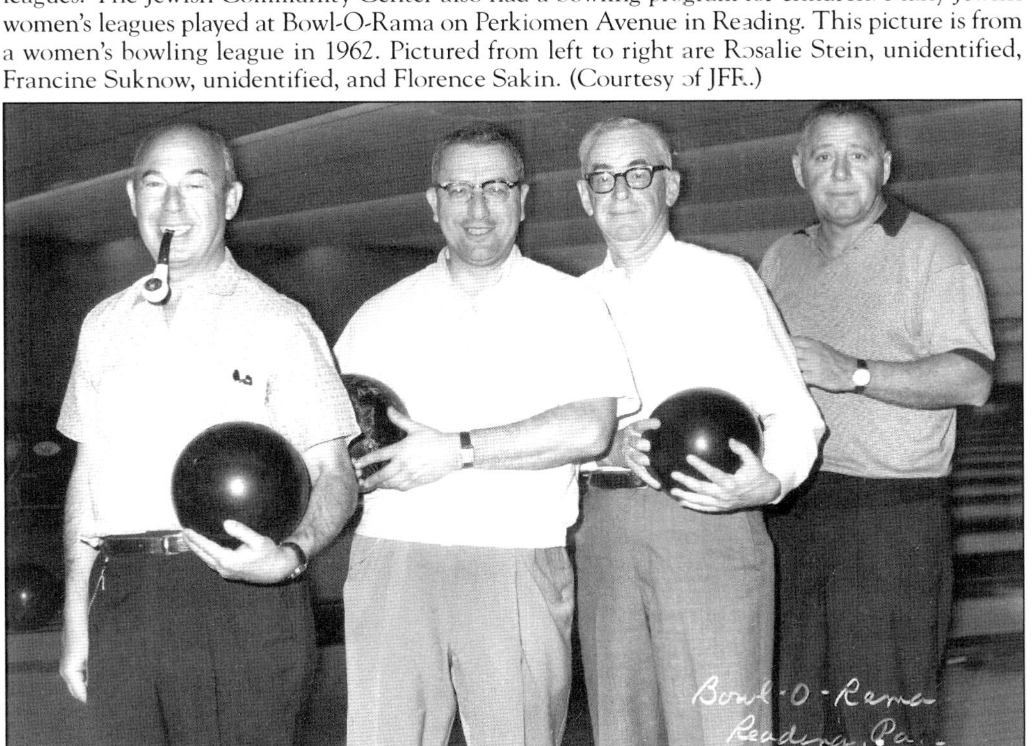

Jewish men's bowling leagues were also very popular at Bowl-O-Rama. This picture is of, from left to right, Irv Bash, Benny Brown, Eli Skaist, and Lester Laufbahn, one of the 1964–1965 men's bowling league teams at the Bowl-O-Rama. At season's end, the league members and their spouses traveled to a variety of Catskills resorts to celebrate the end-of-season awards. (Courtesy of JFR.)

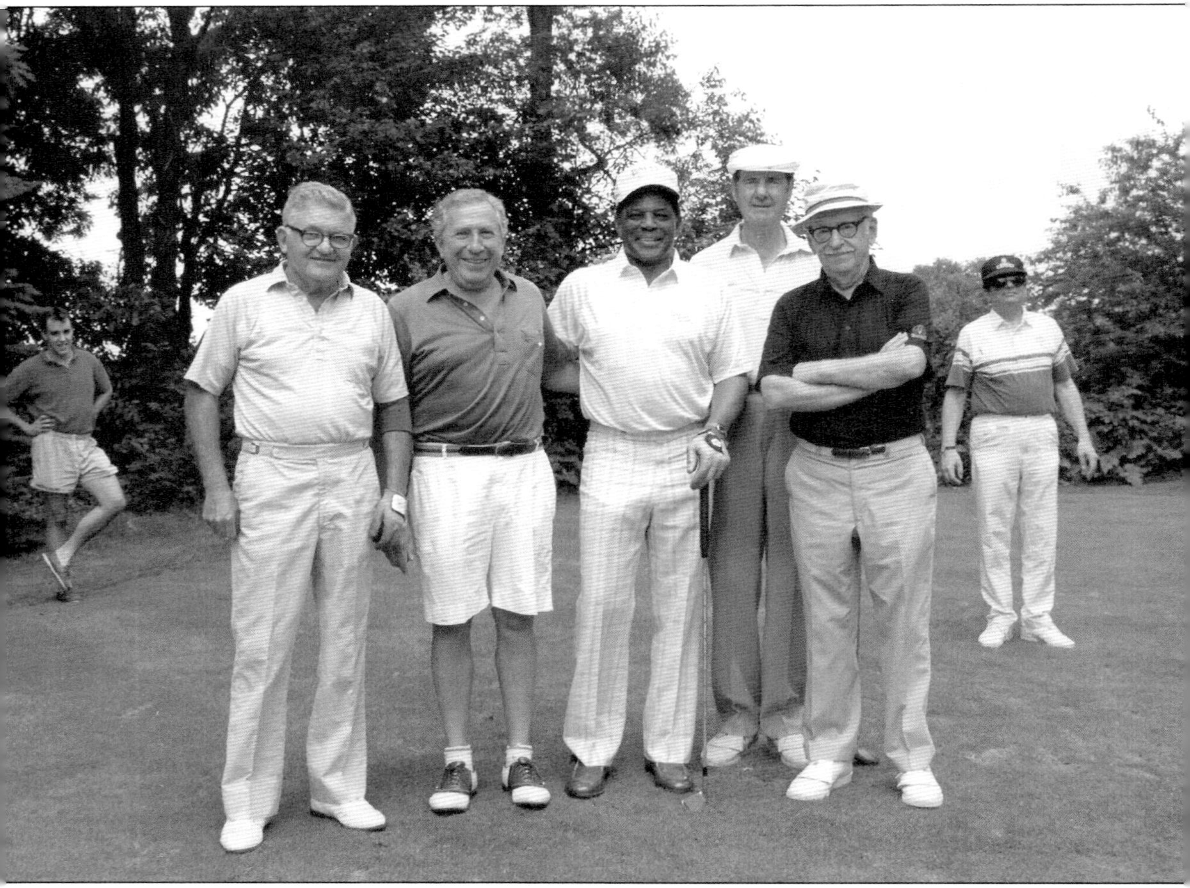

In this picture, Lee Elder, a professional golfer and the first African American to play in the Master's Tournament in 1975, joins local Reading golfers for a game. Pictured from left to right are Norman "Chick" Dunitz, David Blumberg, Lee Elder, Sam Briskin and Eli Skaist. Among the most notable Jewish golfers in Berks County was Herman Imber, a Penn Street merchant who owned the Jeannette Shop. Imber is remembered for consistently shooting his age. Jews from the Reading and Allentown areas formed the Berkleigh Country Club in 1926 because they were not welcome at the more-established clubs. Sam Jacobson was a local Berks County champion. The Sam Jacobson Memorial Tournament held at the Berkleigh was named in his honor. Among his wins were many Berkleigh Championships and the Berks County Senior Golf Championship in 1951. Berkleigh was considered the most challenging golf course in Berks County from the 1930s through 1960s, when Moselem Springs was constructed by Hawley Quier. (Courtesy of Jill Skaist.)

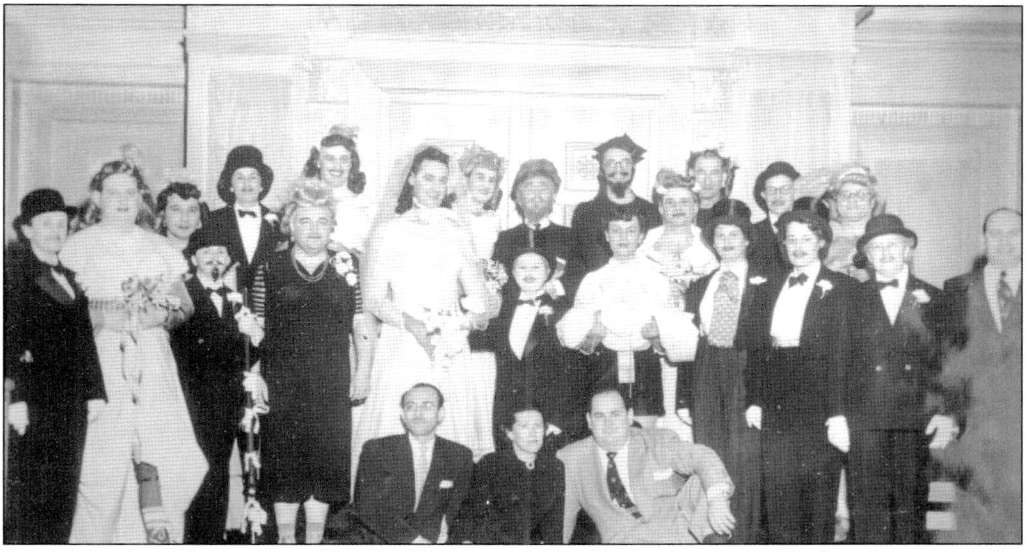

Pictured here is the entire company of a play produced by the Sisterhood of Kesher Zion. The sisterhood often collected popular music of the day or wrote the lyrics and script. Cantor Ben Klonsky (seated left, front row) was the musical director. The plays were often written by Hortense Farber (seated, front center) and Vera Kaplan. (Courtesy of KZ.)

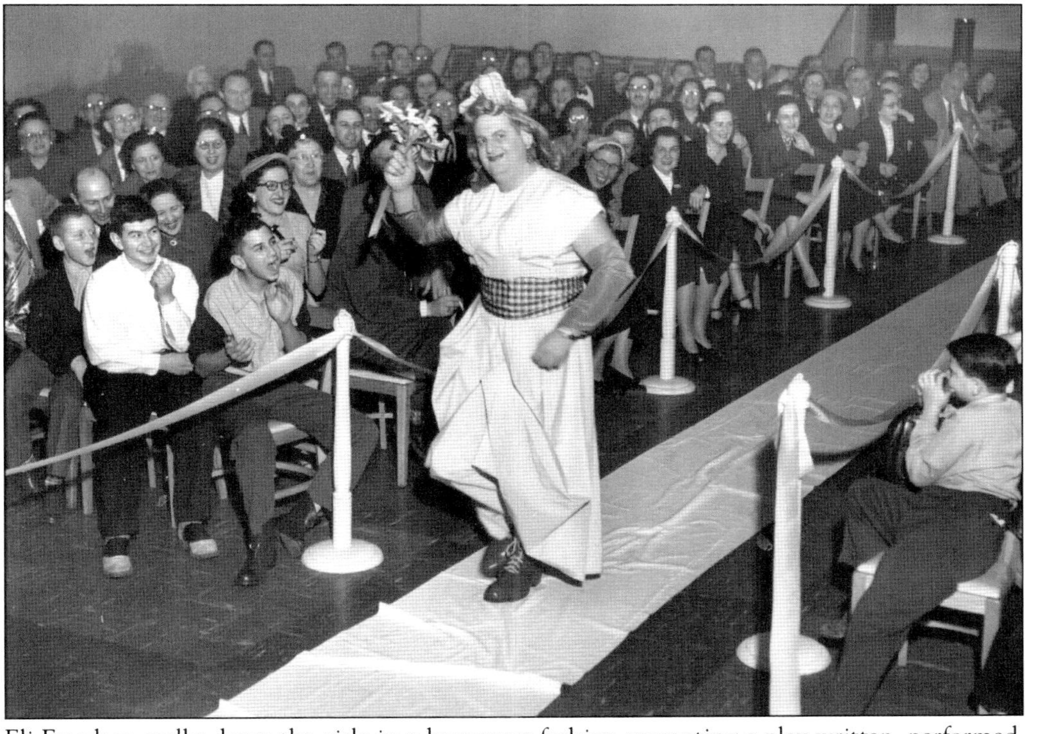

Eli Freedson walks down the aisle in a humorous fashion promoting a play written, performed, sponsored, and organized by Kesher Zion and the Sisterhood of Kesher Zion for the Jewish community. Frances "Honey" Freedson was involved with many performances given by the sisterhood and was a member of the decorations committee. (Courtesy of KZ.)

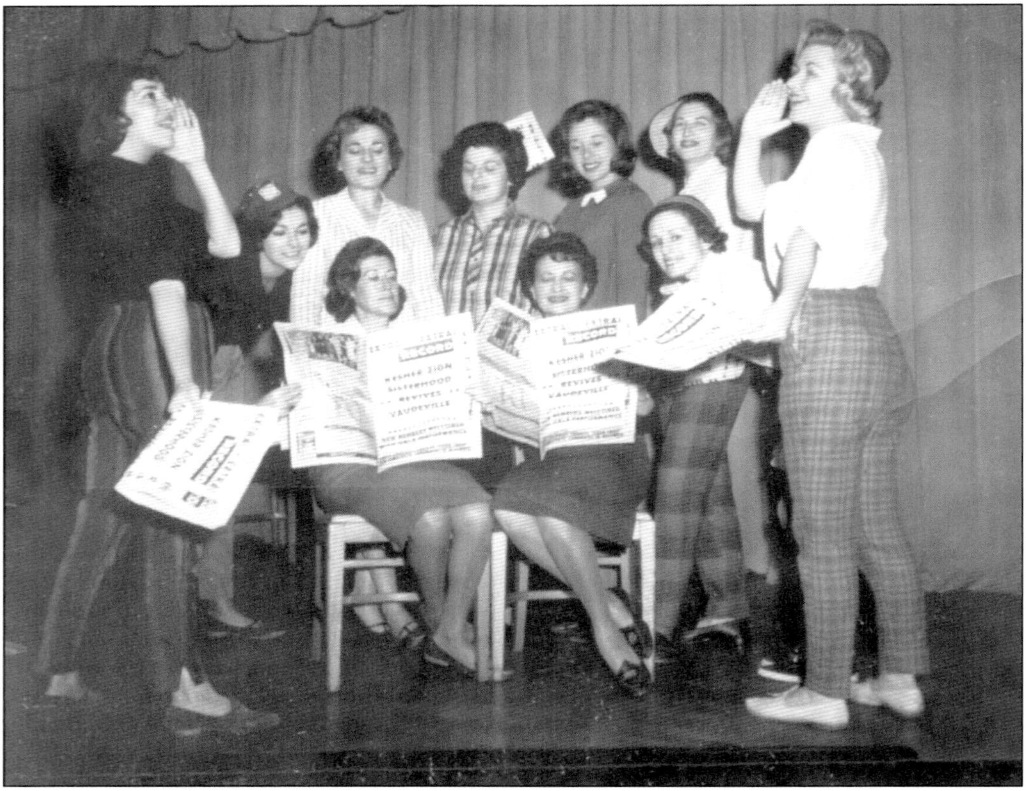

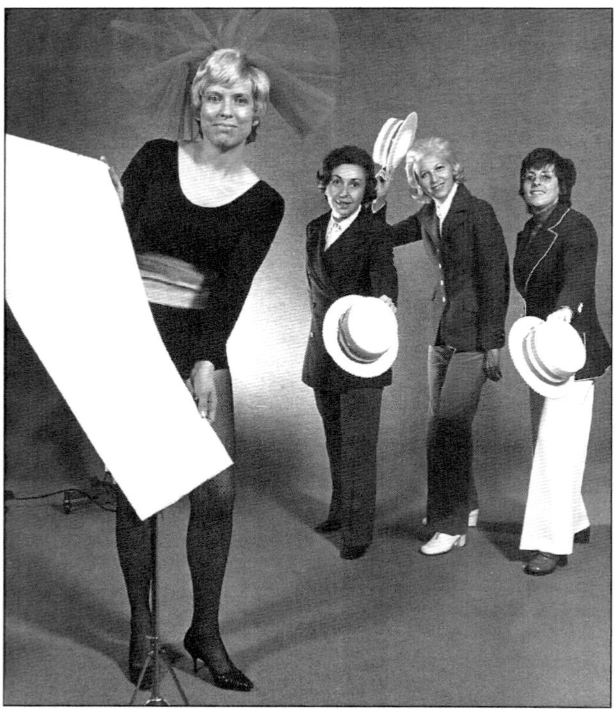

The Sisterhood of Kesher Zion produced and performed countless plays over the years. Pictured here is *Reviving Vaudeville*, performed on November 10, 1960. Some people in the photograph are Barbara Fromm, Evelyn Furman Cooperman, and Charlotte Jacobson. (Courtesy of KZ.)

This is promotional material for one of Kesher Zion's many performances. Today, Kesher Zion and the sisterhood continue to host many musicals and performances. From left to right, the women are Carol Erkes, Judy Hartman, Vi Silverstein, and Betty Hafetz. (Courtesy of KZ.)

Members of Reform Congregation Oheb Sholom performed the musical *Gypsy* in 1997. Congregation member Mike Pardo, who was also cast as the characters Uncle Jock and Phil, designed this flyer. His wife, Eve Pardo, and children, Daniel and Sarah Pardo, were also part of the musical. (Courtesy of Michael Pardo.)

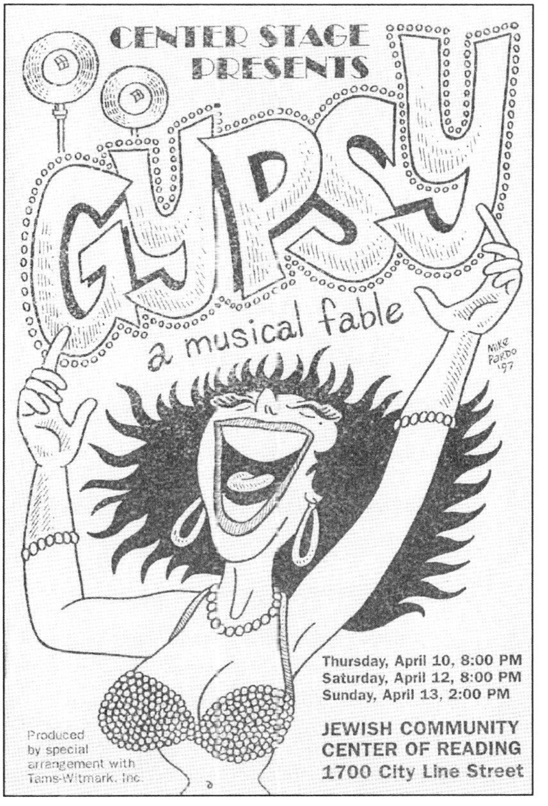

The Night at the Races event was organized at the Jewish Community Center in 1980. The affair was meant to get members of the Jewish community to be more politically involved and encourage them to go out and vote. Pictured from left to right are Sheila Lattin and Marjorie Leisawitz. Sheila and Gary Lattin, a cardiologist, have three daughters, and Marjorie and Alan Leisawitz, an attorney, have three sons. (Courtesy of JFR.)

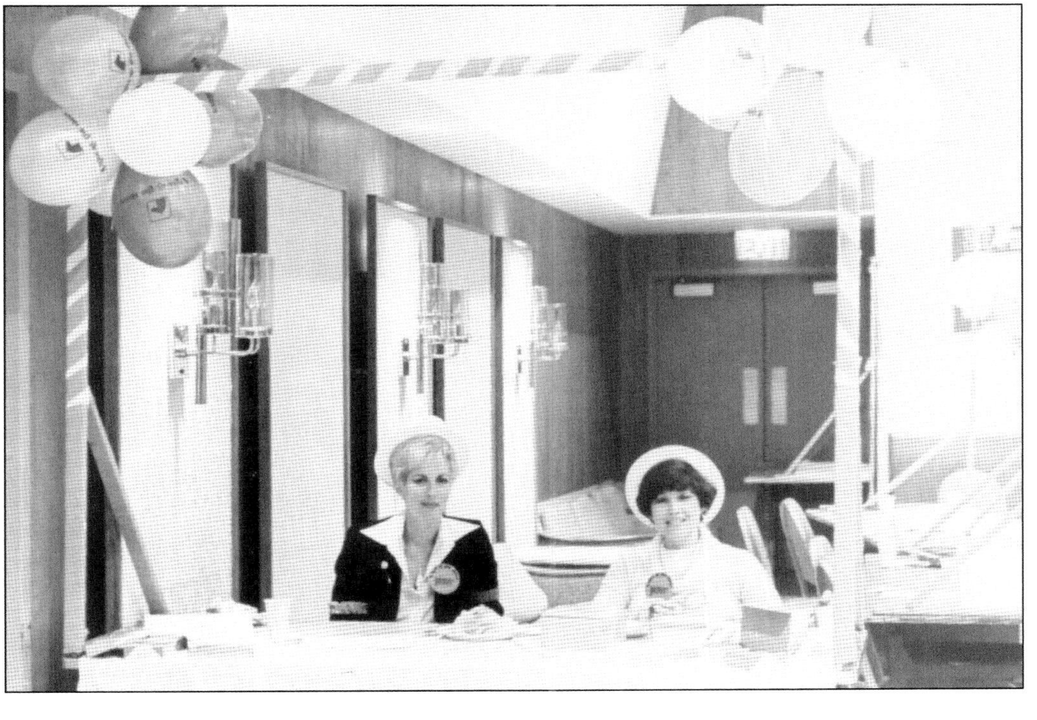

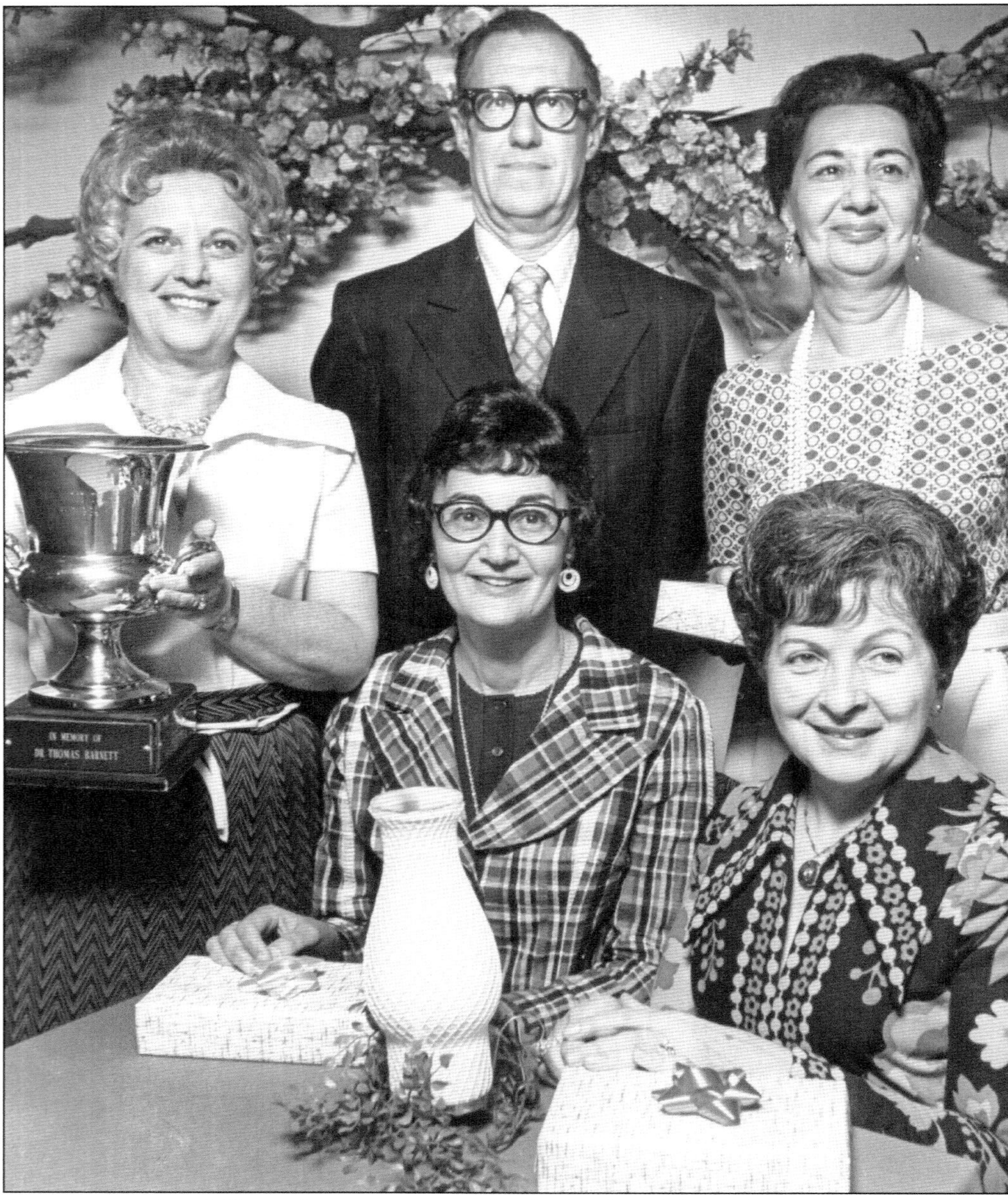

Seen here is the 1972 trophy presentation for the bridge club yearly winners at the Jewish Community Center. In the photograph are, from left to right (seated) Frances Rosenberg and Irma Gibstein Oren; (standing) Edith Mendelsohn; her husband, Milton Mendelsohn; and Dora Rosenberg. Today, there is still a bridge club at the Jewish Community Center, and members meet to play every Wednesday at 12:30 p.m. The American Contract Bridge League sanctions the bridge club. The club is open to members and nonmembers alike as an activity that brings the community together. (Courtesy of JFR.)

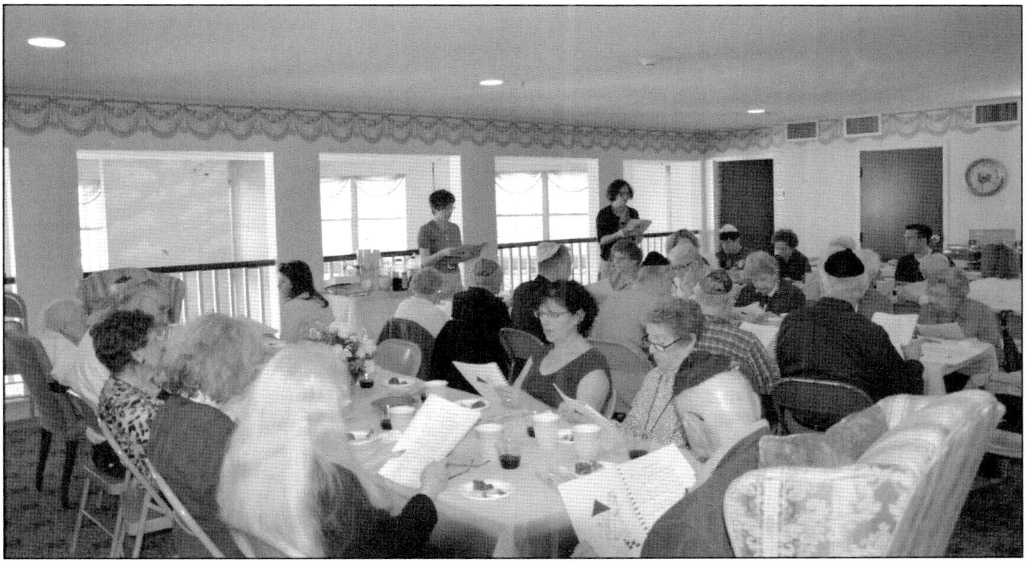

The Friendship Circle for seniors meets every Thursday for lunch and a special program. The name of the organization has changed over the years, but the one constant is that it always meets on Thursdays. The first meeting of the Golden Circle was Thursday, October 11, 1956. Anna Popkin was the chair, and Betty Lou McLean was the group advisor. The 1963 *Centerpiece* refers to the Senior Circle. The opening meeting was on Thursday, October 17. Pictured above is the Friendship Circle Passover Seder held at the Manor at Market Square on Thursday, April 21, 2011. It was led by Sari Incledon, a social worker for the Jewish Family Services. The Seder was also attended by non-Jewish community members. Pictured below, from left to right, are Samuel Silberstein, Ethel Engel, Eileen Kope, Elaine Levine, Gerald Levine, and Betty Ann Sade. (Both photographs by Jeffrey Watts, courtesy of Jeffrey Watts.)

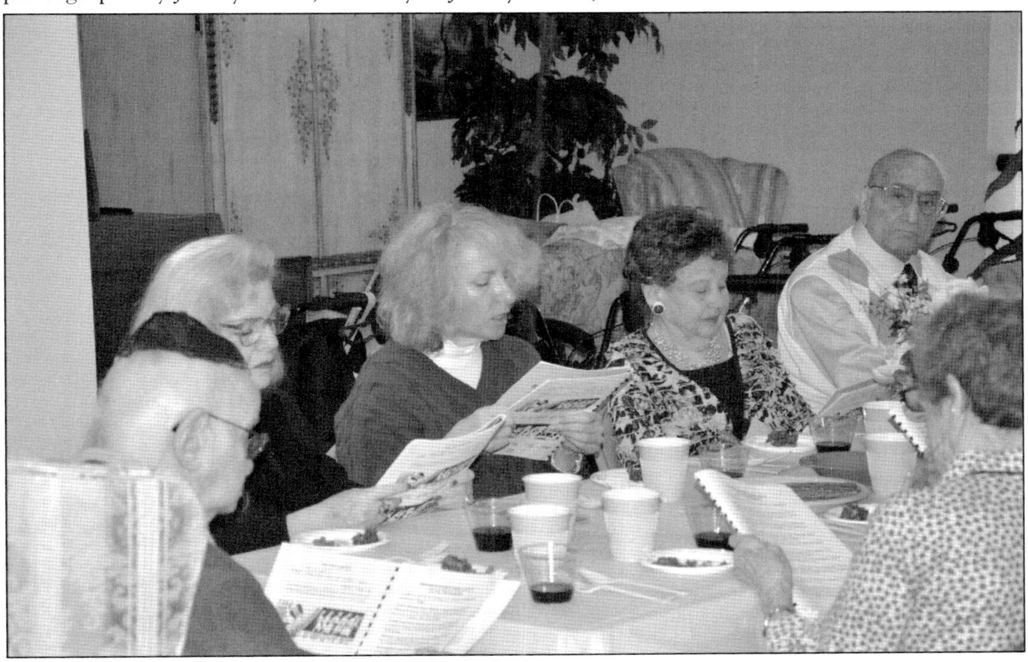